Phädon,
OR
On the
Immortality of the Soul

PETER LANG
New York • Washington, D.C./Baltimore • Bern
Frankfurt am Main • Berlin • Brussels • Vienna • Oxford

Moses Mendelssohn

Phädon,
OR
On the
Immortality of the Soul

TRANSLATED BY
Patricia Noble

WITH AN INTRODUCTION BY
David Shavin

PETER LANG
New York • Washington, D.C./Baltimore • Bern
Frankfurt am Main • Berlin • Brussels • Vienna • Oxford

Library of Congress Cataloging-in-Publication Data

Mendelssohn, Moses, 1729–1786.
[Phädon. English]
Phädon: or, On the immortality of the soul /
Moses Mendelssohn; translated by Patricia Noble;
with an introduction by David Shavin.
p. cm.
Includes bibliographical references.
1. Immortality—Early works to 1800. 2. Socrates.
3. Plato. Phaedo. I. Noble, Patricia. II. Title.
B2691.P42E5 129—dc22 2006034888
ISBN-13: 978-0-8204-9529-3
ISBN-10: 0-8204-9529-8

Bibliographic information published by **Die Deutsche Bibliothek.**
Die Deutsche Bibliothek lists this publication in the "Deutsche
Nationalbibliografie"; detailed bibliographic data is available
on the Internet at http://dnb.ddb.de/.

Cover design by Lisa Barfield

Table of Contents

Acknowledgments

I wish to thank all my friends from the Schiller Institute, including Christoph Mohs, Andreas Andromedas, Rosa Tennenbaum, Hans Peter Mueller, Wolfgang Lillge, Therese Mallory, and Michael and Muriel Weissbach. We spent many delightful hours discussing the *Phädon*'s ideas. Also Steven Douglas, Donald Huff, and Edward Joshie, who gave me moral support and encouragement. Thanks to Ryan Milton who helped me prepare the text.

Translator's Introduction

This present translation is the first to appear since Charles Cullen translated the *Phädon* in 1789, which has recently been republished by Thoemmes Press. Happily, now English readers have a more modern and concise translation, at a time when there is a renewed interest in the history of German philosophy. Also, now they can have a keener insight into Mendelssohn's thinking, with the addition of the "Preface" and "Appendix" to the third edition of the *Phädon*, which is sadly lacking in the Cullen translation,[1] as well as explanatory notes.

This translation is a result of my passion for everything ancient Greek. Since the German writings on ancient Greece, in my opinion, are far superior to anything in English, some time back I set about translating, especially Wilhelm von Humboldt's six essays on ancient Greece, which had not been translated into English, as well as some articles on ancient Greece written by my German friends.

It was only natural that my friend, David Shavin (who provided the notes for this edition and wrote the introduction), turned to me when he was frustrated with the Cullen translation of the *Phädon*. David was involved in a study group of the Schiller Institute, reading aloud and discussing the philosophical ideas of Mendelssohn's *Phädon*, comparing it to Plato's *Phaedo* in the original Greek. It became obvious, with a cursory examination of the original German, that Cullen's translation was wholly inadequate, and that a new modern English translation was needed.

Although the poetic English of Cullen is edifying, the liberties he takes in many cases could arguably be labeled a mistranslation, and the philosophical ideas of Mendelssohn lose some of their pungency and force thereby. It is not just the omission of some of the exchanges of Socrates' interlocutors, the changing of pronouns and verbal tenses, etc. What is worse is the paraphrasing of entire passages, which loses much of the tension and philosophical rigor of the original German.

Compare the following two translations, first Cullen's, and then mine, of the same passage:

> Tell me, Simmias, would we not think it ridiculous if a man, who had never left the walls of Athens, should conclude from his own limited

experience, that day and night, summer and winter, were subject to the same revolutions over all other parts of the globe as they are with us?

What do you think, Simmias? Would we not find a man very ridiculous, who would never leave the walls of Athens, and wanted to conclude from his own experience, that no other form of government was possible than the democratic?[2]

As Humboldt emphasized in the introduction to his translation of the *Agamemnon*, the first requirement of translation is faithfulness to the original text:

This faithfulness must be directed to the true character of the original, and not abandon that to its chance happenings. Generally, every good translation emanates from the simple and unpretentious love of the original, and the study arising from this love, and to which translation must return...I have tried to approach the simplicity and faithfulness just described here in my own work, according to these general considerations. With every new editing I have strived always to remove what didn't plainly exist in the text.

This has been my approach—keeping as closely to the original syntax and punctuation as well as the text, making only those necessary changes for comprehension to the English reader.

Introduction

The *Phädon*—an "American" Project

Plato's *Phaedo* presents the discussions of Socrates in his jail cell, in the final hours before his execution in 399 B.C. During the next five decades, Plato organized a movement in Greece, not by avoiding what injustice and ugliness the Athenian democracy had committed against Socrates, but by having young men come to terms with the depths to which their society had sunk, and so, to forge the requisite internal strength to wrench their society back toward sanity. Plato's Socrates does not simply make good arguments for the immortality of the soul. His actions and his way of thinking and talking, what Friedrich Schiller might call his aesthetic education, conveyed the truth of his arguments. By the end, the readers of the dialogue, as the tearful friends of Socrates in the dialogue, must either become maudlin and sad or change themselves permanently for the better, carrying the spirit of Socrates with them forever. In fact, Plato succeeded in organizing a movement, conveyed through his Academy, that established a classical standard of thought and education, deep enough to wrench the best of culture away from a permanent dark age.

Moses Mendelssohn composed his *Phädon* between the ages of 31 and 37, in the decade before the American Revolution. But he had deep concerns his whole adult life that the quality of thinking in Prussia, and in Europe, had fallen below the level of epistemology and metaphysics established by Gottfried Leibniz several decades earlier—below the level necessary to govern competently. As a young man between the ages of 17 and 24, he himself had to come to terms with the attempted intellectual execution of Leibniz. The strength that he gained—along with his fellow warrior, Gotthold Ephraim Lessing—from the victory over such ugliness prepared him for his *Phädon* project.

The theme of the immortality of the soul was an appropriate subject for Mendelssohn's task: his king and his culture wavered to and fro between the "Scylla" of witty, pleasure-seeking French Enlightenment sophists, and the "Charybdis" of dour, dutiful logistical thinking of the English. Between those who would so lightly cast aside matters of the soul, and those who would too easily separate the soul from this world, Mendelssohn had his mission. He decided to refresh and enrich Plato's *Phaedo* with the powerful culture of Leibniz's treatment of the same issues. And, like Socrates, Mendelssohn did not simply argue for such matters. As eloquent and delightful as his words were, they were one with the example of his life.

Moses Mendelssohn

The story of Moses Mendelssohn is one of those precious and poignant tales, whereby the paradoxes and possibilities of a culture are essentially concentrated in one individual. The modern reader might review the features of the life of Dr. Martin Luther King, in terms of an American republic whose strength was based upon the idea that "all men were created equal," and whose history had reflected an uneven struggle to realize its promise. The possibility of the United States stepping onto the world stage after World War II—not as yet another empire, but as the realization of a higher principle in the development of nations—was ineluctably wrapped up in the solution of the paradox (as Lincoln had put it) of a nation half-slave and half-free. The eloquence and power of King was wrapped up in his very person—as the living testimony that the culture and the country had a vastly underdeveloped potential. So, too, one might most fruitfully approach Moses Mendelssohn.

Born on September 6, 1729 to a Jewish couple in the small Prussian town of Dessau, Moses, son of Mendel, had the prospects of any other bright Jewish child of the previous several centuries.[3] Instead of merely farming another's land or trading goods in small towns' markets, he might be one of the fortunate ones that learned the Torah and the Talmud, and be supported in their life of religious learning. As such, while he would certainly develop his mind in learning Hebrew, he would never learn German, or study at a university, or own property or stray far from the ghetto. Mendelssohn, however, clearly did go beyond his destiny. He would shock and provoke his culture in learning German better than his Prussian King, in grasping philosophy and culture better than the university professors, and in enlarging the best of the culture by his treatment of Plato. A rather slight, somewhat hunch-backed Jew became the towering figure of German culture, that, in fact, laid the basis for the possibility of a German nation—and for the reality of the American republic!

Stars Shine Even over the Ghetto

We shall begin the story by relating how the starry handiwork of the Creator's heavens led Moses out of the ghetto. During the last year of his childhood in Dessau, 1742-43, two major works were published nearby by relatives, the Wulffs, that marked a sort of Jewish Renaissance. First was the famous *More Nevukhim*, or *Guide of the Perplexed*, by Moses Maimonides, which had not been republished in almost two centuries—a mark of the cultural degeneration that had set in during and after the Thirty Years War of 1618-48. The 1742 publication was an important part of re-establishing a more classical sense of Judaism, over some of the mystical, and even outright irrational, trends of the previous century. Since Mendelssohn's teacher, Rabbi David Fränkel, was the editor of the Maimonides' work, young Moses would clearly have been shaped by the project. Then in 1743, the same printing house in nearby Jessnitz followed with David Gans' 1609 treatise, *Nehmad Ve-Na'im*, an astronomical work by a Jewish colleague of Tycho Brahe and Johannes Kepler.[4] Gans had worked with Brahe and Kepler in the famous observatory set up near Prague by the Emperor Rudolph II. In this first publication of the 134-year-old manuscript, there is more than a clue regarding Mendelssohn's family heritage.

David Gans was a student of the hallowed ancestor of Mendelssohn, Moses Isserles, the Rabbi of Cracow in the mid-sixteenth century. After the difficulties of the Spanish Inquisition and the banishment of the Jews in 1492, Isserles (1520–1572) upheld the tradition of Moses Maimonides in locating religion as not being in a perpetual war with reason. In contrast, others, most notably Don Isaac Abravanel, would accommodate their religion to the ugly new, so-called, realities—with all the attendant pressures to import irrationalities into their conception of God.[5] Isserles was an ancestor of Mendelssohn's mother, Bela Rachel Sara Wahl. (Her father, Rabbi Saul Wahl, on his mother's side, was a fifth-generation descendent of Moses Isserles.) This line of the Isserles family immigrated to Dessau in the second half of the seventeenth century. Further, the publishers of the works by Maimonides and by Gans were a part of this same Dessau branch of the Isserles descendants, originally named Wolf, and then Wulff. Moses Mendelssohn is thought to have been named after both the founder of the printing house, Moses Benjamin Wulff, and the teacher of Gans, Moses Isserles.

Gans' *Nehmad ve-Na'im* describes the Brahe/Kepler observatory:

> I have kept for the ending of this book something extraordinary: namely, that in the year 5360 [1600 AD] our sovereign, the noble Emperor Rudolph, may his glory be exalted, eminent in science, wisdom, and knowledge, learned in astronomy, a lover of wise men and a great patron of scholars... [brought Brahe from Denmark] and installed him in a castle called Benatek... with twelve people, all learned in the astronomical sciences. Their task was to manipulate instruments which were larger and more marvelous than any which had ever been seen.

He writes: "Where else can man find the silent echo of the voice of the Creator if not in the contemplation of the stars and their wonderful motions?" Gans contends that the instruction is: "Thou shalt know the Lord thy God," and not "Thou shalt believe the Lord thy God."[6] While Gans' work certainly did not reach the level of Kepler, it must have been an inspiration for the 13-year-old, Moses, as Gans' expressed orientation was a lifelong concern of Mendelssohn.

Finally, Gans' work was prepared for publication by a colleague of Rabbi Fränkel: the Rabbi of Austerlitz, Joel ben Yekutiel Sachs. Though the work was published in Hebrew, a forty-page Latin introduction was added, written by Christian Hebenstreit, the professor of Hebrew at the Leipzig Academy, and a colleague of Johann Sebastian Bach. Within three years, the young Moses began learning Latin, it is said, in order to be able to read works on astronomy. The passion to know God by looking into the handiwork of the stars led Moses to the challenge of learning "Christian" languages.

The Move to Berlin

Rabbi Sachs and Rabbi Fränkel shared more than the works of Maimonides and Gans. They were both students of the famous Chief Rabbi of Berlin, Michel Hasid. Sachs had even become Hasid's son-in-law.[7] Both Fränkel and Sachs moved to Berlin in 1743, soon to assume the positions there, respectively, of the Chief Rabbi and of the Dayyan (Judicial Deputy). That fall, Moses, having just turned fourteen, also left Dessau for Berlin to continue his studies. Later, Mendelssohn's great-grandson, Wilhelm Hensel, the family biographer, described the situation his great-grandfather would have faced there: "The Christians of those times [1740s Berlin] considered the Jews as little their equals in mind and faculties as in our days [1869] the white inhabitants of America regard the negroes." Despite the talent within the Jewish community that Moses had access to, it was not obvious whether the larger European culture would ever benefit from it. At the time, Moses would have pursued both the moral truths of his religious studies and the awe-inspiring beauty of the Creator's handiwork of the heavens, simply for the fruitfulness of the combination of both studies together, without regard to, or opportunity for, professional advancement.

He began studies with Israel ben Moses ha-Levi Samoscz (1700-1772), whose approach to Talmud was enriched with philosophy and astronomy. Mendelssohn could work through the astronomical references in the Talmud, using Samoscz's 1741 *Netsah Yisra'el*, and perhaps Samoscz's (unpublished) astronomical treatise, *Arubot ha-Shamayim*. Samoscz's teaching harkened back to the issues, studies and approach of the happier time of Moses Maimonides and the Arab Renaissance. Samoscz taught at the Jewish school in Berlin established by Veitel Heine Ephraim, but he did at least some of his studies and writings in a library in the house of his patron, the key Jewish figure in Berlin, Daniel Itzig. The Itzigs were another branch of the descendants of Moses Isserles.

Further, Daniel Itzig's wife, Mariane Wulff Itzig, was the daughter of Dessau's Benjamin Elias Wulff, of the book-printing operation mentioned above. The Itzig family would play a central role in support of Mendelssohn's projects all during his life, and afterwards. One of the sixteen Itzig children, Fanny, would introduce Mendelssohn's *Phädon* to Wolfgang Mozart in Vienna.[8] Another Itzig daughter, Blümchen, became the wife of David Friedländer, one of Mendelssohn's closest collaborators. (And a granddaughter, Leah Itzig Salomon, would marry Mendelssohn's son, Abraham, giving birth to the composers Felix and Fanny Mendelssohn.) The Itzig family was known for performing Shakespeare plays in their home. In 1743, Mendelssohn would have found this household, with the resident scholar Israel Samocsz, to be the natural progression from his last year in Dessau.

Astronomy and Culture

By the age of 16, Mendelssohn began the private study of Latin with a fellow Jewish student, Abraham Kisch. It were likely that they both would have been anxious to read the forty-page Latin introduction to the astronomical work by David Gans. Mendelssohn later reported to Friedrich Nicolai that they read some of Cicero's essays, and then studied a Latin version of John Locke's *Essay Concerning Human Understanding*. Following upon this work, Mendelssohn was introduced by Aaron Solomon Gumpertz—Samoscz's prize student, some six years older than Mendelssohn—to the writings of Gottfried Leibniz and Christian Wolff.[9]

Shortly afterwards, in 1746, Samoscz took Mendelssohn with him to audit the philosophy course of Johann Phillip Heinius, a course taught in Latin. Heinius, the Rector at the Gymnasium, was a classicist whose works on Greek philosophy were staples of the Royal Academy's publications. At the time that Mendelssohn was attending his course, Heinius was researching the Pythagorean school of philosophers. (Samoscz and Mendelssohn surely would have read Heinius' 1746 Latin paper on a lesser known disciple of Pythagoras, Oenopidas of Chios.) While Gumpertz had earlier drawn the attention of an Academy member, the Marquis d'Argens, Mendelssohn's earliest known direct contact with the Academy would have been his involvement with Professor Heinius. Mendelssohn had travelled from the Torah and the stars to languages and philosophy and was unlikely to be confined to a ghetto life. However, it was just at this point in Mendelssohn's life that open intellectual warfare was declared at the Royal Academy upon the influence of Leibniz. The next eight years of assaults upon Leibniz would forge Mendelssohn's mental powers and shape his mission in life. In fact, Mendelssohn's life-long alliance with Gotthold Lessing was forged in their successful defense of Leibniz.

Attacks on Leibniz Provoke the Best
for Mendelssohn

In 1746, Pierre-Louis de Maupertuis, the new head of the Berlin Academy, launched a three-fold attack upon Leibniz. In his inaugural lecture, he attempted a mechanistic transformation of Leibniz's concept of "least-action." Shortly afterwards, the Academy announced the new prize contest, on the validity of Leibniz's concept of the "monad." However, in the abrupt schedule for the submission of papers, and in the heavy-handed administration of the contest by Maupertuis' colleague, Leonhard Euler, it appeared that the Academy was somewhat embarrassed by the too obvious prejudice against Leibniz, and the weakness of the prize essay. (The proclaimed winner, J. G. H. Justi, launched his career in government, due to Euler and his faction. Later, in 1761, the senior government official, von Justi, would lead an attempt to try to silence Mendelssohn.) Then, in November and December of 1746, the third attack: a paper by Jean d'Alembert and a presentation by Euler, both to the Academy, argued for an anti-Leibnizian approach to algebraic powers. (Their arguments—effectively for the power in mathematics stemming from the formalisms of numbers instead of stemming from the geometrical powers of the mind—were famously overturned in 1799 by a youthful Carl Friedrich Gauss, who benefited from hearing stories of this period from his professor, Abraham Kästner.) All three of these affairs would have represented a major challenge to the seventeen-year-old Mendelssohn. However, the role of Maupertuis during the next several years of attempts to degrade the conception of "the best of all possible worlds," might well have been the key for Mendelssohn in resolving how he would cleave to truth-seeking, and deal with hypocrisy.

Friendship and Alliance with Lessing

In 1754, Mendelssohn and Lessing jointly authored the pamphlet, *Pope, a Metaphysician!* and distributed it in Berlin the next year. With intelligence, humor and courage, they succeeded in putting an end to the farce at Maupertuis' Academy. Before addressing their victory, it is helpful to examine how they came to this project as two souls with one heart.

First, while it is generally maintained that the two of them did not meet before 1754, it would be better to maintain that they met no later than 1754.[10] Admittedly, little is known of Mendelssohn's activities in general from 1746 to 1754, including with whom he met and when. However, Mendelssohn clearly knew of Lessing's 1749 play, *The Jew*, a play that generated controversy for its presentation of a civilized Jewish character that ran counter to the stock portrayals of Jews. Not only did the author live close by, but the play was based upon Mendelssohn's good friend, Gumpertz. Later, when the play came under attack for its representation of a civilized Jew, Mendelssohn wrote a public letter defending his friend, Gumpertz.

Late in 1748, Lessing, who was several months older than Mendelssohn, had moved to Berlin and taken up residence in close proximity to the Jewish community.[11] He shared the quarters with his older cousin, Christoph Mylius. Lessing had been working closely with Mylius, joining him at the University of Leipzig in 1746, to study with Mylius' professor, Abraham Kästner. They studied the works and methods of both Johannes Kepler and Leibniz, and all three of them were aware of, and concerned about, the 1746 assault upon Leibniz at the Berlin Academy. Mylius and Lessing moved to Berlin shortly after Mylius had won a prize for an astronomical essay at the Berlin Academy in 1748.

In sum, it is not that difficult to imagine how Lessing, as of 1749, might have become acquainted with Gumpertz, given (a) their mutual astronomical interests, (b) the physical proximity, and (c) what Lessing and Mylius would have been able to offer Gumpertz (and Mendelssohn) by way of their studies of Kepler and Leibniz. (Recall that Gumpertz is the one that introduced Mendelssohn to Leibniz.) How Lessing could have become familiar with Gumpertz, but not yet with Mendelssohn, is actually the mystery that would need to be explained. And, finally, even if the two somehow missed making each other's acquaintance before the publication and controversy of Lessing's 1749 play, it would be almost inconceivable that the ensuing controversy would not have precipitated the sort of meetings and discussions that would have involved Mendelssohn.

"Pope, a Metaphysician!"

Regardless, both Lessing and Mendelssohn, from ages 17 to 24, witnessed the hypocrisy of the scientific and cultural elite of Berlin. In 1751-52, the Maupertuis' Academy reached perhaps its ugliest point. A member of the Academy, Samuel König, publicly challenged Maupertuis' reinterpretation and appropriation of the principle of least action. Maupertuis schemed to divert any public discussion over what he had done to Leibniz, by accusing König of quoting from a supposedly nonexistent letter of Leibniz. Maupertuis knew that Koenig was quoting from a copy that he had obtained from an original in the possession of his good friend Captain Samuel Henzi. He also knew that Henzi had been executed in 1749 by the authorities of Berne (Switzerland) for planning a republican revolution and that his papers, including his Leibniz papers, were in the hands of the Swiss authorities. In private letters, Maupertuis expressed his concern over the availability of the Leibniz documents, for his trial of Koenig would fail should the letters appear. (They were never produced, though, since then, they were proven to have existed.) Lessing certainly was following these developments. He had even begun a play with Henzi as the title character.

By April, 1752, Maupertuis' Academy had pronounced König to be at fault. Mendelssohn's older friend, J.G. Sulzer, did not fight the matter openly, writing to a friend: "As Maupertuis has a monopoly of authority, and we are not permitted to speak out against him very loudly, secret bitterness is all the greater, and this causes great harm to the Academy."[12] The actions of the Academy earned it disgrace throughout Europe. Even Voltaire, the longtime collaborator of Maupertuis in their attacks upon Leibniz, found the actions reprehensible. Always willing to seize upon hypocrisy, he skewered his old friend in his *The Letters of Dr. Akakia*, and other pamphlets. This set the scene for the initial Lessing-Mendelssohn collaboration, as the Academy shifted their assault upon Leibniz with an announcement of their new Academy prize essay. The 1755 contest, announced in 1753, invited essayists to consider whether Leibniz's conception of the organization of the universe as the "best of all possible worlds" was basically the same as Alexander Pope's simplified version, "all is good."

Lessing's longtime collaborator, Mylius, departed for America in 1753, sent by their teacher, Kästner. (In 1752, Mylius was the prime exponent of Benjamin Franklin's historic electrical experiments in Berlin. However, Mylius never made it to Philadelphia, as he died at age 31, during a lengthy stopover in London.)[13] It were likely at this point that Lessing would have been open to deepening his collaboration with Mendelssohn. Both Lessing and Mendelssohn found themselves prepared for, and united in, a mission to properly deflate the pretensions of the Academy, in their ostensibly innocent popularization of Leibniz. Their *Pope, a Metaphysician!*[14] was completed in 1754, but was intentionally not submitted to the Academy for the prize. Instead, in 1755, after the Academy had awarded the prize, but before they had published the prize essay, the two published their work as an anonymous pamphlet and circulated it in Berlin. (Of course, the prize had gone to an essay equating Leibniz with Pope.) Their pamphlet made it clear that the joke was on the Academy, and not on Leibniz; and in the process, they created both a new sense of intellectual freedom and a well-intentioned and popular presentation of some of Leibniz's deeper conceptions.

Turning matters right-side up, the pamphlet declared: "The Academy demands an examination of Pope's system, which is contained in the statement, 'all is good'....If I could thus believe that he who conceived of the Academy's competition has, in the words 'all is good', absolutely demanded" that there was systematic thought in Pope, then the Academy's idea of a "system" of thought would have to be investigated. Then, both Pope and Leibniz are examined, with wit and precision. The conclusion posed: "What can one now say to such an obvious proof [just completed] that Pope has borrowed, altogether more than thought of, the metaphysical part of his material." The echo of Maupertuis' borrowing from the least-action concept of Leibniz could not have been missed.

And with a tug of the beard of the Academy, they end the contest. They quote Pope himself, in a letter to Jonathan Swift, on his own status as a philosopher: "I have only one piece of mercy to beg of you; do not laugh at my gravity, but permit to me, to wear the beard of a Philosopher till I pull it off and make a jest of it myself." The pamphlet ends: "How much should he marvel, if he could know of it, that nevertheless a famous Academy has recognized this false beard as the real thing, and put underway the most grave investigation of it."

The *Philosophical Dialogues*

During 1754, while the two worked together on the prize contest essay, Lessing had loaned Mendelssohn a philosophical work by Shaftesbury, written in dialogue form. According to Mendelssohn's son, Joseph, his father told Lessing that he enjoyed the work, but that he himself could write such a work—and Lessing promptly challenged him to do so. Mendelssohn wrote four short dialogues, and Lessing took it upon himself, supposedly without his friend's knowledge, to have them printed in February, 1755, as the *Philosophical Dialogues*. Six years earlier, Lessing's play had modeled the character of a cultured Jew upon Mendelssohn's friend, Gumpertz. Now, Lessing had publicly presented in real life the actual character. Ironically, the influential critic, J. D. Michaelis, who had previously criticized Lessing's *The Jew* for the presentation of such an unlikely and unrealistic character, now wrote that the unknown author of the *Philosophical Dialogues* was so "pleasant" and "sharp-witted" that it was likely written by Lessing. How could Michaelis have imagined that the unlikely and unrealistic character actually existed, and had written the work in question? Both Mendelssohn and Lessing surely must have enjoyed this unintended tugging of the beard.[15]

The opening of the first of Mendelssohn's four dialogues[16] gently mocks Maupertuis. Philopon asks Neophil whether he really means that Leibniz actually had borrowed his conception of the "pre-established" harmony (of soul and body) from another. The theme begs the comparison with the controversy over Maupertuis' borrowing of the Leibnizian concept of "least action," but Mendelssohn takes the dialogue in the direction that Maupertuis could not in real life. In bringing up that Spinoza had come to a similar position prior to Leibniz, Mendelssohn imitates König's contention that Leibniz had developed least action before Maupertuis. However, Mendelssohn develops the dialogue so that the reader's estimation of Leibniz grows in the process of setting the record straight for Spinoza. Mendelssohn is perfectly happy to recast the Maupertuis-Leibniz controversy into a Leibniz-Spinoza controversy, mirroring Maupertuis in the best possible light—as the supposedly new, improved Leibniz. For those who are prepared to entertain the fiction that Maupertuis had surpassed Leibniz, they see a Leibniz in the dialogue take a course that Maupertuis should have, were he actually on the level of Leibniz. Mendelssohn, at twenty-five, was a genius at creating such happy solutions, a master at getting difficult medicine down the victim's throat without it tasting bitter. Lessing must have been struck at just this quality in his friend. We shall see that, years later, his character "Nathan"—modeled upon Mendelssohn—would apply a similar genius in relating the story of "the three rings".

Near the end of the dialogue, Philopon considers the marvelous curiosity: "How wonderful is the makeup of the human intellect! Through erroneous and bizarre principles Spinoza almost stumbles precisely into the view to which Leibniz was led by the soundest and most correct concepts of God and the world." Mendelssohn's readers would break out in smiles in turning around in their minds the multiplicity of truths captured in those two sentences. First, the implied analogy—of Leibniz stumbling around and Maupertuis being the thinker with "the soundest and most correct concepts"—is a hilarious suggestion. But even if, contrariwise, Maupertuis' "erroneous and bizarre principles" caused him to "stumble" into Leibniz's position, then, fine—let Maupertuis' attempt to capture the Leibniz position be taken as one more voice in the revival of Leibniz! Finally, more generally, that whichever analogy is the correct view, it would have to include a world where truth was both universal and also peculiar to "the makeup" of each, unique human intellect. The historical fact that the progress of thinking was social, that there was dependence on other thinkers and progress beyond other thinkers, was itself one more expression of the world-view of Leibniz and Mendelssohn, and not of Maupertuis.

However, the *Philosophical Dialogues* project, a decade before the *Phädon*, also reflected another underlying, abiding concern of both Mendelssohn and Lessing—to transform the German language, the culture, and the population by bridging the gap between profound ideas and impassioned sensibilities. Lessing's announcement of the *Philosophical Dialogues* declaimed against the decay of metaphysics in Germany, due to the inability to convey profound ideas to a wider population without inducing sleep. He wrote: "We, therefore, present to our metaphysical authors these 'Dialogues' as a model and, at the same time, as proof of the possibility of treating subjects of this kind in a graceful, ingenious, and attractive manner." Mendelssohn would carry this approach forward in his great dialogue, the *Phädon*.

The Essay, *On Sentiments*

A few months later, Mendelssohn's essay *On Sentiments* was published. The opening sentence explicitly refers to Shaftesbury's 1709 dialogue, *The Moralists, or a Philosophical Rhapsody*. Mendelssohn has Shaftesbury's character, the English philosopher Theocles, move to 1754 Germany in search of "rigor and fundamentals." There he studied "the immortal writings" of the past century in Germany—an obvious reference to the Leibniz school—but was "more than a little astonished...by the specious and careless manner of our present philosophers...[at] all the gatherings of learned societies...."[17] In a not-so-veiled reference to the current situation at the Berlin Academy, Mendelssohn has Theocles, in a letter to his English friends, relate that "his hopes were betrayed and that even in Germany the philosophical dilettante had gotten the upper hand." Mendelssohn proceeds to treat the interplay of reason and true pleasure in the German language (then little-used for such considerations) in an opening salvo of the war to bring the larger population into the culture.

Mendelssohn's theme in *On Sentiments* was probably taken from the presentations of two like-minded members of the Academy, J. G. Sulzer and Abraham Kästner. Lessing's former professor, Kästner, had authored *Reflexions sur l'origine du plaisir* for his initial contribution to the Berlin Academy—published in the 1749 *Histoire de l'Academie*

Royale. To this, Sulzer responded with his 1751 *Recherches sur l'origine des sentimens agreables et desagreables* in two parts: *Theorie generale du plaisir* and *Theorie des plaisirs intellectuels*.[18] About this time, and by no later than 1755, Mendelssohn became personal friends with Sulzer. Further, Sulzer's next Academy offering, his *Essai sur le bonheur des etres intelligens,* likely was written after Sulzer had read Mendelssohn's *On Sentiments,* for he had Mendelssohn add his critical comments to the work for its (1756) publication. Undoubtedly, Mendelssohn's contribution to this ongoing dialogue of Sulzer and Kästner would have been an essential part of Sulzer's interest in the young man. Amongst the Academy members, Sulzer was probably the one most favorable to Mendelssohn. Much later, in 1771, Sulzer sponsored Mendelssohn for membership to the Academy. However, Frederick the Great never granted the Academy's choice, so Mendelssohn never could accept his position.

Mendelssohn has Theocles write (in the Sixth letter of *On Sentiments*) an allusion to the then-topical ridiculing of Leibniz's conception of the "best of all possible worlds":

> I have never been able to read without astonishment, or rather without a kind of pity, the arrogant declaration of that Frenchman who holds Reaumur's preoccupation with discovering a way to cleanse wallpaper of moths, in higher esteem than Leibniz's efforts to reflect on the system of the best world.

Though Mendelssohn refers to this more obscure attack upon Leibniz,[19] the 1755 audience in Berlin could not have failed to make the connection. Theocles proceeds with an impassioned account as to how Leibniz saved him from

> being completely ruined....Like hellish furies, cruel doubts about providence tortured me; indeed, I can confess, without skittishness, that they were doubts about the existence of God and the blessedness of virtue. At that point I was prepared to give rein to all vile desires....To you, immortal Leibniz! I erect an eternal monument to you in my heart. Without your help I would have been lost forever. I have never made your acquaintance, but in my solitary hours I implored your immortal writings for help, writings which remain to this day unread by the wider world, and it was they which steered me on the sure path to genuine philosophy, to knowledge of my very self and my origin. In my soul your writings have planted the holy truths on which my happiness is based. (Altmann finds in these passages an autobiographical

reflection of Mendelssohn's own intellectual pathway between 1746 and 1754.)

Mendelssohn, by 1755, had forged his adult personality and his mission in life, having taken a measure of the weak points of, and danger to, his society, and having summoned his powers to make himself critically useful to taking the world toward a happier pathway. No little work lay ahead, work that Mendelssohn would accomplish before and after his daily employment in helping to manage a silk factory. His collaboration with Lessing would largely proceed through correspondence, as Lessing had moved from Berlin in October, 1755. Several months later, Mendelssohn would remember: "I enter the garden in which I rarely sought you in vain....[I] remember the night that overtook us when, there in the pavilion, we had become oblivious of all else. Then I call to mind the death of Socrates, which we discussed at that time."[20]

Nicolai and the Aesthetic Education of Germany

By the beginning of 1755, Lessing had introduced Mendelssohn to Friedrich Nicolai, the future publisher of the *Phädon*. (Lessing had known Nicolai from no later than their joint membership in the "Monday Club" of twenty-four intellectuals, including Sulzer.) Mendelssohn's friendship with Nicolai flourished, especially after Lessing left Berlin. The two read and discussed poetry in the same garden where Mendelssohn had discussed Socrates with Lessing, for Nicolai had taken over Lessing's abode at Spandauer Strasse 68. The correspondence amongst the three at this time became famous for their deliberations over tragedy, and over the need to overthrow Aristotle's "cathartic" view of tragedy (whereby the emotions are purged).[21] Mendelssohn focused upon the treatment of Laocoön in the marble sculpture, and its capacity to go beyond the expression of compassion, and to revere the conquering of the pain. Out of these discussions, and Mendelssohn's 1757 *Reflections on the Sources and Connections of Belles-lettres and the Arts*, was prompted Lessing's seminal work, *Laocoön*. From the discussions of 1756 also was born the new literary journal launched in May 1757, and called the *Bibliothek der schönen Wissenschaften und der freyen Künste*. Within two years, Mendelssohn would write at least twenty-one articles for the *Bibliothek*, with a mastery of the poetic sensibilities of German, French, and English.

From 1756 to 1759, Mendelssohn exercised his capacities for writing poetry, learned counterpoint on the piano, and became highly accomplished at his literary critiques. It was Lessing who encouraged his German poetry, while the piano lessons were with J. S. Bach's student, Johann Philipp Kirnberger. The latter served as the court musician for the King's sister, Princess Amalia, and also headed up her music library, where resided, of some significance, the "Musical Offering" manuscript that Bach had presented as a grand puzzle to the King in 1747.[22] Kirnberger later published one of the first sets of solutions for the canons, and it was unlikely that Kirnberger would have failed to bring up this subject with such an adult student of Mendelssohn's intellectual capabilities. Otherwise, Kirnberger was a fanatic for a contrapuntal approach to compositions, and Mendelssohn would certainly have appreciated the rich possibilities of treating voices in dialogue.

Another foreshadowing of Mendelssohn's *Phädon* project was his overlooked, though historic, approach to the possible unity of Jews and Christians in a Prussian polity, centered around the celebration of the miraculous victory at Leuthen. Starting in 1756, Prussia found itself at war against Austria, Saxony, and Russia. Frederick the Great was arrayed against land armies that dwarfed his army, and Berlin was more than a little agitated in the consistent losses of the first two years of battle. At Leuthen, on December 5, 1757, Frederick boldly improvised a novel "double-flanking" action, against an Austrian force attacking according to all the then best-known rules. Berlin rejoiced over the miraculous victory. Mendelssohn composed a special sermon (in Hebrew) that was delivered on December 10, 1757 by the Chief Rabbi, David Fränkel. Mendelssohn then translated his sermon into German, and the text was distributed to the Christian community. Altmann characterized it as "the earliest known specimen of modern Jewish preaching in the German tongue."[23]

Importantly, Mendelssohn deemed it as critical that the population not stand in awe of a simple miracle, but rather think through how the Leuthen miracle occurred. His Leibnizian-flavored argument maintained that men had the responsibility of applying themselves completely to their God-given talents, as God had not dispensed such gifts so that men could simply wait around for miracles. "It is the declared will of our creator, that we should exert that strength and capacity which He has bestowed on us. If ever God alters the course of nature, it is for very great and exalted ends. It is a saying of our rabbis,

'He does as few miracles as possible.'" God acts through "the powers which he has implanted in nature...unless moved by some more sublime and transcendent view....We are to be doing, and make the best use possible of the talents with which he has furnished us."

As Leibniz had put it, God did not produce miracles to fill a gap in the created capacities of man. His miracles were acts of grace, and, as such, more of a celebration of the created world. Leuthen was a miracle of a leader applying himself fully to create new solutions where such had not existed the day before the battle. For Mendelssohn, Jews and Christians did not have to simply separately fete a happy coincidence for both populations in Berlin. The nature of man that had allowed for the creation of the miraculous victory was precisely the quality that existed in humans, independent of their respective approaches to their God, that could make for a republic. Hence, it was not inappropriate for Mendelssohn to lead the Jewish community into the bold action of publishing their Hebrew sermon in German for circulation to their fellow Berliners. It was a type of unique cultural intervention for Berlin, though it would not be as widely known as the *Phädon*.[24]

In 1759, Lessing thought that Nicolai and Mendelssohn should put a sharper edge on their cultural work, ending the *Bibliothek* to found the *Literaturbriefe*. Lessing and Mendelssohn bore the brunt of the writing in the first two years of the new journal. Mendelssohn's initial offering to Nicolai's *Literaturbriefe* of March 1, 1759, warned that even the transmission of Leibniz's thought as a packaged system (e.g., that of Wolff) was insufficient and dangerous. When science was learned too easily, previously discovered truths would be maintained as prejudice, lacking the power of Leibniz's method of analysis situs. In such a sterile environment, the culture would be at the mercy of the yoked opposites of cold logic and irrational feeling states, battling over the possession of the minds of the population.

The following week, Mendelssohn followed up by revisiting the damage that had been done by the 1755 Academy action against Leibniz. The Academy had awarded their prize to such a patently inferior essay, the *Examen de l'Optimisme* by A. F. von Reinhard, that yet more dishonor was cast upon the Academy. Then, from Zurich in 1757, J. H. Waser and C. M. Wieland launched a counterattack on the Academy's actions that fell below the standard of humor and truth displayed in the Lessing and Mendelssohn treatments of 1754 and 1755. In the March 8, 1759 issue of the new *Literaturbriefe*, Mendelssohn intervened to clarify that such counter-attacks were enmeshed in the same level as the Academy actions, and that such serious issues could not be treated so incompetently. Mendelssohn would compose over one hundred of the articles published in the *Literaturbriefe* over the next six years.

Perhaps his most famous article in the *Literaturbriefe* was his review of King Frederick's poetry, the 1760 *Poesies diverses*. Mendelssohn wrote that it would not befit the king's subject to simply extol the king uncritically. Amongst significant praise for the poems' sensitivity and insight, Mendelssohn lamented the loss to the German language that the king took French as the language upon which to speak and concentrate. A people's king should lift up the culture and language of his population. There was more than a little irony, in that a Jew had mastered and defended the German language more thoroughly than the King of Prussia, who ran the country's affairs in French. But Mendelssohn reserved his main criticism for Frederick's adoption of the position against the immortality of the soul. A king who carried the heaviest burden of all, in the midst of the Seven Years' War, who led troops into battle risking their lives for a higher purpose—how could such a one lead men to their death. This wasn't the genius of Leuthen, but one whose immature poetic impulses had been recaptured by the cynical Voltaire. Mendelssohn considered such a picture as equivalent to a square circle. The paradox of Frederick the Great was of abiding concern to Mendelssohn, and it would become the subject of perhaps the most passionate section of his *Phädon*.

Mendelssohn's review was met with a violent response. Nicolai's *Literaturbriefe* was charged with publishing the attack of a Jew upon Christ, and publishing a review that was insulting to the king. Consequently, on March 18, 1762, the journal was put on the index, and so, banned. The leader of the attack upon Mendelssohn, J. G. H. von Justi, was the same fellow who had commenced his career in 1747 as the selected winner of the prize essay contest against Leibniz's conception of the monad. Now, he was an official of some standing in Frederick's government. That the ban was lifted a few days later is a good indicator of the intensity of the battle around Frederick's cabinet.

The *Phädon* Project

The loudest voice for cynicism (and amoral wit) at that time around Frederick's court came from Voltaire's 1759 attack upon Leibniz, *Can-*

dide. Though Voltaire had fled Frederick's court in 1753, he had re-established contact with Frederick late in 1758. Frederick had fallen into some despair and cynicism after the savagery of the Battle of Zorndorf in August 1758, followed by a major loss at Hochkirch in Saxony, where he lost 30% of his 30,000 men. Voltaire sent Frederick a copy of his *Candide*, only feeding his cynicism. In *Candide*, Leibniz is caricatured as a Dr. Pangloss, an out-of-touch philosopher, who moves from one disaster, horror or degradation to another, always proclaiming that this is the best of all possible worlds.

Years later, Mendelssohn recalled how he and Lessing had discussed the situation:

> I recall that my late friend, soon after *Candide* appeared, had the passing idea of writing a counterpart to it, or rather a continuation of it, in which he meant to show by a sequel of events, that all the evils that had been multiplied by Voltaire at the expense of a defamed Providence, in the end turned out for the best, and were found to be in accord with the most wise designs.[25]

While Lessing never wrote this particular sequel, Mendelssohn turned to the matter of the calamity of the execution of Socrates, and the manner in which Plato had chosen to treat that subject. It is not obvious how the unjust execution of a culture's most noble individual could lead anywhere but into a spiral of doom. Plato's Athens had been wracked with sophistry and cynicism, and the artistic challenge of wrenching a society from tragedy became for Mendelssohn an increasingly central focus.

Mendelssohn had fondly recalled his discussions with Lessing on the death of Socrates in the garden in Berlin, prior to 1756. By mid-1760, he was discussing his *Phädon* project with Lessing, to recast Plato's *Phaedo* dialogue through the eyes (or mind, that is) of a Leibniz, to do for modern European civilization what Plato had accomplished for the Greek world. But, first, he prepared the publication of his 1761 *Philosophical Writings*, centered around his newly edited versions of his 1755 *Philosophical Dialogues* and his essay, *On Sentiments*. His preface suggests that, since he is not allowed, as a Jew, to help serve the state during the war, he is reissuing his philosophical works from the victorious war of ideas of 1755.

His new opening for the third of the four dialogues refers to the 1759 *Candide*:

Numesian: Have you read *Candide*, then?

Kallisthen: The most biting satire on our German doctrine of the best world, who wouldn't read it?

Numesian: The author seems to me to have exposed the weakness of this hypothesis quite successfully. Tell me the truth, as German and metaphysically minded as you are, did you not have to laugh?

Kallisthen: Who can deny a Voltaire laughter?

Mendelssohn's character Kallisthen proceeded to quote Lord Shaftesbury: "[W]hat can bear no raillery is suspicious, and a joke that survives no serious investigation is surely false wit." Kallisthen then proceeds to investigate the joke, and finds Voltaire rather shallow. Then, typical of Mendelssohn, the affair serves as a prelude to a deeper discussion of some real difficulties in Leibniz's "best of all possible worlds" concept, to the benefit of the reader, and to one's appreciation of the depth and power of Leibniz's work.

Between 1762 and 1763, Mendelssohn sketched outlines of Plato's proofs of immortality of the soul, translated Plato's *Phaedo* into German, and composed a version of the first part of his *Phädon*. (It certainly should not be discounted that the March 1762 ban on the *Literaturbriefe*, as a measure of deep problems at the court, might have served to catalyze his determination to compose his *Phädon*.) He began the study of Greek under Rector C. T. Damm in 1759, and early on had began to read both Homer and Plato. Within two years, he had a strong mental image of Plato's multi-voiced (contrapuntal) handling of his dialogues. We see this in his (summer 1761) criticism of Jacob Wegelin's translations, *The Last Dialogues of Socrates and His Friends*: "All participants [of the dialogues] speak in one voice; the characters are without life, their ideas without truth, and the speech they utter is unnatural." Mendelssohn had committed himself publicly as to what a translation of Plato had to achieve.

By July 1763, Mendelssohn had completed the first of the three sections of the *Phädon*, which was offered to Isaac Iselin's new journal. Iselin had founded the Patriotic Society of Bern in 1762. The society probably stemmed from his 1755 work, *Philosophical and Patriotic Dreams of a Friend of Humanity*, which had been favorably reviewed by Mendelssohn at the time. Iselin had invited Mendelssohn to join his new Bern group as a corresponding member and had assured Mendelssohn that his metaphysical bent would be totally appropriate for his patriotic organization. That Mendelssohn then thought his *Phädon* project specifically appropriate for their *Journal for Morality and Legislation* underlines again Mendelssohn's commitment—that deep ideas be brought to bear upon politics and worldly affairs.

His letter to Iselin[26] provides further insight on his project. His paper:

> ...represents an idea that I have cherished for many years, namely to write a *Phädon or Dialogue on the Immortality of the Human Soul* in conformity to Plato's design, but truly and definitely borrowing from him not more than the design, which is magnificent. His reasoning is unconvincing, however, and a modern reader finds nothing but obscurity and sophistry where Socrates' friends found light and conviction. Maybe our times are more difficult to satisfy, as some believe to the case, or—as I hold—we have an incorrect understanding of their metaphysical terminology because the critics and lexicographers have to gather the meaning of the words from the poets and historiographers. I resolved, therefore, to make Plato's arguments more emphatic and convincing by minor modifications, and, moreover, to add such arguments as are supplied by modern philosophy. Their number and weight are by no means small. The first part of this project is finished. It advances the proofs for the incorruptibility of the soul. The proofs concerning immortality are to follow in a second section.

Mendelssohn had made the bold conclusion that the meaning of Plato had been partly lost, due to the derivation of the meaning of Greek words from contexts below the level of thinking of Plato. He submitted the first section of the *Phädon* to Iselin that November, but the society folded before the journal was ever published. The rest of the development of the *Phädon*, from 1764 to 1766, became intertwined with Mendelssohn's collaboration with Thomas Abbt, to whom Mendelssohn refers in his "Preface": "He was the one who encouraged me to begin this work again which had been started and set aside for several years."

Thomas Abbt and Shaftesbury's Dialogues

Abbt came to Mendelssohn's attention when in February 1761, in the midst of agonizing warfare, Nicolai published Abbt's *On Dying for the Country*. Mendelssohn wrote on February 11, 1761, to Lessing: "The essay has pleased me so much that I find it wholly unexpected from a professor of mathematics." Mendelssohn's next letter to Lessing, of February 18, 1761, informs him that "I have written...to Herr Professor Baumgarten in order to inform him of my idea to recast and edit the

Phädon." Mendelssohn's great pleasure over Abbt's essay might have led to his decision to inform the respected Baumgarten, and so further commit himself to his *Phädon* project. If so, the wide, positive reception of Abbt's essay would have been a positive indication to Mendelssohn that the deadly serious issue of the war and of the value of human life could be openly dealt with. (Otherwise, Mendelssohn probably knew that Abbt had studied Baumgarten's works, since Abbt was the protégé of Baumgarten's brother.) Abbt's essay electrified a nerve in Prussia, which was then in the sixth year of a brutal and deadly war. It was likely that Mendelssohn was as pleasantly shocked at a math professor's grasp of the sublime, as he would be unpleasantly shocked at the king's published views on death.

Mendelssohn's first letter to Abbt on March 9, 1761, was on the subject of the sublime, in response to Abbt's *Literaturbriefe* comments upon Mendelssohn's treatment of the sublime. (Though Abbt had lectured on math at the University of Halle between 1758-60, he was now a professor of philosophy at the University of Frankfurt, at the ripe young age of twenty-three.) His response to Mendelssohn on March 12, 1761, on the question of suicide reflected Abbt's study of Mendelssohn's *On Sentiments*, and his remarks would find their way into Mendelssohn's new edition of that work, later in the year.[27] Abbt came to Berlin the next month, April, and stayed until October, using his break from the University to meet with Mendelssohn. Along with Nicolai, the trio decided to translate all of Shaftesbury's works into German. Thus, their collaboration began, not to end until Abbt's premature demise in 1766, not yet twenty-eight years of age.

No later than 1754, when Lessing had given him Shaftesbury to read, Mendelssohn had been interested in Shaftesbury's "republican" approach to putting major ideas in a conversational mode, as if anyone who could read could be invited in to figure out the fundamentals of the world. Altmann points out a significant passage in Shaftesbury's *Sensus Communis: An Essay on the Freedom of Wit and Humor*, that Mendelssohn had come to in his translation work: "[The ancients'] Treatises were generally in a free and familiar Stile. They chose to give us the Representation of real Discourse and Converse, by treating their Subjects in the way of Dialogue and free Debate." Altmann, quite properly, connects this passage with Mendelssohn's 1762 response to Abbt, as an insight into Mendelssohn's decision to cease the project of translating Shaftesbury, and to dive more deeply into Plato: "Plato has a manner of writing that combines all the merits of Shaftesbury's style with an inimitable ease of phrasing. His prose, even where it becomes poetic, flows with such tranquil majesty that a non-expert might think the phrase had cost him no effort."

It seems that Mendelssohn had come to the same particular view of dialogue that his hero, Leibniz, expresses through his character Pacidius in the opening to his 1676 *A Dialogue of Motion*:

> When I was with some distinguished men recently, I asserted that the Socratic method of discussion, as expressed in the Platonic dialogues, seemed to me outstanding. For not only are souls imbued with the truth through familiar conversation, but one can even see the order of meditation itself.

Then, the difficulty in accomplishing this is addressed:

> For it is easy to write dialogues, just as it is easy to speak rashly and in no particular order; but to compose a speech in such a way that truth itself might gradually shine out of the darkness, and knowledge might grow spontaneously in the soul, this is really only possible for someone who has himself gone into the reasons very carefully on his own, before taking it on himself to teach others.[28]

This art of organizing a drama of the inner workings of the mind, and to present it as if one had not been digging through the inner workings of the mind, is at the heart of Mendelssohn's art.

The Purpose of Man

From 1764 to 1766, Mendelssohn and Abbt conducted an extensive exploration of the purpose of man, which allowed Mendelssohn to work through ideas for his *Phädon* project. Abbt wrote to Mendelssohn (January 11, 1764), having read J. J. Spaulding's *Determination of Man*, to request Mendelssohn's aid in working through the doubts that Abbt had over Spaulding's too easy solutions. Spaulding's 1748 work had offered a wider reading public a not-so-rigorous version of Leibniz's philosophy. In particular, he had explained that the happiness of others is a pleasure beyond those of the body, or even those of the individual mind; and the fact that God had made us in this fashion shows God to be a virtuous God. (For Spaulding to make such an argument for the insufficiencies of mere pleasure-seeking, or even of mental self-development, in the Berlin of 1748, would have put him into opposition to the "new wave" brought by Maupertuis to the Academy.) When Mendelssohn came to know Spaulding, no later than the mid-1750's, he would have brought to the relationship some respect for Spaulding's earlier public stance. Further, it was likely that Abbt would have known this and could rely upon Mendelssohn to enjoy developing Spaulding's arguments with more rigor.

Spaulding had found great comfort that God had, amazingly but certainly, placed in man the propensity for the welfare of others. The initial thoughts of both Abbt and Mendelssohn were published by Spring of 1764 as [Abbt's] *Doubts* and [Mendelssohn's] *Oracle Concerning the Determination of Man*. Their correspondence on the subject, however, continued for three years, and it served as a major touchstone for Mendelssohn. In his February 1765 letter to Abbt, he writes:

> I meant to continue our correspondence on the vocation [determination] of man. Since I am writing, however, a little work on the immortality of the soul....I mean to fill the second part of it with reflections on our vocation. Hence I want to give myself time to think about it thoroughly. Do continue, dearest friend, to put forward objections and to raise doubts.

Abbt gave voice to existentialist fears, and concerns for how much of humanity was so far from being such a mirror for God. Mendelssohn explained that, as vast as the amount of evil and as extensive the immaturity of the human race, so much also does God allow diversity as part of the larger and greater enrichment of creation. Even a savage forming a concept of a tree is developing a part of God's creation. Certainly, men may not know all the workings and ways of God, and certainly bad things can and do happen, but every human is created with the capacity and the purpose of mirroring the Creator in its development.

In the midst of these deliberations, Mendelssohn's first child, the eleven-month old Sara, died—an event that Mendelssohn would carry with him the rest of his life, even after six other children survived. Two weeks after her death, he wrote on May 1, 1764, to Abbt:

> My friend, the innocent child did not live in vain....Her mind made astonishing progress in that short period. From a little animal that cried and slept, she developed into a budding intelligent creature. One could see the blossoming of the passions like the sprouting of young grass when it pierces the hard crust of the earth in spring. She showed pity, hatred, love, admiration. She understood the language of those talking to her, and tried to make her own thoughts known to others.

Part of Sara's life became entwined in her father's capacity to hold those interchanges in his heart and soul, and so live a larger life. Why it should be that way, Mendelssohn did not claim to know. But whether it were Sara or Socrates, a man owed it to his Creator and to himself to tackle the tasks of life, both easier and harder ones, and fulfill his maximum development allowed by his Creator.

Abbt himself did not live to read Mendelssohn's *Phädon*. On July 22, 1766, Mendelssohn wrote Abbt: "Your questions encouraged me to complete a treatise on the immortality of the soul that I started many years ago. I put my arguments into the mouth of Socrates. Perhaps I run the risk of turning my Socrates into a Leibnizian." In response, Abbt's last letter to his friend, weeks before his own death, was more than poignant: "The count is looking forward to your treatise on the immortality of the soul with burning desire. I too, as you can easily imagine. We are all too deeply interested in this subject."

Abbt had become a councillor to the court of Count Wilhelm of Schaumburg-Lippe at Bückeborg in 1765. It was a small but significant court that would come to play a larger role in Mendelssohn's life. The Count himself represented several generations of proponents of Leibniz.[29] Wilhelm had gained fame as a ballistics officer during the Seven Years War. His small but influential court included J. S. Bach's youngest son, J. C. F. Bach, and the poet, J. G. Herder. Abbt described the deliberations with the Count to Mendelssohn: "My lord has since re-read the *Philosophical Letters*. They pleased him very much, and for six days we talked about Herr Moses." Among other matters, Abbt's premature demise aborted Mendelssohn's plan to leave Berlin and join Abbt in Count Wilhelm's court.[30]

The Reception of the *Phädon*

Phädon oder über die Unsterblichkeit der Seele in drey Gesprächen (Phädon or On the Immortality of the Soul, in Three Dialogues) was published by Nicolai, and was presented at the Leipzig book fair in May 1767. The response was even more electric than Nicolai's earlier success, between 1762 and 1765, in bringing out the first German-language collected volumes of Shakespeare. German readers were responding hungrily to the enrichment of their language with powerful, deep, and complex ideas. The first edition of the *Phädon* was sold out by September. Nicolai would bring out three more editions, those of 1768, 1769, and 1776. During Mendelssohn's lifetime, other publishers would reprint the work eight more times in German, in addition to six published translations. (Mendelssohn is on record with complaints regarding the quality of the Dutch translation of 1769, the French translation of G. A. Junker in 1772, and the Italian translation of 1773. Another French translation of 1772 by Abel Burja, along with Danish and Russian translations in 1779, complete the list. The only previous English translation, that of Charles Cullen, appeared in 1789, three years after Mendelssohn's death.)

A few examples of known responses to the *Phädon* give an indication of the variety and depth. Raphael Levi wrote from Hanover, now eighty-two and re-energized. As a young man, he had lived in Leibniz's household for six years as student and secretary. (The knowledge of the location of Leibniz's grave was due to Levi, as almost everyone else had bowed to political pressure and stayed away from the funeral.[31]) For many years, he taught mathematics and astronomy. Now, in 1767, he was, it appears,[32] surprised that Mendelssohn would attempt to make Leibniz's complex ideas more generally known to a broader audience. Levi also offered to try to replace the departed Abbt in the interrupted correspondence on Spaulding and the purpose of man. Mendelssohn respectfully explained to Levi that, regardless of his conversational tone in the dialogue, he still had required the content to hold to the strict standards of Leibniz's metaphysics. He added that they were both too Leibnizian to differ enough, so as to warrant such a suggested theme of correspondence. However, he made sure to visit Levi in Hanover on both of the occasions that he went to visit Lessing nearby.

Mendelssohn referred again to the Leibnizian core of his *Phädon* in his April 7, 1769 response to the nobleman H. D. von Platen and his questions on the soul. Mendelssohn explained that Leibniz's concept of the monad was the key to understanding the soul and the universe. "I consider these ideas to be both true and great....This philosophy seemed to me, however, too sublime for the purposes I had to pursue in the *Phädon*; there I had to be content merely to touch its hem, as it were."

Many took up the challenge of sorting out where Mendelssohn had diverted from Plato's *Phaedo*, and to what effect. Christian Garve's early review in Nicolai's *Neue Bibliothek der schönen Wissenschaften und der freyen Künste* went into some detail on this. Garve had just graduated that year from the University of Leipzig, a center of Leibniz's influence. Mendelssohn thought Garve's review to be very well thought-out. He explicitly responded to the portion on the law of continuity, in the "Appendix" to the third edition. Goethe, at age twenty-one, was fascinated with this subject, as evidenced by eight pages of his 1770 diary.[33]

Others took umbrage at Mendelssohn's hybrid composition that was neither Plato nor completely new. Mendelssohn had previously addressed this topic in his "Preface" as follows:

> In the third dialogue I had to take my refuge completely in the moderns, and allow my Socrates almost to speak like a philosopher from the eighteenth century. I would rather commit an anachronism, than leave out arguments which can contribute something to convince the reader. In such a way the following mean between a translation and my own composition arose.

His concern for the state of affairs with his king and his culture was deep enough that he perhaps diverted from tradition and dared to fashion a new form. It guided his prolonged deliberations in fashioning his *Phädon*.

Vienna's *Phädon* Circles

Fanny Itzig Arnstein, one of the daughters of Daniel Itzig, took copies of the *Phädon* with her to Vienna. (Earlier, she and the other Itzig children had been on visits to the Mendelssohns' home.) In 1781, she gave a copy to the only lodger in her large Jewish home, a Christian named Wolfgang Amadeus Mozart,[34] who was then in the process of composing his "ecumenical" opera, *The Abduction from the Seraglio*. Mendelssohn's use of Socrates, a so-called pagan, to convey universal truths about the immortality of the soul found a willing ear in Mozart. His use of the Turkish pasha to convey the most "Christian" message of the opera (that of the transforming quality of dispensation, instead of the vicious cycle of revenge) is the same type of compositional choice as Mendelssohn's, as it has the power to uniquely get across the idea to his audience. (Of course, Mozart's opera drew even more heavily from Mendelssohn's friend, Lessing—specifically, his play modeled upon Mendelssohn, *Nathan the Wise*.)

In 1785, the *Phädon* was published in Vienna by Joseph Grossinger,[35] and was reprinted twice more that year. Grossinger's work sheds some light both on the discussions in Berlin with Mendelssohn, and on the interest in Vienna in the remarkable decade of Emperor Joseph II and Mozart, the 1780s. In the "Preface," Grossinger related that Mendelssohn had approved of the Latin translation, called *De Immaterialitate Animae*, which Grossinger had produced the previous year (1784). It represented some of Mendelssohn's post-*Phädon* discussions on the soul. Altmann determined that Grossinger's text had been prepared by Mendelssohn for the sister of Frederick the Great, Luise Ulrike, the widowed queen of Sweden.[36] Mendelssohn had prepared the text subsequent to a prolonged discussion with Luise Ulrike in early January 1772. He evidently valued this addendum, as, in 1774, he provided a copy of the same manuscript for the patrons of his dear departed friend, Abbt—Wilhelm and Marie Eleonora, the Count and Countess of Schaumburg-Lippe.

When Grossinger published the three parts of the *Phädon* in 1785, he also added a new section from Mendelssohn, written no earlier than 1769. After the *Phädon*, Mendelssohn had tackled the writings of Jean d'Alembert, writings that stood in contrast to the view of the soul that Mendelssohn had presented.[37] Mendelssohn knew that d'Alembert, a close collaborator of Maupertuis in the 1746-1747 attacks against Leibniz, had a continuing hold upon Prussia's king, Frederick. In this new, fourth section, Mendelssohn takes issue with d'Alembert's treatment of the workings of God, tracing it to an inherited flaw from John Locke. (Mendelssohn well knew that d'Alembert, Maupertuis and Voltaire all shared a certain Lockean epistemology—one that he rarely avoided taking on.) Locke would have the defect of unthinking matter be remedied by the omnipotence of God. However, Mendelssohn subscribed to Leibniz's view that God does not work in such a fashion so as to make up for the deficiencies in His creation. Perhaps one should enrich one's understanding of substance, rather than starting from dead matter and then trying to infuse it with miracles. Mendelssohn composed a mini-dialogue that revolved around the idea that, as Altmann puts it, "even God could not transform a rosebush into a lemon tree."[38]

Socrates, and One Nation Under God

Within a few weeks of the initial publication of the *Phädon*, the first known objection was sent to Mendelssohn from Duke Ludwig Eugen of Württemburg.[39] Mendelssohn's biography of Socrates included a reference to Socrates' following of the laws of the Creator, "whom he knew in the most vivid manner by the purest light of reason." Mendelssohn had selected the "pagan" Socrates, because he wanted to pose how a human being was virtuous and moral without necessarily being Jewish or Christian. Mendelssohn recognized in Plato the obligation of man to read the starry handiwork from the hand of the Composer of the universe, with the light of the sun being the closest image of the workings of reason. The phrase "purest light of reason" was an exciting way of conveying a Platonic image.

However, the Duke took objection to this approach. His opening objection was that the phrase "purest light of reason" suggests that a human was capable of knowing God supremely.[40] Mendelssohn had no problem in modifying the phrase to "the pure light of reason"—which correction was made, beginning with the second edition. However, in his July 17, 1767 letter to Ludwig Eugen, he chose to address the underlying issue: "I am not disinclined to attribute to the light of reason the capacity of leading man to true virtue....The motivations of reason seem to me entirely sufficient for promoting a steady progression in the love of the good and noble." Ludwig Eugen evidently did not wish to address Mendelssohn's main point, as he simply returned to a general formulation that commended mixing reason with Holy Scripture.

Mendelssohn had chosen the character of Socrates so as to put a powerful question on the table for his society. Without undercutting the truths of the religions of "the book" (that is, Judaism, Christianity and Islam), could the culture rise to a higher level in viewing their God, and in their obligations to their God? In a very short time, the new American republic of the United States would take up this question, of a secular government under God. Just as today, then also there were many who would hear "secular" as "godless materialism," or "under God" as "authoritarian control" —Mendelssohn would be attacked from both sides by those who would not take up the challenge to think through his *Phädon* challenge. In one case, in a similar situation after the 1783 publication of his *Jerusalem*, he was attacked on one side as "a circumcised fellow-believer in the spirit and essence of pagan, naturalistic, atheistic fanaticism" while, on the other side, for allowing his Jewish fanaticism and intolerance to attack atheism. Mendelssohn described the situation as being "in the position of a husband whose wife accused him of impotence and whose maid charged him with having made her pregnant."[41]

The *Phädon*—Theme and Variations

So much for the reception of the *Phädon*. A brief sketch of the remaining major events of Mendelssohn's life suggests that the *Phädon* project did, indeed, play a pivotal role, both for him and for his society. First, he survived the somewhat ugly treatment called the "Lavater affair." In 1769, an enthusiastic theologian, J. C. Lavater, called for Mendelssohn to become a Christian or to refute the arguments for Christianity that were put forward in Lavater's translation of Bonnet's *Contemplation of Nature*. Over two decades, Lavater would alternately bait him and then be overly profuse in his apologies to him. (His first apology included his explanation that he had raised conversion as the proper sequel to the *Phädon*, as he wished to impress the authorities at his Zurich theological school.) Mendelssohn had to deal with the immature mentality of such *schwärmer* outbreaks, but it evidently did tax him severely. He suffered some sort of physical breakdown in 1771, involving temporary paralysis and violent pains along his spine. He would struggle for years to regain the capacity for sustained mental concentration that he had always previously enjoyed.

In the mid-1770s, Mendelssohn launched a sustained effort to translate the Hebrew Torah into German. Characteristically, his idea was that Jews should not sneak into German culture by means of some sort of polyglot mode of communication. Rather, there was great, though overlooked, beauty and culture in the Hebrew Bible; and the problem of so many years in the depressed life of European ghettos had driven Jews below their own culture. The best ideas of both cultures could enrich each other. In both Prussia and Austria, Mendelssohn and his collaborators organized for a Renaissance in Jewish life.[42] When Joseph II of Austria announced his citizenship reforms of 1781, Jews could be citizens and they could run their own Hebrew schools, as long as the schools met certain national standards, including the teaching of German. Mendelssohn's translation team would be at the center of such educational efforts.

Nathan the Wise

Perhaps the happiest outgrowth of the *Phädon* project was Lessing's play modeled upon Mendelssohn, *Nathan the Wise*. During the 1770s, Lessing's position near Hanover for the Duke of Braunschweig featured the supervision of the Bibliotheca Augusta in Wolfenbuettel, where he had access to many of the unpublished writings of Leibniz. Lessing came under increased attack from the religious fundamentalists, and he had met them in battle with a sharpened pen. However, Mendelssohn's visit with Lessing in December 1777—which involved discussions, e.g., on the American Revolution, on whether Freemasonry was a help or a hindrance, and undoubtedly on their cultural strategy—might have consolidated a *Phädon*-based approach in Lessing, turning him toward a higher form of battle. By August 1778, Lessing had discovered the key to his new composition that further developed the issues brought to the fore since the *Phädon*.

At a critical point in *Nathan the Wise*, the Islamic ruler, with pressure from the Christian warrior, asks Nathan, the Jew, to say which of the religions is best. A parable is offered, that of the three rings: A ring, with the special power to make one beloved of man and God, has been passed down through generations, from father to son. There came a time when a father so loved all three of his sons, that he could not decide among them, and had more rings made. When he died, all three sons thought they had the real ring, and they set to quarreling, and finally brought the case to a judge. Nothing could be distinguished amongst the three rings. Lessing alters the resolution at this point. He has the judge observe that, since the brothers are quarreling, none are actually "beloved by man and God." Hence, none could have the real ring. Instead, the only way to make a claim for one's religion would be:

> To prove the virtues of his ring by kindness,
>
> By cordial understanding, charitable acts,
>
> Accepting God's decrees in perfect love.

Lessing's judge continues:

And when in days to come the magic powers

Of these fair rings among your children's children

Brighten the world, I call you once again,

After a thousand thousand years are lapsed,

Before this seat of judgment. On that day

A wiser man shall sit on it and speak.[43]

It was precisely a "Mendelssohnian" sort of Socrates that could gain so much from recognizing what it is that we don't know. Perhaps the human race does not yet know why it is that cultures have the divisions that yet exist. But it also does not know, nor yet experienced, the transformed riches, "After a thousand thousand years are lapsed," of the solutions to these present fissures. However, in fact, the human race was just then, and over the next decade, witnessing the birth of a grand experiment of a secular nation under God. It would even reverberate in the 1780s throughout Europe, including in Mendelssohn's Berlin, in Sonnenfels' Vienna, and the Paris of Benjamin Franklin and LaFayette.

Lessing came under more sustained attacks, and after his death, it would fall to Mendelssohn to assume the burden of the response. Ironically, in Vienna, where the Emperor Joseph II attended Countess Thun's salon (described as a meeting of those who aspired to become "Nathans"), Lessing was even accused of writing the propaganda at the hire of Jews. Amongst his rather pungent retorts to these types of attacks, was the following:

> Should one say: this play teaches...there have been people among diverse nations who disregarded all revealed religion and were good people nevertheless; should one add that it had obviously been my intention to present people of this kind as less repulsive than vulgar Christians generally consider them: I shall have little to object.[44]

But Lessing did not live to see the fruits of his work. Throughout 1780, he was increasingly isolated, and in what would be his last letter on December 19, 1780, to his lifelong friend, he wrote Mendelssohn: "[T]he coldness, with which the world is in the habit of demonstrating to certain people that nothing they do is right, has...a stupefying effect....Alas, dear friend, the scene is finished." He died eight weeks later, barely fifty-two, never witnessing the tremendous victories of the next six to twelve months. Mendelssohn wrote to Lessing's brother, Karl: "I render thanks to Providence for the blessing it conferred upon me by introducing me so early in life...to a man who formed my soul."[45] Mendelssohn did not have to understand all the ways of Providence to be able to recognize this blessing.

Four years later, Mendelssohn still pondered the scene:

> The words used by my unforgettable friend in the last letter still pierce my soul. For as long as I knew him [prior to this last letter]...Lessing had never complained of his contemporaries' ingratitude, of not being treated justly....At all times he was the friend who offered, but did not seek, comfort.[46]

In his 1785 *Morning Studies*, Mendelssohn summarized:

> How dearly our immortal friend had to pay for this magnificent poem in praise of Providence! Alas, it embittered his last days, and it may well be the case that it shortened his precious life. [...I]ntrigue penetrated from studies and bookstores into the private homes of his friends and acquaintances and whispered into everyone's ear that Lessing had insulted Christianity....In reality, his *Nathan*, let us admit it, redounds to the honor of Christendom. The degree of enlightenment and education attained by a people must be high indeed if one of its members can soar to such sublimity of sentiment.

The American Revolution and the Idea of Citizenship

Throughout 1781, in America, France, Prussia, and Austria, a new world was being fashioned—a world Lessing didn't live to see. France had committed to a naval force adequate to entrap the British. Mendelssohn organized Christian W. Dohm, a Prussian ministerial councilor, to write a policy for extending civil rights to Jews. Dohm's *Über die bürgerliche Verbesserung der Juden* (On the Civil Improvement of the Jews) was published in Berlin, in the autumn of 1781. In Vienna, Joseph II organized reforms for Jews and issued the Patent of Tolerance on October 19, 1781. That same day, the world turned upside down on the British, with the surrender of Cornwallis at Yorktown! The reforms imposed national standards of schooling for children, including "better instruction and enlightenment of its youth and its employment in the sciences, arts, and crafts." In Catholic Austria, the "Jewish" reforms were universal, meaning that Protestants also benefited. From Berlin, Dohm observed that Austria's Joseph II believed that "the only means toward [Jews'] gradual improvement consisted in offering [them] the enjoyment of the rights of citizens on condition that the duties of citizens be fulfilled."

In the spring of 1782, with the changed strategic reality after Yorktown, Mendelssohn's "Preface" to the re-publication of *Vindiciae Judaeorum*—published as a supplement to Dohm's treatise—proclaimed: "Thanks be rendered to a kind Providence for having allowed me to reach, at the end of my days, this happy season in which a beginning has been made to consider human rights from a truly universal aspect." Lessing's play, Dohm's treatise, and the Emperor's Edict of Tolerance were not just for Jews, but in addressing the most backward feature of the society at the time, a "least action" political pathway was being fashioned for all men. The Prussian high chancellor chose E. F. Klein (a relative of the previously-cited *Phädon*-advocate, Christian Garve) to work with Mendelssohn on implementing the reforms in Prussia. These Mendelssohn-Klein proposals were before King Frederick II within weeks.

Mendelssohn's next major work, the 1783 *Jerusalem or on Religious Power and Judaism*, was the result of a desperate attack upon the reforms in Vienna and Berlin. First, in the summer of 1782, the actual author of the Edict of Toleration, J. V. Gunther, was arrested, along with the sister-in-law of Fanny Arnstein (the Itzig daughter who had distributed the *Phädon* in Vienna). They were both charged with being "Prussian spies." Then, with Mendelssohn having cause to suspect what was going wrong in Vienna, he received a copy of *"The Searching for Light and Right in a Letter to Herr Moses Mendelssohn occasioned by his remarkable Preface to Manasseh Ben Israel,"* signed by "Your most sincere admirer S***—Vienna." The pamphlet was designed to induce Mendelssohn to believe that his ally, Joseph Sonnenfels, a key policy advisor to Joseph II, had become the new Lavater and had authored a new challenge for him to convert.[47]

Sonnenfels was the grandson of Michel Hasid, the Chief Rabbi of Berlin, who had taught Mendelssohn's teacher, David Fränkel. Hence, though they both had, in a sense, the same grandfather, Sonnenfels had converted and had become a key minister and advisor to Joseph II. That summer, Mendelssohn had sent his collaborator from the Pentateuch-translation project, Herz Homberg, to see Sonnenfels regarding implementing the educational reforms in Austria. This collaboration was targeted by this strange pamphlet, *"The Searching..."*, actually written not by Sonnefels, but by a hired writer named Cranz. It was modeled on the "Lavater affair" but now specifically crafted to make Mendelssohn think that the Emperor's ulterior design was really to convert the Jews. It read:

> [A] great revolution has started for your nation's benefit....You rejoice that at the end of your days you have reached a time when some of the Christians who rule over your nation have begun to become human beings and to recognize the Jews as human beings....You rejoice in the happy revolution in the imperial [Austro-Hungarian] states in which the orphaned children of Israel have found a father in the enterprising Joseph, who accords to them too a portion and an inheritance in his country by placing them on the same level of humanity with the rest of his subjects....One more step and you have become one of us.

It went on to suggest that since reason is prevailing, reason also would have you break with that unreasonable religion, which only commands adherents because the rabbinic law compels such.

Jerusalem was Mendelssohn's response. Mendelssohn's heart-felt, concluding paragraph was written with an eye upon America's 1783 deliberations,[48] as well as upon the reverberations in Europe:

> Brothers, if you care for true piety, let us not feign agreement where diversity is evidently the plan and purpose of Providence....Rulers of the Earth! If it be permitted to an insignificant fellow inhabitant thereof to lift up his voice to you: do not trust the counselors who wish to mislead you by smooth words to so harmful an undertaking. They are either blind themselves, and do not see the enemy of mankind lurking in ambush, or they seek to blind you. Our noblest treasure, the liberty to think, will be forfeited if you listen to them. For the sake of your felicity and ours...do not use your powerful authority to transform some eternal truth, without which civil felicity can exist, into a law, some religious opinion...into an ordinance of the land! Pay heed to the right conduct of men; upon this bring to bear the tribunal of wise laws, and leave us thought and speech which the Father of us all assigned to us as an inalienable heritage and granted to us as an immutable right....Reward and punish no doctrine, tempt and bribe no one to adopt any religious opinion! Let everyone be permitted to speak as he thinks, to invoke God after his own manner....If we render unto Caesar what is Caesar's, then do you yourselves render unto God what is God's! Love truth! Love peace![49]

The Body Dies—Mendelssohn Lives

In 1785, Mendelssohn's *Morning Studies*, a passionate development of Leibniz's ideas, reflected his morning studies with his son, Joseph, and his friends—including the Humboldt brothers, Alexander and Wilhelm. In late 1785, he summoned his strength to compose his long-awaited defense of Lessing, against the over-heated charges of pantheism. The "enthusiast" (or *schwärmer*), F. H. Jacobi, had claimed that Lessing had admitted being a pantheistic Spinozan before he died. Mendelssohn compared this to the silly Academy contest of 1755 that he and Lessing had worked so successfully against. "For the time being, I persist in my astonishment and exclaim: 'Lessing a decided Spinozist!', just as Lessing and I once exclaimed: 'Pope a Metaphysician!'"[50] When he completed his defense, entitled *To Lessing's Friends,* around the New Year, 1786, he personally delivered the text to the printer. His friend, Dr. Herz, related Mendelssohn's words to him:

> "I caught a cold on Saturday...when I took my treatise about the Jacobi affair to [the publisher] Voss. I am glad to have gotten this annoying matter off my mind." He uttered the last sentence with a disgust and ill-humor that were out of character and cut me to the heart. In fact, throughout his life nothing seems to have caused him so much emotional upset...as this matter about his Lessing....There he lay without any prior death-rattle, without convulsion, with his usual friendliness on his lips as if an angel had taken him with a kiss from the earth.[51]

As Mendelssohn's Plato had written of Socrates in Phaedo: "This was the end of our friend, O Echecrates! a man, who among all men we knew, indisputably was the most honest, wise, and just."

Dear reader—You have in your hands a translation of the work that made the person and thought of Moses Mendelssohn into a "beacon of hope and temple of liberty"—a decade before the American Revolution. You have, in a sense, a reflection of the soul of Moses Mendelssohn—which lives over and over again. Please enjoy proving that for yourself.

One

Phädon, or on the
Immortality of the Soul

By

Moses Mendelssohn

Preface to the Third Edition of the *Phädon*

The following dialogues of Socrates with his friends about the immortality of the soul will be dedicated to my friend Abbt.[52] He was the one who had encouraged me to take up this work again which had been started and set aside for several years. While he was still Professor at Rinteln, he revealed his thoughts about Spalding's **Determination of Man**[53] to me in one of his cordial letters. The little essays, which are found in the nineteenth part of the **Letters on Literature**, under the title: **Doubts** and **Oracle Concerning the Determination of Man,**[54] originated from our exchange of letters about this material. I had the fortune to obtain the approval of my friend about some of the most important points, even if I could not satisfy him on every one. With the open-heartedness of a true friend, he poured the most secret feelings of his soul, his entire heart, into my breast. His philosophical considerations received a particular bent through the gentle feelings of a good heart, by means of which they would have kindled the love of truth in the coldest breast. Even his doubts would never fail to discover new vistas, and to put the truth in a brighter light. According to our understanding, I was supposed to compose the following dialogues, and therein lay out the principal theses on which we agreed; and these were to serve as the foundation of our exchange of letters from then on.

But it has pleased Providence, to remove this flourishing genius from the earth before his time. Short and notable was the course of life, which he has completed here on earth. His work **On Merit**[55] will remain for the Germans an incomparable monument of his own merits: compared with his years, this work deserves the admiration of posterity. What kind of fruits could one not hope from such a tree in the future whose bloom was so splendid. He had still other works in progress, which would have increased in perfection, as he would have increased in experience and powers of the spirit. All these beautiful hopes are gone! Germany loses in him an excellent writer, humanity loses a loving sage, whose feelings were as noble, as his understanding was enlightened; his friends lose the most tender friend, and I lose a fellow-traveler on the way to truth, who warned me of false steps.

Following the example of Plato, I have Socrates in his last hours relate the arguments for the immortality of the human soul to his students. The dialogue of the Greek author, which has the name **Phaedo**, has a multitude of extraordinary beauties, which deserve to be used— the best of the doctrine of immortality. I took advantage of its form, ordering, and eloquence, and have only tried to adapt the metaphysical proofs to the taste of our time. In the **first dialogue** I could stay somewhat closer to my model. Various of my arguments seemed to require only a minor change of the style, and other arguments seemed to necessitate a development from their fundamentals, in order to attain the convincing power, which the dialogue of Plato lacks for a modern reader.

The long and intense declamation against the human body and its needs, which Plato seems to have written more in the spirit of Pythagoras, than of his teacher, had to be moderated extensively due to our improved conceptions of the value of this divine creature [the human body]; and nevertheless it will sound strange to many of today's readers. I confess, that I have kept this section simply to pay homage to the winning eloquence of Plato.

From then on I found it necessary to diverge from Plato totally. His proofs for the immateriality of the soul seem, at least to us, so shallow and capricious, that they scarcely deserve a serious refutation. Whether this is due to our better philosophical insight, or stems from our poor insight into the philosophical language of the ancients, I am not able to decide.[56] I have chosen a proof for the immateriality of the soul in the **second dialogue,** which the students of Plato gave, and some modern philosophers adopted from them.[57] It seemed to me not only convincing, but also easiest, to be expressed according to the Socratic method.

In the **third dialogue** I had to take my refuge completely in the moderns, and allow my Socrates almost to speak like a philosopher from the eighteenth century. I would rather commit an anachronism, than leave out arguments, which can contribute something to convince the reader.

In such a way the following mean between a translation and my own composition arose. Whether I have also produced something new, or merely stated in a different way that which is often said, others may decide. It is difficult, in a matter about which so many great minds have reflected, to be thoroughly original, and it is ridiculous to want to pretend to do so. If I would have cited authors, then the names **Plotinus**, **Descartes**, **Leibniz**, **Wolff**, **Baumgarten**, **Reimarus**, et al. would often appear. Then perhaps it would be more obvious to the reader what I have added from my own thinking. But to the mere amateur, it is irrelevant, if he owes an argument to this person or that person; and the scholar knows well to differentiate the "mine" and "thine" in such important matters. I nevertheless ask my reader to be attentive to the arguments which I bring to bear here of the harmony of moral truths, and especially of the system of our rights and obligations. I don't recall, having read them in any other author, and they seem to me to be convincing for those who agree on the principles. The genre of piece has obliged me to insert them as simple grounds for persuasion; but I consider them capable of being elaborated with the rigor of the strictest logic.

I have deemed it expedient to write an introduction on the character of Socrates, who is the main person in the dialogues, in order to refresh my reader's memory of this philosopher. Cooper's *Life of Socrates*[58] has thereby served as my guide, however, the original sources have also been consulted.

The Life and Character of Socrates

Socrates, son of the sculptor **Sophroniscus** and the midwife **Phaenarete**, was the wisest and most virtuous among the Greeks. He was born in the fourth year of the 77th Olympiad, in Athens, into the **Alopecian** clan. In his youth, his father encouraged him in the art of sculpture, in which Socrates must have made no little progress, if the **robed Graces**, which stood on the wall of Athens behind the statue of Athena, are his work,[59] as many assert. Times, in which a Phidias, Zeuxis, and Myron[60] lived, would have granted no mediocre work such a prominent place.

Approximately in his thirtieth year, when his father was long dead, he still pursued the art of sculpture, but from necessity, and without much inclination. **Crito**, an aristocratic Athenian, became acquainted with him, observed his sublime talents, and judged that he could be far more useful to the human race through the use of his mind, than through the work of his hands.[61] Crito took him out of art school and brought him to the wise men of the time, in order to allow beauties of a higher order to be held before him for contemplation and emulation. If art teaches how to imitate life in the lifeless, to make the stone resemble the human form; thus wisdom seeks to imitate the infinite in that which is finite, in order to bring the soul of man, as close as is possible in this life, to its original **beauty** and **perfection**. Socrates enjoyed instruction from and association with the most celebrated people in all the arts and sciences, among whom his disciples named **Archelaus, Anaxagoras, Prodicus, Evenus, Isymachus, Theodorus**, and others.[62]

Crito furnished him with the necessities of life, and Socrates initially pursued **natural philosophy,** which was very much in vogue at that time, with much diligence. He soon decided however, that it were time that wisdom be led back from the contemplation of **nature** to the contemplation of **humanity**. This is the path which philosophy ought to take for all time. It must begin with the examination of external objects, but, with each step that it takes, it should cast a glance back to man, to whose true felicity all its endeavors should be directed. If the motion of the planets, the organization of the heavenly bodies, the nature of the elements, etc., do not have, at least indirectly, an influence on our felicity, then man is not destined to investigate them. **Socrates was**, as Cicero[63] says, **the first who called philosophy down from the heavens, established it in the cities, led it into the dwellings of men, and obliged them to contemplate their deeds and omissions**. Meanwhile, as the originators of innovation are generally wont to do, he went a bit too far, and spoke sometimes of the most sublime sciences with a kind of disdain, which is not befitting to the wise judge of things.

At that time in Greece, as at all times with the rabble, the kind of teachers stood in great esteem, who endeavor to encourage deeply-rooted prejudices and out-of-date superstitions, through all kinds of pretexts and sophistries. They gave themselves the noble name of **Sophists**, which due to their behavior was transformed into a name of disgust. They took charge of the education of the youth, and taught the arts, sciences, moral philosophy and religion, in both public schools and private houses, with general acclaim. They knew that in democratic government assemblies, eloquence was treasured above all, that a free man would gladly listen to mere chatter about politics, and that the appetite for knowledge of shallow minds prefers to be satisfied through fables. Hence, they never failed to skillfully weave together dissembling rhetoric, false politics and absurd fables in their speeches, such that the people listened with amazement, and rewarded them with extravagance. They were on good terms with the priests; for they mutually adopted the wise maxim: **live and let live**. When the tyranny of the hypocrites was no longer able to hold the free spirit of men under its yoke, these seeming friends of truth were commissioned to lead man's spirit astray on the false path, to confuse their natural conceptions, and to nullify all distinctions between truth and falsehood, right and wrong, good and evil, through blinding sophistries. The main principle in their theory was: **Everything can be proved, and everything can be disproved**; and in practice, **one must derive as much advantage from the folly of others, and from his own superiority, as he can**. Of course, they kept this last maxim secret from the public, as one can easily imagine, and entrusted it only to their admirers, who partook of their trade. But the morality which they taught publicly was just as corrupting to the heart of men, as their politics were for the justice, freedom, and felicity of mankind.

Since they were artful enough to entangle their own interests with the prevailing religious system, not only were decisiveness and heroism necessary to put an end to their frauds—even a true friend of virtue might not dare it without the utmost caution. There is no religious system so corrupt, that it does not give to at least some of humanity's duties a certain sanctification which the humanist honors. When he doesn't want to act contrary to his own purpose, he must leave it untouched. From doubt in religious affairs, to carelessness; from neglect of **religious rites**, to the contempt of **all** worship generally; the transition tends to be very easy, especially for minds which are not subject to the rule of reason, and which are ruled by avarice, ambitiousness, or lust. The priests of superstition rely on this deception and take refuge in it all too often, as an inviolable shrine, whenever there is an attack on them.[64]

Such difficulties and obstacles stood in Socrates' way as he made the momentous decision to disseminate virtue and wisdom among his fellow men. On the one hand, he had to conquer the prejudices of his own upbringing, to enlighten the ignorance of others, to battle the Sophists, to suffer the malice, vulgarity, defamation, and abuse of his enemies, to endure poverty, to combat established authority, and what was the most difficult, to thwart the dark horrors of superstition. On the other hand, the weak minds of his fellow citizens were to be taken care of, scandal was to be avoided, and the good influence, which even the most absurd religion had on the morals of the simple-minded, was not to be squandered. He overcame all these difficulties with the wisdom of a true philosopher, with the patience of a saint, with the unselfish virtue of a friend of humanity, with the resoluteness of a hero, at the expense and loss of all worldly goods and pleasures. He sacrificed health, power, comfort, reputation, peace, and finally, life itself, in the most loving way, for the welfare of his fellow man. So powerfully did the love of virtue and justice and the inviolability of the duties to the **Creator** and **Preserver** of things whom he knew by the pure light of reason in the most vivid manner, operate in him.[65]

However, the higher aims of a world citizen did not prevent him from fulfilling his customary duties to his fatherland.[66] In his 36th year, he bore arms against the **Potideans**, the inhabitants of a town in Thrace, who rebelled against their tribute masters, the Athenians.[67] There, he neglected no opportunity to harden his body against all the hardships of war and severity of the seasons, and to exercise his soul in fearlessness and disdain of danger. By general agreement of his rivals themselves, he was awarded the prize of bravery, but gave it to **Alcibiades**,[68] whom he loved. By this he wanted to encourage him to earn such honors from his fatherland in the future through his own deeds. Shortly before, he had saved Alcibiades' life in combat. **Potidea** was besieged in the most severe cold. While others protected themselves from the frost, he remained in his usual clothing, and walked barefoot on the ice. The plague raged in the camp and in Athens itself. What **Diogenes Laertius** and **Aelian**[69] assert is barely believable: that **Socrates** was the only one who didn't get the plague. Without drawing any conclusion from this instance, which could have been a mere coincidence, one can generally say with certainty, that he had a strong and sturdy constitution, which he knew how to maintain through abstinence, exercise, and avoidance of all softness, such that he was inured against all the contingencies and hardships of life. Nevertheless he also didn't neglect to exercise the powers of his soul in the field—he exerted them to the utmost. He was seen at times standing in the same place for 24 hours, with steadfast gaze, immersed in thought, **as if his spirit was absent from his body**, said Aulus Gellius.[70] One cannot deny that these raptures were a predisposition to excessive enthusiasm, [N.B.: the German word, *Schwärmerei*, cannot be sufficiently translated into English. It literally means, "to swarm" like bees and has the idea here of being fanatically enthusiastic for a cause, such that one can go overboard and make mistakes. See Friedrich Schiller's discussion of the Marquis of Posa in his *Letters on Don Carlos*.] and in his life more evidence is found that he was not entirely free from it. However, it was a harmless enthusiasm, grounded neither in pride nor hatred of man, and in the situation in which he found himself, may have been very useful to him. Perhaps the lowly powers of nature aren't sufficient to elevate man to such great thoughts and steadfast resolutions.

After the campaign ended, he returned to his native city, and began to vigorously attack superstitious beliefs and sophistry, and to teach his fellow citizens virtue and wisdom.[71] On public streets, walkways, in baths, private houses, the workshops of artists, wherever he found people whom he believed he could make better, he stopped them, then and there, took up a dialogue with them, explained to them what was right and wrong, good and evil, holy and unholy; talked to them about the providence and government of God, of the means of pleasing Him, of the felicity of men, of the duties of a citizen, head of household, father, etc. [Mendelssohn's note: He was acquainted with

Xenophon in the following manner. He met him in a narrow passage-way. The beautiful and modest manners of the young man pleased him so well, that he held out his cane, and did not want to allow him to go on. Young man! He said, do you know, where the needs of life are to be obtained?—Oh, yes! answered Xenophon.—But do you know also, where virtue and righteousness are to be acquired?—The young man hesitated and looked at him.—So follow me, Socrates continued, I want to show it to you. He followed him, was his most faithful student, and one knows how much he was indebted to him.] All of this never with the overbearing tone of a teacher, but as a friend, who only wants to seek the truth with us. He knew how to initiate it, however, by means of simple-minded, childish questions, from question to question, until the truth was reached, such that his interlocutor believed he discovered the truth himself, and had not been taught. "I take after my mother in this," he used to say jokingly. "She herself doesn't give birth anymore, but she possesses the artistic skill, through which she helps others to bring their offspring into the world. In like manner I perform the office of a midwife for my friends. I ask and question as long as is necessary, until the hidden fruit of their understanding comes to light."[72]

This method of inquiring for the truth was also the most successful in refuting the Sophists. When it came to a detailed discourse, they were insufferable. They had so many evasions, so many fables, so many subterfuges, and so many rhetorical figures of speech at their command that the listeners were dazzled, and believed themselves to be convinced. A general applause usually broke out for them. And one can even imagine the triumphant look, with which such a **teacher** then looked down at his **students**, or **defeated adversaries**. What did **Socrates** do on such an occasion? He applauded along with them. But he ventured a few easy questions somewhat distant from the matter, which the well-educated Sophist regarded as inane, and answered out of pity. Little by little, Socrates crept closer to the essence of the matter, always with questions. In the meantime he always cut off the opportunity of his opponent to ramble on in long-winded speeches. In this way, the Sophists were forced to make their concepts intelligible, to give precise explanations, and to allow the absurd conclusions to be drawn from their assumptions. Finally they saw themselves driven into the corner, so they became testy. Socrates never became so, but tolerated their bad conduct with the greatest composure, and continued to develop their ideas, until finally, the absurdities which followed from the Sophists' axioms, became evident to even the most simple-minded listeners. In such a way the Sophists were made the laughing-stock of their own pupils.

With respect to religion, Socrates appears to have had the following maxim in mind: Any false doctrine or opinion, which obviously led to moral corruption, and thus is contrary to the felicity of the human race, would be spared by him in no way. He challenged it publicly, made it laughable, and showed it in its absurd and disgusting consequences, in the presence of the hypocrites, the Sophists, and the common people. The doctrines of the fable writers were of this type, attributing weaknesses, injustices, shameful lusts, and passions to their gods. With respect to such themes, as well as with respect to false concepts of the divine providence and government of God, also, with respect to the reward of the good and the punishment of evil, he never held back, never even appeared doubtful. He was determined at all times to defend the cause of truth with the greatest courage, and, as the outcome showed, even to die for his belief. A doctrine, however, which was merely false in the abstract, and which could not bring such great harm to morality, as was to be feared from a dangerous fad, he left unchallenged.[73] On the contrary, he publicly professed the prevailing opinion and observed the established ceremonies and religious customs. On the other hand, he avoided any opportunity for conclusive explanations; and when it was not to be evaded, he had a refuge ready: he pled **his ignorance**.

To teach the method benefited him excellently, which as we saw, he had chosen from other considerations. Since he never voiced his teachings with the arrogance of a know-it-all, since he rather asserted nothing himself, but always tried to draw out the truth by questioning his listeners: thus he was permitted not to know what he could not know, or was not allowed to know. The egotism of knowing an answer to all questions has seduced many a great intellect to assert things, which it would have censured in the mouth of another. **Socrates** was far removed from this vanity. Of things which were beyond his comprehension, he confessed with the most naïve frankness: "**This I do not know**"; and when he noticed that traps were laid to coax certain admissions from him, he withdrew himself from the debate, and said: "**I know nothing!**" The oracle at Delphi declared him to be the wisest of all mortals. "Do you know," said **Socrates**, "why Apollo deems me as the wisest man on earth? Because other people, for the most part, believe they know something that they don't know. But I understand and admit, that all that I know, amounts to this, **that I know nothing.**"[74]

Socrates' fame spread all over Greece, and the most respected and educated men from all regions came to him to enjoy his friendly company and instruction. The desire to hear him was so great among his friends that many risked their lives just to be with him daily. The Athenians had forbidden the Megarans to enter their region on pain of death. **Euclides of Megara**, a friend and student of **Socrates**, didn't let that keep him from visiting his teacher. He went at night, disguised in gaudy women's clothing, from Megara to Athens, and in the morning, before it was day, went his 20,000 steps back home again. **Socrates** lived in the utmost poverty and want and wished to be paid nothing for his lessons, although the Athenians were so hungry for learning, that they would have spent great sums, if he had demanded compensation. The Sophists knew better how to exploit this willingness of the Athenians.

It must have cost him all the more effort to endure this poverty, since his wife, the notorious **Xanthippe**, wasn't the most frugal housewife, and he also had to care for children who expected their sustenance from his hand. It is certainly not yet settled, that Xanthippe was of such an ill-tempered nature as is generally believed. The legends that are known to her disgrace arise from later writers, who could only have known them from hearsay. Plato and Xenophon, who had to be the best informed on this subject, seemed to have known her as an average wife, about whom they said neither much good nor much bad. Indeed, one will find in the following dialogues, according to Plato, that she was in jail with Socrates on the last day of his life with their children and extremely grieved over his death. All that is found to her detriment, in these most credible authors, is a passage in the *Banquet* of **Xenophon**,[75] where someone asks Socrates why he took a wife who was so unsociable, whereupon he answered in his customary manner, "He who wants to learn to handle horses, doesn't choose a gentle pack animal for practice, but rather a spirited steed, which is difficult to break. I, because I want to learn to deal with humanity, have chosen for myself a wife who is quarrelsome, precisely for this reason, so as to learn to endure the different moods of men so much the better."[76] In another passage in Xenophon,[77] Socrates' son, **Lamproclus**, complains to his father about the harsh treatment, sullen temper, and intolerable moods of his mother. But from the answer by Socrates it is evident, to her credit, that she, with her quarrelsome temperament, nonetheless observed the duties of a mother conscientiously and loved and took care of her children properly. This testimonial of her husband evidently refutes all the disgraceful anecdotes which were contrived at her expense and through which she was made as an example of a bad wife for posterity. One can believe with good reason, that Socrates' skill in handling men was not practiced in vain with his wife: that he rather through untiring patience, pleasantness, gentleness, and through his irresistible urging conquered the harshness of her temper, won her love, and she was improved in such a way, that she was transformed from a quarrelsome wife into a good housewife and mother, and as her performance before his end demonstrated, became a loving wife. Be that as it may, his poverty must have made his domestic circumstances more difficult for him: since he had to account for his deeds and omissions, not only to himself, but to his whole family, and perhaps a family which was dissatisfied and complaining about his severe frugalness. No one was better informed about the duties of a head of household than Socrates. He knew well, that he was obliged to earn and acquire as much as would be necessary for the honest livelihood of his family, and very often he impressed this natural duty to his friends. But in his case, a higher duty stood in his way, which prevented him from fulfilling that sufficiently. The corruption of the times, and in particular the abject greediness of the Sophists, who sold their corrupt teachings for hard cash, and applied the most disgraceful means to get rich at the expense of the cheated people, imposed on him the obligation to counterpose to them extreme unselfishness, so that his pure and undefiled intentions would be capable of no such evil interpretation. He would rather live in want, and when scarcity weighed too much on him, live on charity, than to justify the filthy avarice of these false teachers of wisdom in some measure, by his example.

He interrupted his benevolent activities, and marched voluntarily again into battle against the Boeotians. The Athenians lost the battle at **Delium**[78] and were decisively defeated. **Socrates** showed his bravery in the fighting as well as in the retreat. "Had every man done his duty as **Socrates**," said the General **Laches** according to **Plato**, "the day certainly would not have been unfortunate for us."[79] As everyone fled, he also retreated, but step by step, and frequently turned back, in order to resist an enemy who was in hot pursuit. He found **Xenophon**, who had fallen off his horse and been wounded, lying on the ground, took him on his shoulder, and carried him to safety.[80]

The priests, Sophists, orators, and others, who promoted such arts for sale, people to whom Socrates must have been a thorn in the side, took advantage of his absence, and tried to whip up people's emotions against him. On his return, he found a self-contained faction, which stooped to the vilest means to harm him. There is reason to believe they hired the comic playwright **Aristophanes** to compose a farce, which was called comedy at that time, to expose **Socrates** to public ridicule and hatred, to whip up the common people, as well as to prepare them, so that if their escapade succeeded, to dare a more decisive one.[81] This farce had the name **The Clouds**. **Socrates** was the main character, and the person playing this role took pains to counterfeit him as he was in real life. Dress, walk, gestures, voice, everything mimicked him realistically. The play itself has been preserved, to the honor of the persecuted philosopher, until our time. Something more insulting can scarcely be imagined.

As a rule, **Socrates** didn't care to visit the theater except when the plays of **Euripides** (which some think, he himself had helped to compose) were performed.[82] Nonetheless, the day that this lampoon was performed, he attended. He heard many strangers who attended ask, "Who is this **Socrates** in the original that was mocked on the stage?" He stepped forward in the midst of the play, and remained until the end of the piece, standing in one place, where everyone could see him and could compare him with the copy. This stroke was deadly for the poet and his comedy. The most farcical incidents had no effect anymore, for the appearance of **Socrates** aroused deep respect and a kind of awe of his fearlessness. The play met with no success. The poet rewrote it, and brought it to the stage again the following year, but with just as little success. The enemies of the philosopher were obliged to postpone the intended prosecution, until a more favorable opportunity.

The war with the Boeotians was scarcely over, when the Athenians[83] had to enlist a new army, in order to check the Lacedaemonian [Spartan] commander **Brasidas**, who had taken several Thracian cities, and among others, the important city **Amphipolis**. **Socrates** didn't let the danger which confronted him in his last absence hold him back from serving his country again. This was the last time he left his native city. From that time, until his death, he never left the region of Athens, and never failed to grant his friendly company to the youth who sought him out, and to instill in them the love of virtue through his teachings and good example. As he was, above all, a great friend and admirer of beauty, he appeared to be mindful of physical beauty in the choice of his friends. A beautiful body, he was wont to say, bespeaks a beautiful soul, and when the soul doesn't meet the expectation, it must have been neglected. Because of that, he then took great pains to make the inside of this person correspond to his well-formed exterior. No one was dearer to him than **Alcibiades**, a young man of uncommon beauty and great talents, who was arrogant, brave, thoughtless, and above all, of fiery temperament. He pursued Alcibiades tirelessly, engaged him in discussion at every opportunity, in order to deter him through friendly admonition and loving rebukes, from the excesses of ambition and sensuality to which he tended by nature. **Plato**, often on these occasions, puts expressions in **Socrates'** mouth which seem almost amorous. On account of this, Socrates was accused, in later times, of a criminal association with young people.[84] But even the enemies of **Socrates**, **Aristophanes** in his comedy, and **Melitus** in his accusation, don't make the slightest mention of it. It is true that **Melitus** accuses him of corrupting the youth, as **Socrates'** answer clearly illuminates, but only in regard to the laws of religion and government, towards which he supposedly made the youth indifferent. Granted also, the corruption of morals at that time had gone so far that this blasphemy against nature was almost accepted as natural. However his enemies would not have remained totally silent about this, if it had not been impossible to publicly accuse the model of chastity and abstinence of such a beastly lechery. If one reads the harsh reproaches which he makes to **Critias** and **Critobulus**,[85] if one reads the testimony the wanton, half-drunk **Alcibiades** gives in Plato's dialogues, the silence of his enemies and slanderers, and the positive testimony of his friends to the other side, leave no doubt, that the accusation was groundless and a punishable slander.[86] The expressions of Plato, as strangely as they ring in our ears, prove nothing more than that this unnatural gallantry was the manner of speaking at that time, as perhaps the most serious man of our time wouldn't abstain from when he writes to a woman, as if falling in love, befriending her.

The opinion of scholars is divided about the guardian spirit [Daemon], which Socrates alleged to possess, and which, as he said, always deterred him from doing anything harmful. Some believe that Socrates, himself, allowed himself a little poetic license here, in order to gain the ear of the superstitious population; but this seems to dispute his usual sincerity. Others understand by this guardian spirit a keen sense of good and evil, which, through reflection, long experience, and constant exercise, became a moral instinct, by virtue of which he could judge and test every act of free will by its probable results and effects, without being able to give an account of it through his judgment. Several instances are found in Xenophon as well as in Plato, however, where this spirit foretells things to Socrates, which cannot be explained by any natural power of the soul. These instances perhaps have been added by his students from good intention. Perhaps also, Socrates, who, as we saw, was disposed to raptures, was weak or enthusiastic enough, to transform this vividly moral feeling, which he didn't know how to explain, into an **intimate spirit**, and to attribute those forebodings to it afterwards, which arise from entirely different sources. Must then an admirable man necessarily be free from all weaknesses and prejudices? In our days, it is no longer popular to mock apparitions. Perhaps, in Socrates' time an exertion of genius was necessary to do that, which he used for a more productive purpose. All the same, it was usual for him to tolerate any superstition, which did not lead directly to moral corruption, as already was recalled above.

The felicity of the human race was his only study. As soon as a prejudice or superstition gave rise to open violence, injury to human rights, corruption of morals, etc., nothing in the world could stop him from defying all threats and persecutions, to profess himself against it. There was a traditional superstition among the Greeks that the spirits of the unburied dead must wander restlessly, for a hundred years, on the banks of the River Styx, before they were allowed across. Those who first established society might have taught this madness to a barbarous people from laudable intentions. However, in the time of Socrates it cost many brave patriots their lives, through a shameful misapplication. The Athenians achieved a decisive victory over the Lacedaemonians at the island of Argos.[87] The commanders of the victorious fleet were prevented from burying the dead by a storm. On their return to Athens, they were publicly accused of the crime of this omission in the most ungrateful way. On this day, Socrates presided in the Senate of the **Prythaneum**, which tended to such public matters. The malice of a few powerful people in the realm, the hypocrisy of the priests, and the meanness of the mercenary rhetoricians and demagogues combined to provoke the blind passion of the people against these defenders of the state. The people pressed vehemently for their condemnation. Even a part of the Senate was duped by this vulgar madness; and the rest didn't have enough courage to oppose the general frenzy. Everyone consented to condemn these unfortunate patriots to death. Socrates, alone, had the courage to defend their innocence. He scorned the threat of the people in power and the rage of the furious rabble, stood entirely alone on the side of the innocent people who were persecuted, and would rather that the anger be directed against him, than consent to such an unholy injustice. Nonetheless, all his endeavors on their behalf ended fruitlessly. He was mortified to see blind passion gain the upper hand, and the Republic inflict disgrace on itself, sacrificing its bravest defenders to an evil prejudice. The following year the Athenians were defeated decisively by the Lacedaemonians,[88] their fleet leveled, their capital besieged. They were brought to such an extreme that they had to surrender unconditionally. It is very likely, that the lack of experienced commanders on the Athenian side was, at least in part, the cause of this defeat.

Lysander, the commander of the Lacedaemonians, who had taken the city, aided and abetted an emerging uprising in the city, transformed the democratic government into an oligarchy, and installed a council of thirty, who were known by the name of the Thirty Tyrants. The cruelest enemies could not have been able to rage in the city, as these monsters raged. Under the pretext of punishing political criminals and rebellion, the most righteous people in the city were robbed of their lives or their fortunes. Plunder, robbery, and banishment, the latter publicly, the former secretly and treacherously, were deeds by which they characterized their government. How **Socrates**' heart must have bled to see **Critias**, who had formerly been a student, in the leadership of these monsters! Yes, that **Critias**, his former friend and pupil, now proved himself to be an open enemy, and sought the opportunity to prosecute him. The wise man had once harshly rebuked him for his swinish and unnatural lechery, and since that time, the degenerate bore a secret grudge, which now sought an opportunity to erupt.

When he and Charicles were appointed legislators, in order to find a reason to indict Socrates, they established a law that no one should be allowed to teach rhetoric. They heard that Socrates had slandered them and that he had let it be known on various occasions, that it would indeed be incredible, if shepherds made the flocks entrusted to them smaller and thinner, and nevertheless should not be regarded as bad shepherds; but it would be even more incredible, if the leaders of a state made the citizens fewer and worse people, and yet should not be regarded as bad leaders.

They sent for him, showed him the law, and forbade him to engage in conversation with the young people, period.

"Is it permitted," replied Socrates, "to ask you about this or that in this ban which isn't quite clear to me?"

"Oh, yes!" answered one.

"I am ready," he rejoined, "to abide by the law, and fear only to break it out of ignorance. I beg, therefore, for a clearer explanation: Whether by rhetoric, it is understood, an art by means of which one speaks correctly, or speaks incorrectly? If it is the former, then I must refrain from saying anything about how one should speak correctly; but, if it is the latter, then, I must instruct no one about how he should speak incorrectly?"

Charicles was enraged, and said: "If you don't understand this law, we will make it clearer to you, and absolutely forbid you to speak with young people."

"So that I also know how I have to conduct myself in this," said Socrates, "specify for me, how long men are considered young by you?"

"As long as they can't sit in the council," answered Charicles, "that is, as long as they don't have mature understanding, namely until 30 years of age."

"But, if I want to buy something," replied Socrates, "that a younger man under 30 years old has to sell, shall I not ask, how much it costs?"

"This is not forbidden to you," said Charicles, "but sometimes you ask about things, which you know the answer to quite well: refrain from such questions anymore!"

"What about answering," said Socrates further, "if a young man asks me, where Charicles or Critias live, may I answer him?"

"Yes, yes," said Critias, "but refrain from the worn-out examples and similes of leather tailors, room servants, and blacksmiths."

"Presumably," replied Socrates, "also the ideas of justice, holiness, piousness, etc, which I am accustomed to explain by these examples?"

"Entirely correct!" answered Charicles. "And above all things, speak not of shepherds. Pay attention to that, or I fear, you will also make 'the herd' smaller."[89]

Socrates paid as little attention to their threats, as he did to their absurd law, which they had no authority to establish, and which was directly against common sense and natural law. He continued his efforts to improve virtue and justice with untiring zeal. Even so, the tyrants didn't dare attack him directly. They tried roundabout ways, and

sought to embroil him in their injustices: They assigned him, together
with four other citizens, to bring **Leon of Salamis** to Athens, to exe-
cute him. The others assumed the task; but Socrates declared that he
never would offer his hands to commit an injustice.[90]

"So do you then," said Chariclas, "want to have liberty to speak
what you please, and not suffer for it?"

"**Every possible evil**," he answered, "**would I suffer for it,
only not this: to do injustice to someone**." Chariclas was silent,
and the rest looked at each other. These liberties would have cost Socrates his life, if the people hadn't tired of the cruelty of these tyrants,
provoked a rebellion, slain their highest-ranking leaders, and driven
the rest of them away from the city.

Under the re-established democratic government, the old enemies
of Socrates, the Sophists, priests, and orators, found the long-wished-
for opportunity to prosecute him with better luck, and finally to do
away with him. **Anytus**, **Melitus**, and **Lycon** are the three unforget-
table names, who, to their disgrace, lent themselves to the execution of
this shameful scheme.[91] They spread the slander among the people:
Socrates allegedly taught Critias the principle of tyranny, which he so
recently exercised with such extreme cruelty. Anyone who knows the
gullibility and inconstancy of the rabble, will not wonder why the
Athenians believed in such an obvious lie, even though everyone knew
what had passed between Socrates and the tyrants. A few years before
this,[92] Alcibiades, who possessed great talents, but a very wild character, had smashed the statue of Hermes in the company of other mis-
chievous youths, and had openly mocked the Eleusian mysteries, and
then, because of this wild behavior, had to flee from his homeland.[93]
Now this was stirred up again, and spread by the enemies of Socrates,
that he had taught contempt of religion to the young men. Nothing
was more contrary to the teaching and conduct of Socrates than such a
heinous act. No matter how superstitious it might have been, he had
always honored the public worship of God; and, regarding the
Eleusian mysteries, he advised his friends to be initiated in them; even
though at the same time he had his own reasons for not doing so.
There are good reasons to believe, that the great mysteries of Eleusis
were nothing other than the doctrines of a true natural religion, and a
rational interpretation of myths. When Socrates himself refused to accept the initiation, it is probable that he did so, in order to retain the
freedom to spread these secrets with impunity, which freedom the
priests would have taken away from him through the initiation.[94]

When the slanderers believed they had sufficiently prepared the people by the malicious dissemination of rumors of this type, **Melitus** brought a formal charge against Socrates to the state authority, who immediately informed the people. The law court of the **Hellenes** was convened, and the usual number of citizens was chosen by lot to judge the accused. The charge was that **Socrates acts against the law, in that he: 1) doesn't worship the gods of the city and wants to adopt a new deity, and, 2) corrupts the youth, to whom he teaches contempt of everything holy. His penalty is death.**[95]

His friends brought him well-thought-out speeches for his defense.[96]

"They are very beautiful," he said, "but for an old man like me, skills of this type are not befitting."

"Will you not even draft something for your defense?" they asked him.

"The best defense that I can make," he answered, "is that I never did anything unjust in my life to anyone. At different times, I began to think of a defense speech, but God always prevents me from it. Perhaps it is his will, that I die an easy death this year before the frailty and illness corresponding to old age comes, and neither to my friends nor to myself should become a burden."[97] There are those who have wanted, for some time, to find in these words the evidence that Socrates was faint-hearted, and would fear the inconvenience of old age more than death. It requires more than a little gumption to want the reader to imagine this!

On the day publicly appointed for this trial, Melitus, Anytus, and Lycon appeared, the first for the poets, the second for the people, and the last for the orators. They stepped up to the podium, one after the other, and delivered the most venomous and slanderous speeches against Socrates. After they were done, he stepped up in their place, without trembling or hesitating, without attempting to move the judges to pity by presenting a heart-rending spectacle, according to the custom at tribunals at that time; but, in a composed and confident manner, which was befitting to his wisdom. He delivered an unrehearsed and unprepared, but manly and forceful speech, in which he refuted without bitterness all the slanders and malicious rumors which had been spread against him. He shamed his accusers, and showed the contradictions and absurdities in their own accusations. He met his judges with the necessary respect, but spoke in such a confident and deliberate tone of his virtue, that his speech was interrupted frequently by murmurs of discontent. He concluded with the following words:

"Don't be angry, Athenians! that I, contrary to the custom of the accused, don't speak to you in tears, or have my children, relatives, and friends appear in a pathetic parade, in order to arouse your sympathy. I have refrained from this, not from pride or defiance; but, because I consider it ill-mannered to implore a judge, and to want to win him over, in any other fashion than through the righteousness of my case. The judge is committed by oath to judge according to the law and justice, and to let his sympathy as little as his anger determine his sentence. Therefore, we defendants act against the law and justice, if we try to make you break your oaths through our laments, and act contrary to the respect due to you, if we think you capable of it. I will, in no way whatsoever, owe my deliverance to such means, which are neither just, nor fair, nor god-fearing; especially because I have been accused by **Melitus** of impiety. If I try to make you perjure yourself by my begging, this would be the most convincing proof that I don't believe in God; therefore, this defense itself would convict me of atheism. But, no! I am more convinced than all my prosecutors of the existence of God, and submit myself here to God and to you, to be judged according to the truth, and to be sentenced, in a manner which you deem best for you as well as for me."[98]

The judges were extremely displeased by this composed and fearless being, and interrupted Plato, who stepped forward after him, and began to speak. "Athenians, although I am the youngest," began Plato, "of those who climbed up to this place".—"**Climb down!**" they shouted out to him, and would not let him continue his speech. Socrates was found guilty by a majority of 33 votes.

It was the custom in Athens, that condemned persons had to impose a certain punishment upon themselves—such as a fine, imprisonment, or banishment—to confirm the justice of the verdict, or rather to admit their crimes. Socrates was supposed to choose; but he wanted in no way to be so unjust as to find himself guilty.

"If I am supposed to say frankly, what I believe I have earned, so know, Athenians! I believe, in return for the services I provided to the Republic, that I am more than worthy to be supported by public funds in the **Prytaneum**."[99] He consented, on the urging of his friends, nevertheless, to a small fine but didn't want to concede to their pooling together a larger sum among themselves.

The judges deliberated over which penalty they should impose on him, and the malice of his enemies brought it to pass, that he would be condemned to death: "You were very hasty in your judgment, Athenians!" said Socrates, "and, thereby, have given to the mud-slingers in this city material to reproach you, that you took wise Socrates' life, for they will call me wise, even if I am not, in order to be able to criticize you all the more. Had you waited a little while longer, I would have died without your help. You see how close I am to death already. I mean you hereby, you, who have adjudicated death to me! Do you possibly believe, men of Athens! that words to charm and persuade you would fail me, if I was of the opinion, that one should grovel, do anything and say anything, in order to receive a favorable judgment? Certainly not! If I succumb, it is not from a lack of words and ideas, but from a lack of shamelessness and degeneracy, to say such things to you, which you want to hear, but which are indecent for a righteous man to say. Howling, wailing, and other such groveling means of persuasion, which you are accustomed to from others, are totally unworthy of me. I had resolved, at the very beginning, to lose my life, rather than save it through ignoble means. Because I believe, that neither I, nor another is justified, whether before the court or in war, to grovel, to do **anything**, in order to escape death. How often does a man in battle not have an opportunity to save his life, if he throws away his weapon and begs for mercy, from the one who pursues him? And so, there are many occasions in life, where death, indeed, can be avoided, if one is only shameless enough to do and say **anything**, which is required for this. To escape death, men of Athens! is not so difficult, but to escape shame is far more difficult, because it is quicker than death. Hence, it also follows, that I, a slow, old man, am grabbed by the slowest; on the contrary, my accusers, who are quite sprightly and lively, will be overtaken by a very **quick shame**. I go to the death, to which you have sentenced me, and they to the shame and dishonor, to which truth and justice condemn them. I am satisfied with the verdict; presumably, you are also. Therefore, things go just as they should, and I, for my part, also find the ways of destiny herein just and worthy of praise."[100]

After he had frankly stated a of number of truths without anger to the judges, he turned to those who had voted for his acquittal, and talked to them with a kind of contemplation about life, death, and immortality, which might have been tailored to the mental capacity of the general public at that time. But, when he was alone with his students and trusted friends, he allowed himself to go over this material with greater thoroughness. Our readers will be entertained in the following dialogues with more mature thoughts of this philosopher. Therefore we spare them that exoteric philosophy.

He was led into prison, which, as Seneca[101] says, lost its shame through the presence of this man, in that there can be no prison, where a Socrates is. On the way, he met a few of his students, who were completely inconsolable about that which had befallen him. "Why do you weep?" the wise man asked them. "Has nature not sentenced me by my birth likewise to my death? If death snatched me from a true and beneficial good, then I, and those who love me would have cause to lament my fate. However, since I leave behind nothing here below but misery and suffering, on the contrary, my friends should wish me happiness on my trip."

Apollodorus, who is described as a very kind-hearted man of somewhat weak mental capacity, could not accept that his teacher and friend had to die so **innocently.**"**Good Apollodorus**," said Socrates, smiling, as he laid his hand on his head, "**would you rather that I should die guilty?**"[102]

For the rest of what passed in the prison, and in the last hours of the dying Socrates, the reader will learn in the following dialogues. But we ought not omit a discussion with Crito, from which Plato made a separate dialogue.[103] A few days before the execution of Socrates, Crito came to him in prison before dawn, found him in sweet sleep, and quietly sat next to his bed, so as not to disturb him. When Socrates awoke, he asked him, "Why so early today, friend Crito?" Crito informed him that he had gotten a report that the next day the death sentence would be carried out. "If it is the will of God," answered Socrates with his usual composure, "so be it. However, I don't believe that it will happen tomorrow. Just now, even as you came to me, I had a pleasant dream. A woman of uncommon beauty appeared to me, in a long white robe, called me by my name, and said: **In three days, you will arrive in your fertile Phthia.**"[104] A graceful allusion! by means of which he intimated that he longed for the life to come as in Homer the angry Achilles longed for a way out of the camp, and to return to **Phthia**, his fatherland. But Crito, who had an entirely different intention, revealed to his friend that he had bribed the guard, and arranged everything necessary to abduct him from prison at night; and that it depended at this point only on Socrates, if he wanted to escape a disgraceful death. He also sought to convince him, through the strongest exhortations, that this was his responsibility and duty. Since he knew of Socrates' love for his fatherland, he pointed out to him how he was obliged to prevent the Athenians from shedding innocent blood; he further asserted, that he must do this for his friends, who, besides their sorrow of his loss, would also remain exposed to shameful gossip that they had neglected his liberation. Finally, he did not refrain from painting a very moving picture of the misfortune of his helpless children, who would be deprived of his fatherly instruction, example, and protection. To this Socrates answered: "My dear Crito, your friendly concern is praiseworthy, and to be accepted with thanks, if it is consistent with common sense. But if it is to the contrary we must be much more wary. We should first consider if your proposal is just and in agreement with reason or not. I have always accustomed myself, to argue nothing, except what I, after thorough consideration, regarded as the best. I see no reason why I should deviate from what have been my lifelong rules until now, just because I am now in the situation in which you see me: They still appear to me in precisely the same light, and therefore, I cannot do otherwise than to continue to treasure and honor them." After he refuted Crito's false premises, and showed him the duty that a reasonable man owed to his country and the laws, he continued, "If I now were of a mind to escape, and the republic together with her laws appeared, in order to ask me: 'Tell us, **Socrates**, what do you want to do? Don't you realize, that your conduct is preparing our destruction, the laws and the whole state? Or, do you believe that a state can continue to exist, and not necessarily be destroyed, where the judgment of the court has no power, and where any private person can thwart it?' What can I answer to this, my worthy one? Perhaps, that an injustice is done to me, and I don't deserve the sentence that has been passed on me? Shall I answer in this way?"[105]

Crito: "By Jupiter, yes, O **Socrates**!"

Socrates: "But if the laws retorted: 'What, **Socrates**, have you yourself not made a pledge to us to sanction all the verdicts of the republic?' I would be in a quandary over this question; but they would continue: 'Don't let this confound you, **Socrates**! but just answer; you are, indeed, a friend of question and answer. State what displeases you about us and the republic, such that you want to destroy us? Are you displeased with the laws of marriage, by which your father married your mother, and brought you to the world; are you displeased with these?'

" 'Not at all!' I would answer.

" 'So, perhaps you object to our ways of educating and bringing up the children? Is the institution not praiseworthy, which we made for this purpose, and which enabled your father to educate you in music and gymnastics?'

" 'Very praiseworthy!' I would have to answer.

" 'You acknowledge therefore, that you have us to thank for your birth, your upbringing, and your schooling; and consequently, we can consider you, as well as each of your predecessors, as our son and subordinate.

'If that is the case, we ask: Are your rights equal to ours, and are you authorized, to do everything to us, that we do to you, to repay with the same coins? You don't presume to have an equal right with your father, not an equal right with your commander, if you have one: to make them endure everything which you suffered from them, to offend them with words and deeds, if they had affronted you somehow; and you want to have an equal right with your fatherland, and with the laws? Will you consider yourself authorized to rebel against us, whenever we make a ruling against you? to wreak destruction on the laws, on your fatherland, which always stands by you? and you believe yourself to act justly? you, you who earnestly devote yourself to virtue? Is your wisdom so faulty, that you do not even see, that your father and mother and ancestors are far from being as sacred, are not to be honored as highly, are not as holy, to both the gods and to all men who are in their right mind, as your fatherland?'

"They continue in these tones, and add in conclusion: 'Consider, **Socrates**, if you don't conduct yourself toward us inequitably? We have sired, reared, and educated you; we have allowed you, and every Athenian citizen, as far as it was in our power, to participate in all the benefits which social life can provide, and nonetheless, we granted you, and everyone who settled in Athens, permission to depart with his belongings, and to repair to wherever he wants, if, after a sufficient trial, our national constitution is not agreeable to him. The gates of Athens stand open to anyone who doesn't like the city, and he can take his possessions with him unhindered. But, whoever has seen how we do things, and how we administer justice and the law, and nevertheless remained with us, tacitly entered into a contract, to be pleased with everything that we command him; and if he is disobedient, then he commits a threefold injustice: He is disobedient to his parents, disobedient to his good rearing and teachers, and he violates the contract, which he entered into with us.'

"Dearest friend Crito! I believe I hear this speech, as the Corybantes[106] imagine they hear the sound of the flutes, and the voice rings so loudly in my ears, that I can hear nothing else over it." Crito went away convinced, although reluctantly, that reason had disapproved of his proposal.

Two

Phädon, or on the Immortality of the Soul

Dialogues

First Dialogue

Echecrates, Phädon, Apollodorus, Socrates, Cebes, Crito, Simmias.

ECHECRATES: My **Phädon**, were you with Socrates yourself the very day he took the poison in prison, or has somebody related it to you?

PHÄDON: I myself, Echecrates, was there.

ECHECRATES: What did he say before his death? How did he die? If only someone would tell me everything in detail! The Phliasian citizens seldom come to Athens, and it has been a long time since a visitor came from there who could have delivered such news to us.[107] This much we have heard: Socrates drank the poison and is dead; not the least more of the circumstances.

PHÄDON: Nothing of his death sentence?

ECHECRATES: Oh yes! Someone related that to us. We were surprised, that after he was convicted, he was still allowed to live so long. How did this happen, Phädon?

PHÄDON: Entirely by accident, **Echecrates**. It just happened that the ship, which the Athenians send to **Delos** annually, was crowned with a wreath the day before his conviction.

ECHECRATES: And this ship...?

PHÄDON:...is supposed to be, as the Athenians say, the same vessel in which **Theseus** once had taken seven pairs of children to Crete and back again unharmed. It is said that the city made a vow to Apollo at that time, to send him grand presents to **Delos** every year in this ship, if these children would return without harm; and since that time Athens has still always kept her word to the god.

When the sacred ship is ready to depart, the priest of Apollo hangs a wreath on the ship's stern, and immediately the festival of the **Theory**[108] commences. This festival lasts until the ship arrives at **Delos**, and has come back from there again, within which time the city is purified, and no one may be publicly executed according to the law. If the ship is delayed by adverse winds, the condemned can thereby gain a long delay.

As I already said a little while ago, fate decreed that the crowning of the ship with a wreath happened one day earlier, before Socrates was condemned; and this is why a fairly long time passed by between his conviction and his death.

ECHECRATES: But the last day, **Phädon**! How was it there? What did he say? What did he do? Which friends were with him in his hour of death? Or would the Archons[109] allow no one to be with him? And did he depart this life without having a friend with him?

PHÄDON: By no means! There were many present.

ECHECRATES: If you are not too busy, Phädon, relate to me what took place there. I am very eager, to find out all the circumstances of this important event.

PHÄDON: And I am just as willing to report it to you. I am never too busy, when it comes to talking about Socrates. What is more delightful, than to call Socrates to mind, to talk about him, or to hear others speak about him?

ECHECRATES: Your listeners,[110] **Phädon**, are of the same way of thinking. Therefore tell everything, as precisely and in as much detail as is possible for you.

PHÄDON: I was present, friend! but it was paradoxical for me. I felt no pity, no such oppression, as we usually feel when a friend fades away in our arms. Socrates appeared blissfully happy to me, worthy of envy, Echecrates! so gentle, so tranquil was his demeanor in his hour of death, his last words so calm. I thought his conduct was not that of a mortal man, who wanders down before his time to the shadows of Orkus; but like an immortal, who is confident to be as blissful where he goes, as anyone has ever been. Therefore, how could I have the feeling of anxiety, with which the sight of one dying usually cripples our soul? However, our teacher's philosophical conversation didn't have the pure delight at that time to which we were accustomed. We experienced a strange, never felt mixture of pleasure and grief; since the enjoyment was constantly interrupted by the foreboding feeling that: **"Soon we will lose him forever."**

We in attendance were all in this peculiar state of mind, and the contradictory effects showed just as strangely on our faces. One moment we laughed, then tears would pour down our faces. Frequently a smile appeared on our lips, and hot tears welled up in our eyes. But Apollodorus exceeded us all. You know him, and his sensitive nature.

ECHECRATES: How could I not know it?[111]

PHÄDON: He exhibited the strangest agitations. He felt everything far more fervently: He was ecstatic if we smiled, and when our eyes were bedewed, his swam in tears. We were almost moved by him more than by the sight of our dying friend.

ECHECRATES: Who were those present?

PHÄDON: Of the people of our town: **Apollodorus, Critobulus**, and his father Crito, Hermogenes, Epigenes, Aeschines, Antisthenes, **Ctessippus, Menexenus,** and still a few others.[112] **Plato**, I think, was sick.

ECHECRATES: Were foreigners also there?

PHÄDON: Yes, also Thebans; **Simmias, Cebes**, and **Phädondas**, and from Megara; **Euclid**, and **Terpsion**.[113]

ECHECRATES: What! were not **Aristippus** and **Cleombrotus** there!

PHÄDON: Oh no! It is said they were detained in Aegina at that time.[114]

ECHECRATES: Otherwise no one else took part?

PHÄDON: I can't recollect anyone else.

ECHECRATES: Now, my dear! what kind of discussions occurred there?

PHÄDON: I will relate it to you from the beginning to the end. As long as **Socrates** sat in prison, we were accustomed to visit him daily. We usually gathered in the courthouse for this purpose, where his sentence was pronounced (because the courthouse is very close to the prison) and entertained ourselves with conversation until the door to the jail was opened, which usually doesn't happen very early. As soon as the door opened, we went to Socrates, and frequently spent the whole day there with him. We arrived on the last morning earlier than usual, since we heard the evening before, as we were going home, that the ship from **Delos** arrived, and decided to be as early as possible that last time.

When we all met, the jailor came to us who was responsible for opening the prison door, approached us, asked us to disperse, and not to go into the jail until he would call us. For the Eleven Men[115], he said, are now taking the chains off of Socrates, and are telling him that he must die today. Not long afterwards he came to call us. As we went in we found Socrates, just unfettered, lying on the bed. Xanthippe, you know her, sat next to him in quiet grief, and held her child in her lap. When she caught sight of us, she began, in a womanly fashion, to lament out loud. **"Oh! Socrates! You see your friends today, and you, friends, see Socrates today for the last time!"** and a torrent of tears followed these words. Socrates turned to **Crito**, and said "Friend, see that she is taken home."

Crito's servants led her away: she went and wailed, and pitifully beat her breast. We stood dazed. Finally Socrates raised himself in the bed, bent the leg which had been fettered, and while he rubbed the wounds with his hand, he said: Oh my friends! What a strange thing it seems to be, which one calls pleasure! how marvelous! At first glance it is the opposite of pain, as no person can acquire pain and pleasure simultaneously from something, and nevertheless no one can have one of these sensations, without immediately thereupon feeling the opposite, as if they were attached to each other in an infinite loop.[116] If **Aesop** had observed this, he continued, perhaps he would have invented the following fable: "The gods wanted to unite the contending sensations with one another: but as this cannot be done, they tied a fast bond between them; and since then they follow hot on the heels of each other." So it fares now with me. The chains caused me pain, and now, since they are gone, the pleasant sensation follows.

By Jupiter! **Cebes** chimed in, good that you remind me, Socrates! It is said that you composed some poems here in prison, namely, that you turned Aesop's fables into poems, and started with a hymn to **Apollo**. Many ask me, and in particular the poet **Evenus**,[117] what gave you the idea you to compose poetry now, since you never have done so before? If I shall give **Evenus** an answer, when he asks me again: (and ask he certainly will), tell me, what I should answer him?

Tell him, O Cebes, replied **Socrates**, nothing but the truth: that I composed these poems without the intention of surpassing him in rank in the art of poetry; for I know how difficult this is. But I composed them simply because of a dream, which I resolved to follow in all its possible interpretations, and therefore to try my powers in this type of music also, in the poetic art. It happens as follows. In times past I often had a dream, which appeared in many forms, but always gave me the same command—**take up the subject of music and apply yourself to it**! Up until now I only regarded this exhortation as an encouragement and stimulation, as when one calls out to a runner in a race. The dream, I thought, doesn't command me to do anything new, for philosophy is the most splendid music, and I myself have always been concerned with this; therefore it merely wants to encourage my eagerness, to encourage my love for wisdom so that it doesn't grow cold. Now however, after my sentence had been pronounced, and the festival of **Apollo** delayed my death for a while, the thought came to me, perhaps if the dream didn't order me to apply myself to popular music,[118] and I had enough leisure, not to let this thought vanish fruitlessly. I began with a song of praise to the god, whose festival was celebrated at that time. But afterwards it dawned on me, that he who wants to be a poet, must deal with inspiration, not logical reason. However, a song of praise isn't born of inspiration. Since I possess no gift of writing poetry myself, I used other people's inventions and turned some fables of **Aesop**, which came to my hands first, into verse.

This is the answer, my **Cebes**, you can give to Evenus. Send my compliments to him also, and if he is wise, so may he soon follow me. Apparently, I will depart yet today by the command of the Athenians.

And you wish this to **Evenus**? asked **Simmias**. I know this man very well, and as far as I can judge him, he won't thank you for this wish.

Eh? challenged Socrates, is **Evenus** not a philosopher?

Yes, I think so, said **Simmias**.

Then certainly he will gladly follow me, answered **Socrates**, he and every man who deserves this name, philosopher. Certainly he will not commit suicide; for this is not permitted, as is known to everyone.

While he said this, he put both feet down from the bed to the ground, to continue the conversation in this position.[119]

Cebes asked: How is this to be understood, **Socrates**? It is not allowed, you say, to take one's own life, and nevertheless everyone who is a philosopher should gladly follow a dying man? Why?

Cebes, said **Socrates**: you and Simmias, you have both heard the philosopher **Philolaus**,[120] has he never said anything to you about this?

Nothing in detail, my **Socrates**.

Well! I have heard various things about the subject, and will gladly communicate them to you.[121] I think, he who wants to travel, has reason to inquire himself about the condition of the country where he plans to go, in order to form a correct idea of it. This discussion is therefore appropriate to my present circumstances, and what could be more important to take up today until the sun goes down?

By what means does one prove, asked **Cebes**, that suicide is not permitted? **Philolaus** and other teachers have impressed upon me in many ways that it is forbidden, but nobody has taught me more about it.

All right! So get ready to know more about it. What is your opinion, Cebes! I maintain that suicide is absolutely forbidden in all possible cases. We know that there are people, for whom it would be better to be dead, than to live. Now it may seem strange to you, that the sacredness of morality should require of these unfortunate people that they not take their lives themselves, but that they await God's charitable hand.

May a voice of Jupiter explain that! answered **Cebes** laughing.

And, nevertheless it is not so difficult, to do away with this apparent inconsistency through reason. What is usually said in the mysteries, **that we men on earth were posted like the sentries, and therefore may not leave our posts, until we are replaced**, seems to me somewhat beyond reach and incomprehensible. But I have some rational arguments, which are not difficult to grasp.[122] I believe that we agreed on the assumption that there are gods (let me now say God, for whom do I have to dread?).[123] **God is our Proprie-**

tor, we His property, and His providence procures what is best. Are these propositions not clear?

Very clear, said **Cebes**.

A bondsman, who lives under the provision of a good lord, acts criminally, if he defies the intentions of his lord. True?

Certainly!

Perhaps if a spark of righteousness glows in his bosom, it must be a true joy to him, to see the wishes of his master fulfilled through him, and the more so, if he is convinced of the state of mind of his lord to include his own welfare in these wishes?

Incomparable! my **Socrates**.

But how? **Cebes**, when God constructed the skillful structure of the human body, and implanted a rational being in it, did he have good or bad intentions?

Without doubt good intentions.

For He must deny His essence, the self-subsisting good, if He could associate evil intentions with His acts and omissions; and what is a God, who can deny His nature?

An absurdity, **Socrates**, a mythical god, to whom credulous people attribute changeable forms. I remember very well the reasons with which you disputed this blasphemous error on another occasion.

The same God, **Cebes**, who constructed the body, has also equipped it with powers, which strengthen, preserve and defend it from too premature destruction. Shall we also assert that this power of preservation has the maximum good intention as its aim?

How can we do otherwise?

As faithful bondsmen therefore, it must be a sacred duty for us, to allow the intentions of our Proprietor to thrive to their maturity, not to forceably obstruct their course, but rather to allow all our actions of free will to agree with them most perfectly.

That is why I have said, my dear **Cebes**, that philosophy is the most excellent music,[124] for it teaches us to direct our thoughts and actions, in such a way that they, as far as is possible, agree with the intentions of the Supreme Proprietor. But if music is a science, which brings the weak in harmony with the strong, the harsh with the soft, and the disagreeable with the agreeable: then certainly no music can be more admirable and excellent than philosophy, which teaches us, not only to tune our thoughts and actions with each other, but also to tune the actions of the finite with the designs of the infinite, and the thoughts of the inhabitants of the earth with the thoughts of the All-

Knowing in a great and wonderful harmony. Oh **Cebes**! should the presumptuous mortal dare to destroy this delightful harmony?

He would deserve the abhorrence of the gods and men, my dear **Socrates**!

But also tell me this, my dear friend! Are the powers of nature not servants of the Deity, to carry out His commands?

Certainly!

They are also prophets, who proclaim the will and the intentions of the Deity for us far more correctly than the entrails of the sacrificial victims; for that is unquestionably a decree of the Almighty, to where the powers created by Him are aimed. True or not?

Who can deny this?

Therefore, as long as these prophets indicate that the preservation of our lives belongs to the intentions of God, we are bound by duty to order our voluntary actions accordingly, and have neither justification nor right to do violence to the powers that preserve our nature, and to disturb the servants of the Highest Wisdom in their function. This duty is incumbent upon us, until God, by the self-same prophets, sends the explicit command for us to forsake this life, just as He sent it to me today.[125]

I am completely convinced, said **Cebes**. But now I comprehend so much the less, my dear **Socrates**, how you could have said before, that every philosopher must gladly want to follow a dying man. If it is true, as you now assert, that we are a possession of God, and that He provides for our welfare: this statement seems absurd. Eh? should a reasonable man not grieve, if he must forsake the services of a Sovereign, who is his best and most benevolent provider? And if he also could hope to be liberated by death and to be his own master: how can the ignorant ward flatter himself, to be better off under his own command, rather than under the command of the Most-Wise Guardian? I should think, it is rather a gross misunderstanding, if one chooses to be in absolute freedom, and will not tolerate the best Sovereign to rule over him. He who possesses reason, will always submit with pleasure to the oversight of another, whom he believes to be capable of better insights than himself. Therefore, I would draw just the opposite conclusion of your opinion. The wise man, I would say, must grieve when he dies, but the fool rejoices.

Socrates listened to him intently, and seemed to take delight in his astuteness. He then turned to us, and said, **Cebes** can give trouble to one who wants to argue with him. He has constant subterfuges.

But this time, said **Simmias**, **Cebes** seems not to be wrong, my dear **Socrates**!

Truly, what can move a wise man, to remove himself from the good provision of the All-Wise Keeper without discontent?—And if I am right, **Socrates**, **Cebes** directs his objections properly against your present conduct, by which you so calmly, so willingly, not only abandon us all, to whom your death falls so painfully, but also alienate the control and care of such a Ruler, whom you have taught us to revere as the wisest and most benevolent Being.

So, said **Socrates**, I have been accused, as I hear? Therefore I will probably have to officially defend myself?

Certainly, said **Simmias**.

Good! replied **Socrates**: I will endeavor to organize my present defense speech better, than the one which I delivered before my judges.[126]

Listen, **Simmias**, and you **Cebes**! If I didn't have hope, there, where I am going, firstly to always be under the same most gracious Provider, and secondly, to meet the souls of the departed, whose company is to be preferred to all friendship here below: if this were not the case, it would be a folly to esteem death so little, and to run willingly into its arms.

But I have the all-comforting hopes that both will not fail me. The latter I dare not maintain with absolute certainly, but that the providence of God will also rule over me in the next life, this friends! I state it as confidently, as certainly, as I have ever maintained anything in my life. This is why it doesn't sadden me that I shall depart; for I know that death is not the end for us. Another life follows, and indeed such a one, that, as the old adage insures, will be far happier for the virtuous, than for the wicked.

What? said Simmias, my dear Socrates! Will you take this comforting guarantee locked in the innermost part of your soul with you? Or will you not begrudge a doctrine to us also, which is so comforting? It is just to share such a heartfelt good with your friends, and if you convince us of your opinion, then your defense speech is complete.

I will try it, he replied. But let us first hear **Crito**, who seems to have wanted to say something for a long time.

I? nothing my dear, answered Crito. The man who is supposed to bring you the poison, won't leave me alone: I should ask you not to talk so much. Speaking will heat you up too much, he says, and then the drink won't work so well. Previously, he had to prepare a second or third drink of poison, for people who didn't refrain from talking.

Let him, in the name of the gods! said Socrates, go and see to his duty. Let him keep the second drink ready, or the third, if he deems fitting.[127]

I expected this answer from you, said Crito, but the man will not cease—

Oh! forget him! replied Socrates. I have to give my judges here an account, why a man, who has grown gray in the love of wisdom, must be of good cheer in his last hours, because he can expect the greatest blessedness after death. With what reasons, **Simmias** and **Cebes**! I assert this, I will try to explain—

Perhaps the fewest people know, my friends! that he who truly devotes himself to the love of wisdom, uses his entire lifetime to become more familiar with death, in order to learn to die. However, if this is the case, what an absurdity would it not be, to direct all his wishes, all his efforts to a single goal, in his entire life, and yet to grieve, when the long desired goal was finally reached?

Simmias laughed: By Jupiter! he said, **Socrates**! I must laugh, even though I am so little inclined to do so. What you say here may not seem so very strange to the common people, as you think. In particular the Athenians could tell you: how it is well known to them, that the philosophers have learned to die gladly; and therefore they actually let them die, because they know well that this is what they longed for.

I would concede everything to you Simmias! but I don't grant that the Athenians comprehend this. They don't know what kind of death it is, about which I talk, and to what extent the philosophers deserve it. But they are of no concern to us. I am talking now with my friends.[128] Is death not something that can be described and explained?

Certainly! answered **Simmias**.

Is it anything else, than the separation of the body and the soul?— Is this not called death, when the soul leaves the body, and the body leaves the soul in such a manner, that they have nothing in common with each other anymore, and each remains for itself? Or do you know how to explain more clearly, what death is?

No, my dear!

Just consider, friend, if it occurs to you also as it does to me. What do you think? Does the true lover of wisdom indulge himself in so-called sensuous pleasures, and in particular strive for extravagant food and drink?

Nothing less than such things, answered Simmias.

Will he be fixated on sex?

Just as little!

And with respect to the rest of the physical comforts of the body? Will he, in his dress, for example, look to finery and luxury, or will he be content with what is necessary and disregard that which is unnecessary?

Whatever one can manage without, said Simmias, is of no concern to the wise.

Don't we actually want to say, continued **Socrates**, that the philosopher tries to dispose with all unnecessary concerns of the body, in order to be able to pay more attention to the soul?

Why not?

Therefore he differentiates himself from the rest of humanity, in that he doesn't allow his soul to be fettered completely by the concerns of the body, but tries to wean his soul partly from the companionship of the body?

It seems so.

The majority of people, Oh **Simmias**! will tell you, that he who doesn't want to enjoy the pleasures of life, doesn't deserve to live. They call this longing for death, if one renounces sensual pleasure and abstains from all carnal lusts.

This is the truth, **Socrates**!

I am taking this argument farther. Doesn't the body often hinder the one who loves wisdom in thinking, and will he be able to expect notable progress in wisdom, if he has not learned to transcend sensuous objects?—I'll explain myself.—The impressions of our eyes and ears are just as they are sent to us from objects, merely discrete sensations, still not truths; for these truths must first be derived from them through universal principles of reason. Must they not?

Certainly!

Also as discrete sensations they are not to be completely trusted, and the poets sing with righteousness when they say that the senses are deceptive and comprehend nothing clearly. What we hear and see is full of confusion and darkness. However, if both of these senses can grant us no clear insights; the rest of the less accurate senses are not to be mentioned.

Of course not.

Now, how must the soul begin, if it wants to be worthy of the truth? Where it depends upon the senses, it is deceived.

Right!

Therefore the soul must think, reflect, judge, infer, invent; and as much as possible, through these means, to penetrate the true essence of things.

Yes!

But what is most conducive to reflection? I think, when we don't feel so to speak, when we neither see nor hear, and don't recall pleasant or unpleasant sensations, which make us think of our bodies. Then the soul withdraws its attention from the body, quits its association with the body as much as possible, to collect itself, in order to take into itself, not the phenomenon of the sensuous, but its essence, not the impressions which sensuous objects make on us, but to behold that which they truly embody.

Right!

Once again, an opportunity, by which the soul of the wise flees from the body, and as much it can, must try to distance itself from it.

So it seems!

In order to make the matter still clearer: are the words **Maximum Perfection** a mere idea, or does it mean an actual being, which is present outside of us?

Certainly a real, independent, unlimited being outside of us, which existence must preferably approach, my **Socrates**!

And the Maximum Good, and the Maximum Wisdom? Are these also something real?

By Jupiter! Yes! These are inseparable attributes of the All Perfect Being, without which nothing can exist.[129]

Who has taught us to know this Being? Indeed, with corporeal eyes, we have never seen it?

Certainly not!

We have also not heard it, not felt it; no external sense has ever led us to a conception of wisdom, goodness, perfection, beauty, the power of thinking, etc., and nevertheless we know, that these things that are outside of us are real, and are real in the highest degree. Can no one explain to us, how we came by these conceptions?

Simmias said, the voice of Jupiter, my dear **Socrates**! I will refer once again to it.[130]

Eh? My friends! if we heard an exquisite flute playing in the next room, would we not run in, to know the flute player who was able to delight our ears so much?

Perhaps not now, laughed **Simmias**, since here we hear the most splendid music.

When we consider a painting, continued **Socrates**, we wish to know the hand of the master, who has composed it. Now, the most excellent picture lies in ourselves, which the eyes of the gods or men have ever seen, the picture of maximum perfection, goodness, wisdom, beauty, etc. and yet we have never even inquired about the artist who drew this picture?

Cebes replied: I remember once to have heard an explanation from **Philolaus**, which perhaps clarifies the matter.

Will **Cebes** not allow his friends, replied **Socrates**, to share in this legacy of the blessed **Philolaus**?

If these friends, said **Cebes**, wouldn't rather hear the explanation from a **Socrates**. So be it!—**Philolaus** said, the soul has not acquired any of its incorporeal conceptions from the external senses, but has acquired them through itself, while it observes its own actions, and thereby gets to know its own nature and attributes.—To make this clearer, I have often heard him tell a story: Let us borrow from Homer, he used to say, the two casks which stood in Jupiter's foyer, but at the same time let us ask the liberty, to fill them, not with fortune and misfortune, but the one to the right with true being, and the one to the left with deficiency and non-being.—Whenever the allmighty Jupiter wants to create a spirit, he draws from these two barrels, casts a glance on eternal fate, and prepares, according to fate's proportion, a mixture of being and deficiency, which contains the complete foundation of the future spirit. From thence a wonderful similarity is found between all types of spiritual beings, for they are all created from the same barrels, and differ only in the mixture. Therefore when our soul, which is nothing other than such a mixture of being and deficiency, observes itself, it acquires a conception of the nature of spirits and their limits, of possibility and impossibility, perfection and imperfection, of understanding, wisdom, power, intention, beauty, justice and a thousand other incorporeal things, about which the external senses would leave it in the most profound ignorance.

How incomparable! replied **Socrates**. See, **Cebes**! You possess such a treasure, and you were going to let me die without sharing it with me!—But let us see how we want to enjoy this treasure yet before the hour of death. **Philolaus** said: The soul recognizes its kindred spirits, in so far as it observes itself. Does it not?

Yes!

And it reaches for and obtains conceptions of incorporeal things, in so far as the soul analyses its own faculties, and gives each a particular name, in order to be able to differentiate them more clearly?

Certainly!

But if it wants to form an idea of a being superior to itself, a daemon, e.g., who will supply it with the conception?

Cebes was silent, and **Socrates** continued: If I have grasped the meaning of **Philolaus** correctly, the soul certainly can never form an idea of a thing of a superior nature than itself, or form an idea of a thing of higher ability than it possesses itself; but it can generally grasp the possibility of a thing, which has more being and less deficiency in parts than it, that is, which is more perfect than it; or have you perhaps heard otherwise from **Philolaus**?

No!

And of the Maximum Being, of the Maximum Perfection the soul has not more than this glimmer of a conception. It cannot grasp the essence of the same in its full extent; but it thinks of its own essence, that part which has truth, goodness, and perfection, separates it in thought from deficiency and non-being, with which it is mixed, and comes thereby to a conception of an entity, who is pure being, truth, goodness, and perfection.—

Apollodorus, who until now had softly repeated every word of Socrates, broke into rapture, and repeated out loud: **who is pure being, pure truth, pure goodness, pure perfection**.

And **Socrates** continued: Do you see my friends! how far the man who loves wisdom must distance himself from the senses and their objects, if he wants to grasp what is true felicity to grasp, the All Maximum and Most Perfect Being?[131] In this quest for ideas he must close his eyes and ears, and pay no attention to pain and sensual pleasure, and if possible, forget his body entirely, in order to focus himself all the more completely on the capacities of his soul and its inner activity.

The body is to his understanding not only unnecessary for this inquiry, but also a burdensome companion; for now the lover of wisdom seeks neither color nor greatness, neither tones nor motion, but an entity, which can produce all possible colors, greatnesses, tones, and motions, and, what is still more, thinks of all possible spirits most clearly, and can bring them forth in all imaginable orders. What a cumbersome companion is the body on this journey?

How sublime! cried **Simmias**, but also how true!

The true philosophers, said **Socrates**, who take these reasons into consideration, could not have any other opinion, and say to one another: "Look! here is a false path, which leads us always further away from the goal, and frustrates all our hopes. We are certain, that the knowledge of the truth is our only wish. But as long as we trudge here on the earth with our body; as long as our soul is encumbered with this earthly scourge, we cannot possibly flatter ourselves, to see this wish completely fulfilled. We should seek the truth. Alas! the body allows us little leisure for this important undertaking. Today its maintenance requires all our care; tomorrow it is attacked by diseases, which disturb us once again; then follow other bodily concerns, love, fear, longings, desires, whims, and follies, which constantly divert us, which lure our senses from one vanity to another, and let the true object of our wishes, that is wisdom, languish in vain. What provokes war, revolt, quarrels, and discord among men? What other than the body, and its insatiable desires? For greediness is the mother of all unrest, and our soul would never crave after worldly possessions, if it didn't have to care for the hungry appetites of the body. We are occupied most of the time in such a way and seldom have leisure for philosophy. Finally, if one also obtains some leisure time, and prepares himself, to embrace truth; the disturber of our felicity, the body, stands in our way, and offers its shadow to us, instead of the truth. The senses hold their shadow images before us, against our will, and fill the soul with confusion, darkness, inertia, and utter foolishness: and the soul is supposed to think competently in this general turmoil and reach the truth? Impossible! We must therefore await the blessed moments, in which stillness without and peace within provides the happy opportunity, to take our attention totally away from the body, and to look towards the truth with the eyes of the spirit. But how rare, and how short are these blessed moments! —

We see clearly, that we will never reach wisdom, the goal of our wishes, until after our death; during one's life there is no hope of it. For the soul can't know the truth clearly, as long as it resides in the body, so we must assume one or the other; either, we shall never know the truth, or we shall know it after our death, because then the soul leaves the body, and is probably far less hindered in its progress to wisdom. But if we are to prepare ourselves in this life for that blessed knowledge, in the meantime, we must not grant more to the body's desires and lusts than what is necessary, and must, as often as possible, meditate, until it pleases the Almighty to set us free. Then we can hope, freed from the follies of the body, to behold the source of truth, the Maximum and Supreme Being, with pure and holy senses, while we perhaps see others near us enjoying the same felicity. But it is not allowed, that the unholy touch Holiness itself."—This language, my dear **Simmias**! may be used by those who truly desire wisdom among themselves, when they discuss their concerns with each other, and they must also cherish this opinion, which I believe; or do you think otherwise?

Not otherwise, my **Socrates**!

But if this is also the case, my dear! doesn't such a person, who follows me today, have great hope, that where we are going is better than anywhere else, to attain that which he has struggled for so much in the present life?

Certainly!

Therefore, I can begin my journey with good hope today, and every lover of truth can follow suit, if he reflects, that no free entry to the mysteries of truth is granted to him without purification and preparation.

This cannot be denied, said Simmias.

However, this purification is nothing other than the detachment of the soul from sensuous things, and to meditate in a sustained way regarding the nature and the attributes of the soul itself without admitting anything into it which is not soul, to mislead it; in short, the endeavor, in this life as well as in the future life, to free the soul from the chains of the body, so that it can contemplate itself unimpeded, and thereby may arrive at the knowledge of the truth.

Certainly!

The separation of the body from the soul one calls death.

Of course.

The true lovers of wisdom, therefore, take great pains to approximate death, in order to learn to die: do they not?

It appears so.

Then would it not be highly absurd, if a man, who studied nothing in his entire life, other than how to die, if such a man, I say, wanted to grieve at the end, because he sees death approach. Would it not be ridiculous?

Without a doubt.

Therefore, **Simmias**, death is never terrifying to true philosophers, but must always be welcome.—The companionship of the body is burdensome to them at all times; for if they want to fulfill the true goal of their being, they must try to detach the soul from the body, and as it were, to focus on the soul. Death is this separation, the long-desired liberation from the companionship of the body. What an absurdity, therefore, to tremble when death is imminent, to grieve! We must rather journey to death confidently and cheerfully, where we have hope to embrace our love, I mean wisdom, and to become free of the burdensome companion who has caused us so much sorrow?—Eh? common and ignorant people, who are robbed by death of their mistresses, their wives or their children, wish nothing more passionately in their sorrow than to leave the world and to be able to descend to the objects of their affection, or their desires: and these people, who have definite hope, to see their loves nowhere in greater brilliance than in the next life, should these people be totally afraid? should these people tremble? and rather not start the journey with joy? Oh no! my dear! nothing is more preposterous, than a philosopher, who fears death.

By Jupiter! entirely excellent, exclaimed Simmias.

To be trembling and full of fear, when death beckons, can this not be taken as an unfailing sign, that one loves not wisdom, but the body, wealth, honor, or all three together?

Entirely infallible.

To whom belongs the virtue, which we call manliness, more than the philosophers?

To nobody!

And temperance, this virtue which exists in the readiness to tame his desires, and to be restrained and modest, in everything he does, is it not to be found primarily in him who doesn't pay attention to his body, and simply lives and immerses himself in philosophy?

Necessarily, he said.

All others' manliness and moderation will seem absurd to you, when you observe them more closely.

How so? my Socrates!

You know, he replied, that the majority of men consider death as a very great evil.

Right, he said.

If therefore these, so-called courageous and manly people, die fearlessly, it happens simply out of fear of a still greater evil.

Not otherwise.

Therefore, all such manly ones, except the philosophers, are fearless only from fear. But is fearlessness stemming from fear not the highest paradox?

This is not to be denied.

It is the same with respect to temperance. From intemperance they live temperately and abstinently. One might consider this impossible, and nevertheless it is completely the case with this irrational temperance. They abstain from certain sensual pleasures, so that they may enjoy others, which are dearer to them, in greater excess.

They are masters over certain sensual pleasures because they are slaves to others. Question them, they will certainly tell you, that to allow themselves to be ruled by their desires, would be intemperance; but they themselves have achieved the command over certain desires in no other way than by slavery to other desires, which are still more excessive. Can we now not call this to a certain degree to be temperate from intemperance?

So it seems.

O my dear **Simmias**! to exchange one sensuous pleasure for another sensuous pleasure, one pain for another pain, and one fear for another fear, as it were, like money, to change a large bill for a lot of small change: this is not the way to true virtue. The only currency which has value, and for which one must give up all others, is wisdom. With this one acquires all the remaining virtues: bravery, temperance, and justice. In general, wisdom is the source of true virtue, true mastery over the desires, over feelings of loathing, and over all passions: but without wisdom we achieve nothing, only an exchange of passions for a wretched shadow of virtue, which has to serve as a slave to vice, and in itself leads to nothing healthy or true within the soul. True virtue is a sanctification of morals, a purification of the heart, not an exchange of desires. Justice, temperance, manliness, and wisdom, are not an exchange of one vice for another. Our forefathers, who instituted the **Teletes**,[132] or the **feast of perfect atonement**, apparently must have been very wise men; for they wanted to give us the understanding through these mysteries, that he who leaves this earth unatoned and unsanctified, has to bear the harshest punishment. However, the purified and atoned will dwell among the gods after death. Those who deal with these mysteries of atonement, are accustomed to say: **There are many who carry the sacred implements of Dionysius, but few are inspired**: and in my opinion, one understands under the concept "inspired ones," those who dedicated themselves to wisdom. I have spared nothing in my life, but have striven ceaselessly, to be one of those inspired ones; whether my efforts have been fruitless, or to what extent my intention has succeeded, I shall know best there, where I am going, and God willing, in a short time.—

This is my defense, **Simmias** and **Cebes**! this is why I leave my best friends here below without grief, and tremble so little with the immanence of death. I believe to find better friends and a better life there, than I leave here behind, even though so few of greatest multitude of men will consider this belief to be true. If my present defense speech is a better address than that which I delivered before the judges of the city, I am completely satisfied.

Socrates finished speaking, and **Cebes** began to speak: It is true, **Socrates**! You have completely justified yourself; but what you claim about the soul must seem unbelievable to many; for in general men argue,[133] that the soul is nowhere to be found anymore, as soon as it leaves the body, but is dissolved and annihilated immediately after death. It rises, like a mist, or like a fine vapor, out of the body into the air above, where it dissipates, and entirely ceases to be. If it could be accounted for, that the soul can exist by itself, and must not necessarily be connected with the body: then the hopes which you postulate would have a great probability; because as certain as it can become better for us after death: as certainly the virtuous person also has reasonable hopes, that it actually will be better for him after death. But even the possibility is hard to grasp, that the soul can still think after death, that it still would have will and powers of reason. This therefore, my **Socrates**, still requires some more proof.

You are right, **Cebes**! replied **Socrates**. But what is to be done? Do we possibly want to consider, whether we can find a proof, or not?

I am very eager, said **Cebes**, to hear your thoughts about this.

At least the one, replied **Socrates**, who hears our discussion, even if he were a comic poet, can not reproach me, that I busy myself with foolish whims, which neither are necessary nor relevant. The inquiry, which we now will undertake, is rather so important, that every poet will gladly give us permission to implore the assistance of a divinity, before we proceed to the task.

He was silent, and sat a long time engrossed in thought; then he said: my friends! to seek the truth with a pure heart, is the most worthy worship of the one God, who can give us assistance.[134] Therefore, to the subject! Death, oh **Cebes**! is a natural change of the human condition, and we will now investigate what happens in this change with respect to body of man as well as to his soul. Shall we?

Right!

Would it not be advisable first to generally explore what a natural change is, and how nature is accustomed to bring forth this change not only in regard to man, but also with respect to animals, plants, and lifeless things? I think, in this way we will come closer to our goal.

This is a happy idea, answered **Cebes**; we must therefore first search for an explanation, of what **change** is.

I think, said **Socrates**, we say a thing has changed, when among two opposite determinations, which can belong to it, the one ceases, and the other actually begins to exist. For example, beautiful and ugly, just and unjust, good and evil, day and night, sleep and waking, are these not opposite determinations, which are possible to one and the same thing?

Yes.

When a rose wilts and loses its beautiful form: don't we then say, it has changed?

Certainly!

And if an unjust man wants to change his conduct, must he not adopt an opposite conduct, and become just?[135]

How else?

Also conversely, if something is supposed to exist through a change, its contrary must have been there shortly before. So it becomes day, shortly after it was night, and in turn night, shortly after it was day; a thing becomes beautiful, large, heavy, important, etc. after it was ugly, small, light, unimportant: not so?

Yes!

Therefore a change generally means nothing else than the exchange of **opposite** determinations, which are possible to a thing. Should we leave it at that explanation? **Cebes** still seems undecided.—

A detail, my dear **Socrates**! I have some doubts about the word opposite. I cannot believe that directly opposite states can follow one another immediately.

Right! replied **Socrates**. We likewise see, that nature in all its changes knows to find an intermediate state, which serves as a transition, likewise, to go from one state to the opposite. For example, night follows the day, by means of evening twilight, as the day follows the night, by means of the morning dawn: Is this not so?

Certainly.

The large becomes small, mediated by decrease, and the small in turn becomes large, mediated by increase.

Right.

Even if also in certain cases we give this transition no particular name: still there is no doubt, that it must actually be existent, if a state would alternate in a natural way with its opposite: for must not a change which is supposed to be natural, be produced by the powers which lie in nature?

How could it be called natural otherwise?

But these powers are always working, always active: for if they fell asleep even for a moment, only the Almighty could awaken them to act. But should we call this natural, what only the Almighty can do?

How could we? said **Cebes**.

What the natural powers therefore produce now, my dear! they have been working on since time immemorial. They were never idle, but their effect became visible gradually. The power of nature, for example, which changes the times of day, is working already now, to lead night to the horizon after some time, but it makes its way through midday and evening, which are the transitions from the birth of the day until its death.

Right.

Even in sleep itself the vital powers work towards the future awakening, as they prepare the awakened state for future sleep.

This is not to be denied.

And generally, if a state is supposed to follow its contrary in a natural way, as such things happen with all natural changes: then the constantly active powers of nature must have already worked on this change previously, and have made the previous state pregnant, as it were, with the future state. Doesn't it follow from this, that nature must take all intermediate states with it, when it wants to alternate a state with its contrary?

Entirely undeniable.

Ponder it well, my friend! so that afterwards no doubt enters your mind, that you conceded too much to me at the beginning of the argument. We require three things for every natural change: a previous state of the thing, which is to be changed, a state which follows, which is opposite to this, and a transition, or the state in between both, which charts the course for nature from one to the other so to speak. Is this granted?

Yes, Yes! exclaimed **Cebes**. I can't imagine, how could I be able to doubt this truth?

Let us see, replied **Socrates**, whether the following will seem just as undeniable to you? I think, **all changeable things cannot remain unchanged for even a moment**, but while time hastens forward without rest, and the future constantly effects the past, time also changes at the same instant everything changeable, and manifests everything changeable constantly under a new form. Are you not of this opinion also, **Cebes**?

It is at least probable.

It seems indisputable to me. For every changeable thing, if it is a reality, and not a mere notion, must have a power to do something, and an ability to be acted upon by something. Now it may act or be acted upon, then it becomes something other than it was before; and since the powers of nature are never at rest; what could hinder the stream of the transitory in its course for one moment?

Now I am convinced.

The truth is not harmed by the fact that certain things often seem unchanged to us for a long time; just as a flame always seems the same to us, and nevertheless it is nothing other than a stream of fire, which rises upwards from the burning body without ceasing, and becomes invisible. Our eyes often see colors as unchanging, and nevertheless new sunlight constantly alternates with the previous rays of the sun. However, if we are searching for the truth, we must judge things according to reality, not according to how they appear to the senses.

By Jupiter! replied **Cebes**, this truth opens a new vista into the nature of things, which puts us in a state of awe. My friends! he continued, while he turned towards us, won't **Socrates** reveal all kinds of important things to us, if he applies these arguments to the soul!

I still have to establish one proposition, replied **Socrates**, before I arrive at that application. That which is changeable, we have admitted, cannot remain unchanged for a moment, but, just as time that has passed becomes older, so the past series of alterations that depend on each other must also grow older. Now consider, **Cebes**! Does one find two moments in time which are the closest to each other?

I still do not understand, said **Cebes**, what you want to say.—

An example will make my thoughts clearer. When I say the word "**Cebes**" aloud, don't two syllables here follow on each other, between which no third is encountered?

Right!

These two syllables therefore are the closest to each other.

Right!

But in the idea which we connect to the word, are there here also two parts which are the closest to each other?

I think not![136]

And you think rightly; because the parts of the idea form a continuous whole and can't be severed; on the other hand the syllables are separable, and follow in a discontinuous series one on the other.

This is perfectly clear.

Therefore, I ask about time: is it to be compared with the spoken word, or with the idea? Do the moments of time follow in a continuous, or a discontinuous order on each other?

In a continuous order, answered **Cebes**.

Certainly, **Simmias** replied; for we know time by the succession of our ideas; therefore how is it possible, that the nature of the succession in time and in ideas shouldn't be one and the same?

There are therefore no two moments, which are so close together that there is nothing between them?

No, said **Cebes**.

And since the changes continue in equal steps with time, also there are no two states, which are the closest to the other?

It appears so.

It certainly seems to our senses as if the changes happen in a discontinuous fashion; but in reality the succession of change is continuous; and one can put two states as close to each other as one wants: there is always still a transition in between, which connects them with each other, which leads nature on the path from one to the other.

I comprehend this all very well, said **Cebes**.

My friends! exclaimed **Socrates**, now it is time for us to draw near to our goal. We have compiled reasons, which supposedly argue for our eternity, and I promise myself a decisive victory. But shall we not, according to the custom of the generals before a battle, review our forces once more, in order to be acquainted with their strengths and weaknesses all the more precisely?

Apollodorus begged Socrates for a brief recapitulation of the argument.[137]

The propositions, said **Socrates**, whose truth we no longer dispute, are these:

1) For every natural change, three things are required: 1) a state of a changeable thing, which ceases, 2) another state, which is to take its place, and 3) the middle state, or the transition, so that the change doesn't happen suddenly, but gradually.
2) What is changeable doesn't exist for a moment without being actually changed.
3) The succession of time proceeds in a continuum, and there are no two moments, which are closest one to one another.
4) The succession of the changes coheres with the succession of time, and is therefore so constant, so indivisible, that one can specify no states which are closest to one another, or between which one could not find a place of transition. Are we not agreed on these points?

Yes, said **Cebes**.

Life and death, my dear **Cebes**, replied **Socrates**, are opposite states: are they not?

Certainly!

And dying is the transition from life to death?

Certainly!

This great change presumably touches the soul as well as the body; for both beings exist in this life in the most intimate connection.

Apparently.

Observation can teach us what happens to the body after this important event; for that which is extended remains present to our senses; but how, where and what the soul will be after this life can only be discerned by reason; for through death the soul has lost the means to be present to the human senses.

Right!

Shall we not, my dearest!, first pursue the visible through all its changes, and afterwards, where possible, compare the invisible with the visible?

That seems the best path which we can take, replied **Cebes**.

In every animal body, **Cebes**!, constant divisions and combinations take place, which aim partly at the preservation, partly at the destruction of the great machine [the body].[138] Already when animals are born, death and life begin to struggle with each other as it were. Everyday experience demonstrates this.

What do we name the condition, asked **Socrates**, in which the animal changes aim more to the preservation than to the destruction of the body. Don't we call this condition **health**?

How else?

On the contrary, the animal changes, which cause the dissolution of the great machine, increase through illnesses, or also by aging, which can be called the most natural illness.

Right!

The decay increases gradually by imperceptible degrees. Finally the structure falls to pieces, and dissolves into its smallest parts. But what happens? Do these parts cease to undergo changes? Are they entirely lost?

Apparently not, answered **Cebes**.

Impossible; my most worthy one! replied **Socrates**, if what we agreed upon is true: for is there a mean between being and not-being?

No way.

Therefore being and not-being would be two states which immediately follow on one another, which must be the closest to each other: however we have seen that nature can produce no such changes, which happen suddenly and without transition. Do you still remember this proposition well?

Very well, said **Cebes**.

Therefore nature can produce neither being nor annihilation?

Right!

Therefore nothing is lost with the dissolution of the animal body. The disintegrated parts continue to exist, to act, to suffer, to be combined and separated, until they change through infinite transitions into parts of another composition. Some become dust, some become moisture, the former rises into the air, the latter passes into a plant, wanders from the plant into a living animal, and leaves the animal, to serve as nourishment for a worm. Is this not in accord with experience?

Completely, my **Socrates**! answered **Cebes** and **Simmias** at the same time.

Therefore we see, my friends!, that death and life, in so far as they concern the body, are not as distinct in nature, as they appear to our senses. They are links in a continuous series of changes, which are connected with each other in the most intimate way through successive transitions. There is no precise moment, where one could say: **Now the animal dies**; as little as one can pinpoint the precise moment: **Now it became sick,** or **now it became healthy again**. Certainly the changes must seem separated to our senses, since they become noticeable to us only after a fairly long interval of time; but we know enough that they cannot be so in fact.

I now recall an example which will shed light this statement. Our eyes, which are limited to a specific zone of the earth, very clearly differentiate the morning, afternoon, evening and midnight, and it appears to us as if these points of time were separate and distinct from the others. But whoever considers the whole earth, knows very clearly, that the revolutions of day and night follow continuously on each other, and therefore every moment of time—morning and night, midday and midnight is joined together.

Homer has the freedom, as a poet, to assign the times of the day according to his gods' functions: as if the times of day really would be separate epochs to someone who is not limited to a narrow district on the earth, and rather it would not be at every moment of time morning as well as evening. The poets are permitted to do this; but to comply with the truth, Dawn with her rosy fingers must constantly hold the gates of heaven open, and drag her yellow cloak unceasingly from one place to another, just as the gods, if they only want to sleep at night, must sleep constantly or not at all.—

So the days of the week, considered as a whole, don't allow differentiation; for that which is continuous and unified is divided into particular and separate parts only in the imagination and through the deception of the senses. But the understanding sees very well, that one doesn't have to stop where there is no actual division. Is this clear, my friends?

Very much so, replied **Simmias**.

It is the same case with the life and death of animals and plants. In the course of the changes, which the same thing undergoes, judging by our senses, an epoch begins at the time, when the thing becomes noticeable to our senses as a plant or as an animal, and we call this the sprouting of the plant, and the birth of the animal. The second point of time, there, where the animal or plant movements elude our senses, we call death; and the third, when finally the animal or plant forms disappear and become invisible, we call the decay, the decomposition of the animal or the plant. However, in nature all these changes are links of an unbroken chain, gradually unfolding and enfolding the same thing, which clothes and unclothes itself in forms without number. Is there still anything doubtful herein?

It seems not, replied **Cebes**.

When we say, continued **Socrates**, the soul dies, we must assume one of two things: Either all its powers and abilities, its actions and sufferings suddenly cease, they disappear as it were in an instant; or like the body, it undergoes gradual transformations, innumerable changes of appearance, which proceed in a continuous series, and in this series there is an epoch, where it has ceased to be a human soul, but has become something else, just as the body, after countless transformations, ceases to be a human body, and becomes dust, air, plant, or a part of another animal. Is there is a third case in which the soul can die other than **suddenly** or **gradually**?

No, answered **Cebes**. This division exhausts the possibility completely.

Good, said **Socrates**. Therefore, those who still doubt if the soul can be immortal, may choose, whether they are concerned, that the soul may disappear suddenly, or gradually cease to be what it was.

Does **Cebes** want to take up their side and make this choice for them?

The question is, whether they would accept the choice of their advocate. My advice would be that we consider both cases; because if they reject my choice, and declare themselves on the other side: there might be no one here tomorrow, who could refute them [since you will be gone].

My dear **Cebes**!, retorted **Socrates**, Greece is a sprawling empire, and even among the barbarians there must be many for whom this inquiry lies close to their heart.[139] So be it! Let us examine both cases. The first was: **Perhaps the soul dies suddenly, disappears in an instant.** This type of death is possible in itself. But can it be produced by nature?

No way: if what we granted before is true, that nature can produce no annihilation.

And have we not granted this correctly? asked **Socrates**. Between **being** and **not-being** is a enormous abyss, which cannot be bridged by the nature of things which act gradually.

Entirely correct, replied **Cebes**. But what if the soul was annihilated by a supernatural force, by a deity?

Oh my dearest!, exclaimed **Socrates**, how happy we are, how well provided for, if we have to fear nothing but the **immediate** hand of the only Miracle Worker! What we were anxious about, was, whether the nature of our soul as such is not mortal, and this anxiety we are

trying to overcome by reason; but if God, the all good Creator and Preserver of things, will destroy the soul by a miracle? No **Cebes**, let us
rather fear the sun would change into ice, before we will fear an evil
act from the self-subsisting Good, **annihilation by a miracle**.

I didn't take into consideration, said **Cebes**, that my objection was
so close to sacrilege.

The one kind of death, sudden annihilation, doesn't terrorize us
anymore, **Socrates** continued; for it is impossible in nature. But consider also the following, my friends. Assume that it were not impossible, the question is, when? at what point in time should our soul
vanish? Presumably at the time, when the body no longer needed it, in
the moment of death?

Apparently.

But we have seen, that there is no definite moment, where one can
say, **now** the animal dies. The dissolution of the animal machine has
already started long ago, before its effects were visible; for it never
lacks in such animal movements, which are contrary to the preservation of the whole. They gradually increase, until at last all the movements of the parts don't harmonize anymore to one unified goal—each
one has adopted its own particular goal: and then the machine is dissolved. This happens so gradually, in such a continuous process, that
every state can be called a boundary condition of the previous and following states, an effect of the previous state and a cause of the following state. Have we not accounted for this?

Correct!

Therefore, if the death of the body is also supposed to be the death
of the soul: there must be no moment at which one can say, **now** the
soul vanishes; but gradually, as the movements in the parts of the machine cease to harmonize towards one unified goal, the soul must di-
minish in power and internal activity also. Does it seem to you not
thus, my **Cebes**?

Completely so!

But look! what a wondrous turn our inquiry has taken! It seems
like a statue of my great-grandfather Daedalus,[140] to have rolled away
by an internal mechanism from its previous place.

How so?

We have assumed that our adversaries were concerned that the
soul would suddenly be annihilated, and wanted to see, whether this
fear would be reasonable or not. After that we examined, at which
moment it might be annihilated: and this inquiry itself brought us to

the contrary of the hypothesis, namely that the soul is not suddenly annihilated, but gradually diminishes in internal power and activity.

So much the better, answered **Cebes**. So this assumed opinion has disproved itself as it were.

We therefore have to examine only this, if the internal powers of the soul aren't able to die away as gradually as the parts of the machine separate themselves.

Correct!

Let us follow these faithful companions on their journey, body and soul, who are also supposed to have death in common with each other, in order to see where they remain in the end. As long as the body is healthy, as long as the majority of the movements of the machine aim to the preservation of the whole, the sense organs also function properly, the soul also possesses its full power, perceives, thinks, loves, abhors, conceives and wills. Does it not?

Indisputable!

The body becomes sick. It manifests a visible discord between the movements that proceed in the machine, as its many parts don't harmonize any more to preserve the whole, but have entirely individual and conflicting goals. And the soul?

As experience teaches, in the meantime it becomes weaker, perceives indistinctly, thinks falsely and often acts against its own self-interest. Well! I will continue. The body dies: that is to say, all its movements now don't seem to aim towards the life and preservation of the whole anymore; but internally probably still a few weak vital movements of life proceed, which still provide the soul with some murky images: therefore the power of the soul must limit itself to these movements until it perishes entirely. Is this not true?

Certainly.

Decomposition follows. The parts which had one common goal until now and have made one single machine, now acquire entirely different goals, and become various parts of entirely different machines. And the soul, my **Cebes**? Where will we leave the soul? Its machine is decomposed. The parts, which are still left of it, are not **its** parts anymore and form no whole, which could be infused with soul. There are no organs of the senses, no more instruments of feeling, anywhere by means of which it could obtain a sensation. Shall therefore everything in it be barren? Shall all its sensations, its imaginations, its desires and aversions, appetites and passions vanish, and leave behind not the slightest trace?

Impossible, said **Cebes**. What would this be other than a total annihilation, and no annihilation, we have seen, exists in the ability of nature.

Therefore what is the remedy, my friends? The soul cannot perish in eternity; for the final step, one may postpone it as long as possible, would still always be a leap from being to nothingness, which neither can be established in the nature of a discrete thing, nor in the continuum. Therefore the soul will continue and be eternally existent. If it should exist, it must act and be acted upon; if it should act and be acted upon, it must have concepts, for to feel, think, and will are the only actions and sufferings which can befit a soul. Concepts always begin from a sensuous perception, and from where should sensuous perceptions come, if no tools, no organs of the senses exist?

Nothing seems more correct, said **Cebes**, than this sequence of conclusions, and nevertheless it leads to an apparent contradiction.

One of the two must be the case, continued **Socrates**: Either the soul must be annihilated, or it must still have conceptions after the decomposition of the body. One is predisposed to consider both these cases as impossible, and nevertheless must one of them actually be true? Let us see if we can find a way out of this labyrinth! On the one hand our spirit cannot be annihilated by natural means. On what is this impossibility based?—Don't give up, friends! follow me through the thorny paths; they lead us to one of the most splendid regions which has ever delighted the mind of man. Answer me! Has a proper conception of power and natural change not led us to the conclusion, that nature can produce no annihilation?

Correct!

From this perspective, there is therefore absolutely no hope of a way out, and thus we must turn around. The soul cannot perish, it must continue, to act, to suffer, and to have conceptions after death. Here the impossibility confronts us that our spirit, without sensuous impressions, is supposed to have conceptions: but who can verify this impossibility? Is it not simply our experience that we never could have the ability to think without sensuous impressions here in this life?

Nothing else.

But what kind of reason do we have, to extend this experience beyond the borders of this life, and to absolutely deny nature the possibility, to let the soul think, without this body, which has sense organs. What do you think, **Simmias**? Would we not find a man very ridiculous, who never had left the walls of Athens, and wanted to conclude from his own experience, that no other form of government would be possible than the democratic?[141]

Nothing would be more absurd.

If a child could think in the mother's womb, would it be possible to persuade it, that one day, it would be cut from its umbilical cord, and would enjoy the refreshing light of the sun in the free air? Would it not believe itself rather to be able to prove from its present circumstances the impossibility of such a situation?

So it seems.

And we, in the infantile state of mankind, do we think any more reasonably, if we, imprisoned in this life, want to be able to account by our experiences what likewise is possible for nature to do after this life?—One single look into the inexhaustible multiplicity of nature can convince us of the unreasonableness of such a conclusion. How poor, how weak the soul would be, if its capability couldn't reach beyond our experience!

Admittedly!

Therefore with good reason we can reject this experience, in so far as we contrast it with the agreed-upon impossibility, that our spirit should to perish. Homer rightly has his hero call out: **In truth! in the house of Orkus the soul still moves, although its corpse doesn't come with it**. The conception, which Homer creates of Orkus for us, and of the shades which wander down there, indeed seems to not quite coincide in general with the truth; but this is certain, my dears! Our spirit triumphs over death and decay and leaves the corpse behind, in order to fulfill the purposes of the Almighty in a thousand changing forms. It rises above the dust, and continues, according to other **natural**, but **celestial** laws, to contemplate the works of the Creator, and to entertain thoughts about the power of the infinite being.[142] But ponder this, my friends! If our soul still lives and thinks after the death of its body, will it not also there, as in this life, strive towards felicity?

Probably, I think, said **Simmias**; but I don't trust my conjecture anymore, and wish to hear your reasons.

My reasons are these, replied **Socrates**; When the soul thinks, it must alternate its concepts with other concepts, it must prefer one concept and not the other, which means it must have a will; but if the soul has a will, what can its purpose be other than the highest degree of well-being, to strive for felicity?

This was clear to everybody.

But how? continued **Socrates**: in what does the well-being of a spirit exist, which has no more care for the needs of its body? Food and drink, love and lust can no longer please it; what delights its feelings, palate, eyes and ears in this life is unworthy of its attention; barely a weak, perhaps rueful memory of passions remains to it, which it enjoyed in the company of its body. Will the spirit seek those in particular?

As little as a person born deaf seeks beautiful music, said **Simmias**.

For example will the goal of its desires be a great fortune? How can this be possible in a situation, where, apparently, no property can be possessed, no worldly goods can be enjoyed?

Love of fame is indeed a passion, which, apparently, can still abide in the departed spirit; for it seems to depend little on the needs of the body. But in what can the bodiless spirit invest, which would give it priority? Certainly not power, not riches, also not nobleness of birth: for all these follies it leaves behind with its body on earth.

Admittedly!

Therefore nothing remains to it, which could give it priority, but wisdom, love of virtue, and knowledge of the truth. In addition to this noble love of fame, the spiritual, pleasant sensations are restored to it, which the soul enjoys even on the earth without its body—beauty, order, symmetry, and perfection. These sensations are thus innate to the essence of a spirit, and they can never leave it. Therefore, he who has bestowed care on his soul while on earth, he who has exercised himself in wisdom, virtue, and the feeling of true beauty, has the greatest hopes, likewise to continue in these practices after death, and to approach the most sublime First Principle step by step, which is the source of all wisdom, the embodiment of all perfections, and is above all beauty itself. Remember, my friends, those enraptured moments which you enjoyed, whenever your souls, transported by spiritual beauty, forgot the body along with its needs, and surrendered themselves entirely to perceiving that which is heavenly. What shudders! What enthusiasm! Nothing but the nearer presence of a deity can exite these sublime raptures in us. Likewise, in fact, every concept of a spiritual beauty is a glance into the essence of the Godhead; for the beauty, order, and perfection, which we perceive, is a weak impression of Him, who is self-subsisting beauty, order, and perfection. I remember, to have argued these principles on another occasion clearly enough[143], and will presently draw only this consequence from them: If it is true, that after this life, wisdom and virtue constitute our ambition, and striving for spiritual beauty, order, and perfection constitute our desires: thus our continued existence becomes nothing other than an uninterrupted contemplation of the Deity, a heavenly delight, which, as little as we grasp it now, rewards the noble sweat of the virtuous with infinite usury. What are all the toils of this life compared to such an eternity! What is poverty, contempt, or the most humiliating death, if we can thereby prepare ourselves for such a felicity! No, my friends! he who is conscious of living righteously, cannot possibly be troubled, when he commences the journey to eternal felicity. Only he who offends the gods and man in his life, who wallows in bestial lust, or sacrifices human beings to honor deities, and takes delight in other depravities, may tremble at the threshold of death, since he can cast no glance into the past without regret, and no glance into the future without fear. But I, thanks be to the Deity!, have to make none of these reproaches to myself since my entire life I sought the truth with fervor, and have loved virtue above all; thus I rejoice to hear the voice of the Deity, who calls me hence, in order to enjoy the light of heaven, which I have striven for in this darkness. But you, my friends! Consider well the grounds for my hopes, and if they convince you, bless my journey, and live thusly that death may call you away from here someday, not drag you away by force. Perhaps the Deity will lead us one day in transfigured friendship into each other's arms. Oh! With what rapture then would we remember the present day!

Second Dialogue

Our teacher had finished speaking, and walked back and forth in the room, engrossed in thought; we all sat and were silent, and reflected on the matter. Only **Cebes** and **Simmias** spoke quietly with each other.

Socrates looked around, and asked: Why so quiet? my friends! Shall we not learn what could be improved in the principles of reason which were asserted? I know very well that they still lack perfect clarity in some respects. If you are discussing other things now, that's fine; but if you are talking about the subject which we have in mind, reveal all your objections and doubts to us, so that we may examine them collectively, and either resolve them, or share the doubts with you.

Simmias said: I must confess to you, **Socrates**! That we both have objections to make, and have been urging each other for a while to present them, because we both would like to hear your refutation, but we each shy away of being a burden to you in your present calamity.

When **Socrates** heard this, he smiled, and said, "Ah, O **Simmias**! how difficult will it be for me to be able to convince other men that I don't consider my circumstances so unfortunate, since you, friends, still cannot believe me, and now are worried, that I might be more annoyed and disagreeable now than I have been formerly. It is said about the swans, that close to their end, they sing more delightfully than in their whole life. If these birds, as is said, are consecrated to Apollo, then I would say that their god let them feel a foretaste of the bliss of that life to come in the hour of death, and that they take delight in this feeling, and sing. It is the same with me. I am a priest of this god: and in truth!, he has imprinted on my soul a premonition of the bliss after death, which drives away all unhappiness, and allows me to be far more cheerful close to my death, than in my whole life. Therefore, disclose your doubts and objections to me without reservation. Ask what you have to ask, as long as the Eleven Men still permit it.

Good! replied **Simmias**, therefore, I will begin, and **Cebes** may follow. I have only one more thing in mind to bring up before we start:

If I raise doubts about the immortality of the soul, it is not to contradict the truth of this divine teaching, but rather to challenge the ability to prove it rationally, or more so to contest the way which you have chosen, oh **Socrates**!, to convince us of it through reason. For the rest, I embrace this comforting doctrine with all my heart, not only as you have presented it to us, but in such a way as has been handed down to us by the most ancient philosophers, leaving out some falsifications, which have been added by the poets and inventors of fables. Where our soul finds no reason for certainty, there it trusts the comforting opinions, like the vessels on the bottomless sea, which lead it securely under the cheerful sky through the waves of this life. I feel that I cannot contradict the doctrine of immortality, or of God's judgment after this death, without raising infinite difficulties, without seeing everything, which I regarded as true and good, shaken to its foundation. If our soul is mortal, then our reason is a dream, which was sent by Jupiter, to deceive us wretched ones; thus virtue lacks all the brilliance, which makes it divine in our eyes.[144] Then the beautiful and the sublime, moral as well as physical, is not an imprint of divine perfection; (for nothing perishable can grasp the weakest ray of divine perfection); and so we, like the cattle, have been put here to seek food and die. So it will be the same in a few days, whether I have been an ornament or a shame to creation, whether I have troubled myself to increase the number of blessed people or the wretched ones. Thus the most confused mortal has the power to even revoke the rule of God, and a dagger could cut the bond which connects men to God. If our spirit is perishable, the wisest lawgivers and founders of human societies have deceived us, or themselves; thus the whole human race has come to an understanding, so to speak, to foster a falsehood, and to worship the swindlers who fabricated such an untruth. Thus a state of free, thinking beings is not superior to a herd of dumb cattle, and man, I am horrified to behold him in this lowliness! And man, robbed of the hope for immortality, is the most wretched animal on earth, who, reflecting on his misfortunate situation, must fear death and despair. Not the most-kind God, who takes delight in the felicity of his creatures, but a sadistic being must have bestowed man with virtues, which only make him more pitiable. I can't express, what oppressive anguish overcomes my soul, when I put myself in the place of the wretched people, who fear annihilation. The bitter reminder of death must embitter all their joys. When they want to enjoy friendship, when they want to know truth, when they want to practice virtue, when they want to worship the Creator, when they want to fall into a rapture about beauty and perfection: at these moments the horrible thought of annihilation arises, like a specter, in their soul, and throws them into despair. A breath which is missing, a pulse which stops, robs them of all these glories: the being who worships God becomes dust. I thank the gods, that they liberate me from this fear, which would interrupt all the pleasures of my life with the stings of a scorpion. My conceptions of divinity, of virtue, of the dignity of man, and of the relationship in which he stands to God, allow me to doubt no more about man's determination. The hope of a future life resolves all these difficulties, and brings the truths, which we are convinced of in various ways, into harmony again. This hope sanctifies the Deity, establishes virtue in its nobility, gives beauty its brilliance, gives pleasure its attraction, sweetens misery, and even makes the plagues of this life worthy of worship in our eyes; as we compare events here below with the infinite series of consequences, which are provoked by them. A doctrine, which stands in harmony with so many known and established truths, and by means of which we so easily resolve an array of difficulties, finds us very much inclined to accept it; it needs almost no further proof. For though, from these reasons, taken individually, perhaps none have the highest degree of certainty in themselves, nonetheless, taken together, they convince us with such a winning power, that they reassure us completely, and dispel all our doubts. But, my dear **Socrates**!, The difficulty is, to have all these reasons present with the vividness whenever we wish, in order to survey their harmony with clarity. We need the assistance of this doctrine of immortality at all times, and in all circumstances of this life; but not all times and circumstances of this life grant us the serenity and thoughtfulness of the soul, to remember all these reasons vividly, and to feel the power of truth, which is interlaced in their connection. Whenever we either don't imagine a part of the doctrine at all, or don't imagine it with sufficient mental vividness, the truth loses its strength, and the serenity of our soul is in danger. But if that path, which you, oh **Socrates**! pursue, leads us through a simple series of irrefutable arguments to the truth: then we can hope to secure the proof for ourselves and always remember it. A series of clear conclusions can be recalled more easily in thoughts, than that congruence of truths, which to a certain extent demands its own state of mind.[145] For this reason I have no misgivings to set all the doubts before you, which the most determined opponent of immortality could assert. Where I have understood you correctly, your proof was approximately the following: the soul and body exist in the most intimate connection; the latter is gradually dissolved into its parts, the former must either be annihilated, or still have ideas. Nothing can be annihilated by natural powers: therefore through natural means our soul can never cease to have concepts. But suppose, my dear **Socrates**! if I were to prove through similar reasons, that musical harmony would have to continue when the lyre was smashed to pieces, or that the symmetry of a building still must exist, even if all the stones were ripped apart from each other, and crushed to dust? Harmony, as well as symmetry, I would say, is something isn't it? One would not deny me this; the former exists with the lyre and the latter with the building in precise connection: one must also admit this. If we compare the lyre or the building with the body, and harmony or symmetry with the soul: then we have proved that the playing of a stringed instrument must last longer than the strings, the elegant proportions would have to last longer than the building. But this is highly absurd in regard to harmony and symmetry; since they indicate the manner of the composition: they cannot endure longer than the composition itself.

The same can be asserted about health: It is an attribute of the body made up of members, and is found nowhere else, than where the functions of these members aim to the preservation of the whole; health is an attribute of the composition, and disappears, when the composition is dissolved into its parts. There is apparently a similar circumstance with life. The life of a plant ceases, as soon as the movements of its parts tend toward the dissolution of the whole. The animal has the advantage over the plant of having the organs of sense and perception, and finally man has the advantage of reason over both. Perhaps this feeling in the beast, and even man's reason, are nothing other than attributes of the composition, as well as life, health, harmony, etc., which, according to their nature and circumstances, cannot last longer than the compositions, from which they are inseparable. If the art of structure is sufficient to give life and health to plants and animals, perhaps a higher art could bestow feeling upon the animals, and reason to man.[146] We, as mankind in its infantile state, grasp the former as little as the latter. The ingenious structure of the most insignificant leaf surpasses all human reason, and contains mysteries, which will still mock the diligence and brilliance of all future generations: and we want to stipulate, what can be achieved by the organization of nature, and what cannot? We want to set limits on the omnipotence or the wisdom of the Creator? We must necessarily do one or the other, I would think, if our insignificance in regard to the Creator, shall decide, that the art of the Almighty himself couldn't create an ability to feel and to think by the formation of the smallest speck of matter.

You see, my dear **Socrates**! what is still lacking to your students for complete, rock-solid conviction. If the soul is something which has life, which the Almighty created outside the body and its structure and is connected with it: so it is correct, that the soul must continue after death and have ideas; but who can guarantee that? Experience seems rather to state the opposite. The ability to think is composed with the body, grows with it and undergoes similar changes with it. Every illness in the body is accompanied by weakness, disorder, or incapacity in the soul. Especially the functions of the brain and intestines exist in such intimate connection with the effectiveness of the ability to think, that one is very inclined, to derive both from one source, and therefore to explain the invisible by the visible; as one attributes light and heat to a single cause, because they correspond so much in their changes.

Simmias was silent, and **Cebes** began to speak. Our friend Simmias, he said, seems only to want to possess with certainty that which had been promised to him, but I, my dear **Socrates**!, would like to have more than you promised to us. If your proofs are defended against all objections, still nothing more follows from them, than that our soul continues after the death of our body and has ideas; but continues how? perhaps in a swoon, in a faint or as in sleep. The soul of one sleeping must not be entirely devoid of conceptions. The objects all around must affect his senses through weaker impressions, and provoke at least weak sensations in his soul, otherwise stronger and stronger impressions will not be able to awaken him. But what kind of conceptions are these? An unconsciousness, without recollection, an irrational state, in which we remember nothing of the past, and which we also never recollect in the future. Now if our soul should sink into a kind of sleep or state of lethargy with its separation from the body, and never awake again, what would we have gained by its continuation? A being without reason is still farther distant from the immortality for which you hope, as the felicity of the animal is distant from the felicity of a mind who knows God. If that which befalls the spirit after death concerns us, and should already arouse fear or hope here below in us: so we who are conscious of ourselves here in this life, must still keep that awareness of self in that life after death and be able to remember the present. We must compare that which we will be, with that which we are now, and be able to make a judgment about it. Yes, where I have understood you correctly, my dear **Socrates**!, you expect a better life after death, a greater enlightenment of the understanding, nobler and more sublime movements of the heart, than has been the lot of the most altruistic mortal on earth: what is the reason for this flattering hope? The lack of all consciousness is not an impossible state for our soul: daily experience convinces us of this. How, if such a state without consciousness should continue in eternity after death?

Certainly you have shown us a little while ago, that everything changeable must be in a continuous process of change, and a ray of hope shines from this doctrine, that my anxiety would be unjustified. For if the series of changes, which are forthcoming to our soul, progress infinitely, it is extremely probable, that the soul would not be destined to sink away into eternity, and to constantly lose more and more of its divine beauty, but that, at least with time, it also will rise and again resume the level, on which it stood previously in creation, that is, to be a contemplator of the works of God. And a higher degree of probability isn't necessary to encourage us in the assumption that a better life is at hand for the virtuous. In the meantime, my dear **Socrates**!, I wish to see this point touched upon by you as well, because I know that every word that you speak today, will be indelibly engraved deeply in my soul, never to be forgotten.

We all listened attentively, and as we afterwards confessed, not without displeasure that a doctrine, of which we believed ourselves to be very convinced, was made doubtful and uncertain to us. Not only this doctrine, but everything which we knew and believed, seemed to us at that time to become uncertain and indecisive, since we saw, that either we didn't have the capacity to distinguish truth from falsehood, or that truth and falsehood couldn't be distinguished from each other.

ECHECRATES: My dear **Phädon**! That you and your friends thought so doesn't surprise me at all. This was what I was thinking while I listened to you.[147] The reasons of **Socrates** had convinced me totally, and I seemed certain, that I would never be able to doubt them; but Simmias' objection made me doubtful again. I remember, that I formerly was of the opinion, that the power to think could be an attribute of the composition, and could have its foundation in a delicate organization or harmony of the parts. But tell me, dear **Phädon**, how **Soc-**

rates took in these objections? Did he become as annoyed about this as you, or did he encounter them with his usual gentle temper? And did his answer satisfy you and your friends, or not? I would like to hear all of this in as much detail as possible from you.

PHÄDON: If I ever admired **Socrates**, my dear **Echecrates**!, it was certainly on this occasion. That he had a refutation ready is nothing unexpected from him. What seemed admirable to me, was first, the kind-heartedness, friendliness, and gentleness, with which he took in the immature reasonings of these young people, then how quickly he noticed what kind of impressions the objections made on us, how he hastened to help us, how he, as it were, called us back from the escape, encouraged us to fight, and directed the argument himself.[148]

ECHECRATES: How was this?

PHÄDON: I will relate it to you. I sat to his right, next to the bed, on a low chair, so he was a bit higher than I. He touched my head, and stroked my hair, which hung down my neck, as he was accustomed occasionally to play with my curls: Tomorrow, he said, **Phädon**!, May you strew these locks over the grave of a friend.

So it seems, I answered.

Oh! do it not, he answered.

Why do you say that? I asked.

Yet today, he continued, we must both cut our hair, if our beautiful doctrinal edifice dies away, and we are not in a position to awaken it again.[149] And if I were in your place, and one would have undermined my doctrine: I would, like any Argive, make a vow, not to let my hair grow again, until I had vanquished the opposing arguments of **Simmias** and **Cebes**.

The old adage is, I said, **Hercules himself can do nothing against two.**

Then call me your Iolaus to help, because it is still daylight, he replied.

Good! I said, I will call upon you to help; not like Hercules helped his Iolaus, but as Iolaus helped Hercules.[150]

That's a diversion, he replied. Above all things we must be careful of taking a certain false step.

Which false step? I asked.

That we not become **haters of reason**, he said, as certain people become **haters of men**. No greater misfortune could befall us than this hatred of reason. As a matter of fact, hatred of reason and hatred of men originate in a similar way. The latter arises, by and large, when one initially puts blind trust in someone and esteems him highly as a totally faithful, sincere, and righteous man, but then finds out, that he is neither sincere nor righteous, especially if this happens to us repeatedly, and occurs with respect to those whom we have considered as our best and truest friends. Then one becomes unhappy, projects his hate on all people indiscriminately, and thinks no one is capable of the least righteousness anymore. Have you not noticed that it usually happens that way?

Very often, I answered.

But is this not shameful? And doesn't this mean wanting to have benefit from human society, without having the least insight into human nature? Whoever isn't entirely without reflection, easily finds herein the middle road, which in fact also contains the truth in itself. Totally good or evil men are only very few. Most men retain approximately the middle between both extremes.

What are you saying? I asked.

As for instance, he said, in respect to the largest and smallest, or the remaining attributes. What is rarer than a man, dog or other creature, which is very large or small, very fast or very slow, extraordinarily beautiful, ugly, black, white, etc? Have you not also noticed, that in all these things, the most extreme on the two sides is encountered rarely and seldom, and the mean on the other hand most frequently?

I think so, I said.

Don't you mean, he replied, if a prize would be awarded for the most extreme worthlessness, that very few men would deserve the prize?

Likely, I answered.

Very likely, he continued. However in this point between reason and between the human race is found much more a dissimilarity than a similarity: and I have been led by your questions to this digression. The similarity then is to be seen though, when someone regards some conclusion to be true and coherent, without proper inquiry and without insight into the nature of human reason, and shortly after believes to find the same conclusion to be false again—now he would like it to be true or false as such: particularly if this happens often, as we saw previously in the case of friendship. Then he fares like those certified conjurers, who defend and refute as long as one wants, until they imagine themselves to be the wisest among mortals, the only ones, who perceived that reason, as well as all remaining things on earth, contain nothing certain and sure; but that everything sways to and fro on the whirlpools of the sea of Euripus, and doesn't remain in its previous place for a moment.[151]

It is true, I said.

However, my dear **Phädon**, he continued, suppose that the truth as such is not only certain and unchangeable, but also not entirely incomprehensible to man, and that it would tempt somebody through such pretences by reasons and counter-reasons which cancel each other. Further, suppose that he would not blame himself and his own incompetence, but out of indignation rather blamed reason itself, and the rest of his life hated and detested all rational principles, and would allow all truth and knowledge to be distant from him. Would the misfortune of this man not be lamentable?

By Jupiter! I answered, very lamentable.

We must therefore first try to avoid this error, and convince ourselves, that the truth itself not be uncertain and variable, but that our understanding would be too weak on occasion, to hold fast to the truth and to master it; therefore we must double our powers and our courage and always venture new attacks. We all are obliged, my friends! you for the sake of your life ahead, and I on account of my death.— Yes, I have an additional motivation, which might seem more plaintive than truth loving to the mentality of common, ignorant people. When these people have something doubtful to investigate, they trouble themselves little about what attributes the thing in itself has, as long as they make their point and their opinions are applauded by those present. I will be different from these people only in one particular point. To convince the persons present of my opinion is only my secondary objective. My foremost concern is to convince myself, that my opinion is in accord with the truth, because I find the greatest benefit thereby. For look, dearest friend! I draw the following conclusion: If the doctrine which I present is well-reasoned, then I do well to convince myself of it; but if there is no more hope left for the departed, I gain at least this consolation, that I am not troublesome to my friends before my death by lamenting. I please myself at times with the thought, that everything which would bring the whole human race true comfort and benefit, if it were true, already for this reason has a great likelihood that it be true. If the skeptics turn against the doctrine of God and virtue, and say it is a mere political invention, which had been thought up for the betterment of human society: then I would like to shout to them: Oh! my friends! Conceive of a concept of teaching, which is so indispensable to the human race, and I'll wager that it be true. The human race is summoned to society, as every member is summoned to felicity. Everything, which can lead to this end in a universal, certain, and constant manner, has been indisputably chosen by the Wisest Creator as a means and has been produced. These flattering images contain so much consolation, and show us the relationship between the Creator and man in the most refreshing light.[152] Therefore I wish nothing so much, as to convince myself of its truth. Nevertheless, it wouldn't be good if my ignorance concerning this should continue still longer. No! I will soon be liberated from it.

In this state of mind, **Simmias** and **Cebes**! I turn to your objections. You, my friends!, if you want to follow my advice, look more to the truth than to **Socrates**.[153] If you find that I remain faithful to the truth, give me approval; where not, oppose me without the least reservation: so that I not, because you respect me so much, deceive you and myself, and part from you like a bee, who leaves its stinger behind.

Well now, my friends! Be attentive and remind me, where I would omit something of your reasons, or would state them inaccurately. **Simmias** grants that our ability to think is either created for itself, or must be produced through the composition and formation of the body: Has he not?

Right!

In the first case, namely if the soul be considered as an incorporeal thing created for itself, he further endorses the series of rational conclusions, by which we proved, that the soul cannot cease with the body, and absolutely cannot pass away in any other way, than by the almighty nod of its Creator. Is this still granted, or do any among you still hesitate?

We all agreed willingly.

And that this all-good Creator never would annihilate any work of his hands: as much as I recall, also no one has doubted this.

Nobody.

But **Simmias** fears this: Perhaps our power to feel and think is not an existence created for itself; but, like harmony, health, or the life of the plants and animals, is the attribute of a skillfully formed body: was it not this, about which you were anxious?

Exactly this, my **Socrates**!

We want to see, he said, if that which we know of our soul, and can experience as often as we want, doesn't make your anxiety impossible. What happens with the skillful formation or composition of things? Are not certain things brought closer together, which previously were distant from each other?

Certainly!

They were previously in combination with others, and now are combined among themselves, and form the component parts of the whole, which we call a **composition**?

Good!

Through this combination of the parts, depending on the manner in which these component parts are next to each other, first a certain order comes into being, which is more or less perfect.

Correct!

So then also the powers and efficacies of the component parts are changed more or less by the composition, having been restrained one moment, the next moment accelerated by action and reaction, and then altered in their direction. Is this not true?

It seems.

The Creator of such a composition sometimes looks at the parts one moment solely as they exist next to each other: for example, at the proper proportion and symmetry in architecture, where nothing other than the order of the parts existing next to each other comes into consideration; the next moment however his design turns to the changed efficacy of the component parts, and the power which results from their composition, as with some engines and machines.[154] There are some cases, where one sees clearly, that the artist has directed his design to both, to the order of the parts and to the modification of their efficacy at the same time.

The human artist, said Simmias, seem to have done so perhaps somewhat rarely, but the Creator of nature seems to have always connected these designs in the most perfect composition.

Excellent, replied **Socrates**; nevertheless I will not pursue this secondary consideration any further. Only tell me this, my **Simmias**! Through composition, can a power arise in the whole, which doesn't have its foundation in the efficacy of the component parts?

What do you mean, my **Socrates**!

If all parts of matter, without action and resistance, would lie inert next to each other, would the skillful ordering and transposition of the parts, be able to produce any motion, any resistance—generally a power in the whole?

· It seems not, answered **Simmias**; no active whole can be composed of inactive parts.

Good!, he said, we can therefore accept this axiom. But, nevertheless, we notice that concord and symmetry can be found in the whole, even if every component part has neither harmony nor symmetry in itself. How is this possible? No individual tone is harmonic: and nevertheless many tones together constitute a harmony. A well-proportioned building can consist of stones, which have neither symmetry nor regularity. Why can I compose a harmonic whole from dissonant parts, an extremely regular whole from irregular parts?

Oh! this difference is obvious, replied **Simmias.** Symmetry, harmony, regularity, order, etc. can't be conceived without multiplicity: for they represent the proportions of different impressions, as they present themselves to us together and in relationship with each other. Therefore, a combination belongs to these concepts, a comparison of manifold impressions, which together constitute a whole, and therefore they cannot possibly belong to the particular parts.

Continue, my dear **Simmias**! exclaimed **Socrates** with an inner pleasure about the astuteness of his friend. Also tell us this: If every single tone would not make an impression on the ear, would a harmony be able to arise from many tones?

Impossible!

Also with symmetry: Every part must have an effect on the eye, if what we call symmetry is supposed to come into being from many parts.

Necessarily.

Therefore, we see here that no efficacy can come into being in the whole, the basis of which is not encountered in the component parts, and that everything else which doesn't flow from the attributes of the elements and the component parts, such as order, symmetry, etc. are sought solely in the manner of the composition. Are we convinced of this proposition, my friends?

Completely.

Therefore, in every composition, even in the most skillful composition of things, there are two things to consider: first, the sequence and order of the component parts in time or space; thereafter, the connection of the original powers, and the way in which they express themselves in the composition. Certainly the actions of the simple powers are limited, determined, and changed by the ordering and position of the parts, but a power or efficacy whose origin is not sought in the fundamental parts can never be obtained by the composition. I dwell here a little on these subtle basic considerations, my friends!, like a competitive runner who paces himself while running around the track many times, so at the end he can sprint with increased drive, to swing around the goal and to be victorious, when the gods have decided to give him fame and glory. Consider it with me, my dear **Simmias**!, if our ability to perceive and to think should not be a being created for itself, but is supposed to be an attribute of the composition: must it not either, like harmony and symmetry, result from a certain position and order of the parts, or, like the power of the composition, have its origin in the efficacy of the component parts?

Certainly, as we have seen, no third can be conceived.

In regards to harmony, we have seen, for example, that each particular tone has nothing harmonious, and the concord would simply exist in the contrasting and comparing of different notes? Is this not true?

Correct!

The same can be said about the symmetry and regularity of a building: it exists in the combination and comparison of many discrete irregular parts.

This cannot be denied.

But this comparison and contrasting, is it anything else than the action of the ability to think? And is it to be encountered anywhere in nature outside of the thinking being?

Simmias didn't know what he was supposed to answer to this.

In unthinking nature, continued **Socrates**, individual sounds, individual stones follow on and next to each other. Where is harmony, symmetry, or regularity here? If no thinking being intervenes, who collects the various parts together, juxtaposes them, and perceives a concord in this comparison, then I don't know how to find them; or do you know, my dear **Simmias**!, how to seek out their trace in soulless nature?

I must confess my inability to answer, was his reply, though I have in mind where this is going in a moment.

A happy omen!, exclaimed **Socrates**, when the adversary suspects his own defeat. Meanwhile, answer me cheerfully, my friend!, for you have no small part in the victory which we hope to obtain over you: Can the origin of a thing be explained from its own effects?

In no way.

Order, symmetry, harmony, regularity, generally all proportions, which require gathering together and contrasting of the manifold parts, are effects of the capacity to think. Without the addition of the thinking being, without comparison and contrasting of the manifold parts, the most regular building is a mere heap of sand, and the voice of a nightingale, not more harmonic than the creak of a night owl. Yes, without this action, no whole exists in nature which consists of many separate parts; since these parts have its own existence each for itself, and they must be contrasted to each other, compared, and considered in connection, if they should form a whole. The thinking capacity, and this alone in all of nature, is able, through an inner activity, to make comparisons, combinations, and contrasts a reality: therefore the source of everything compound, of number, greatness, symmetry, harmony, etc. in so far as they require a comparison and contrast, must be sought solely in the ability to think. And since this is granted, thus this ability to think itself, this cause of all comparison and contrast, cannot possibly originate from its own functions, cannot possibly exist in proportion, harmony, symmetry, cannot possibly exist in a whole, which is composed from parts existing separate from each other. For all these things assume the actions and functions of the thinking being, and can't become real in any other way, than by it.

This is very clear, answered **Simmias**.

Since every whole which exists of parts which are separate from each another, assumes a combination and comparison of these parts, this combination and comparison must be the function of the imaginative capacity: thus, I cannot place the origin of this imaginative capacity itself in a whole which consists of such separate parts, without allowing a thing to originate through its own operations. And such an absurdity, even the writers of fables have still never yet dared, as far as I know. No one has yet located the origin of a flute in the harmony of its notes, or the origin of sunlight in the rainbow.

As I perceive, my dear **Socrates**!, now the last vestige of our doubt is gone.

Meanwhile, the rest is especially important to ponder, he answered, if I don't tax your patience with these thorny inquiries.

Always dare, friend!, exclaimed **Crito**, to test the patience of these people. You have not spared my patience the least, when this morning I insisted on the implementation of a proposal—

Say nothing of a thing, **Socrates** interrupted him, which now is absolutely certain.[155] We have to investigate things here, which still seem to be subject to doubt. Indeed no more of this, that our power to feel and to think should be sought in the situation, structure, order, and harmony of the components of the body. This we have rejected as impossible, without violating either the omnipotence or the wisdom of God. But perhaps this thinking ability is one of the activities of the composition, which are essentially different from the position and formation of the parts, and nevertheless are to be encountered no-where else than in the composition? Is this not the last vestige of doubt, which we dispute? My worthy **Simmias**!

Right!

We will therefore suppose this case, **Socrates** continued, and ac-cept, that our soul is an **efficacy** of the composition. We have found, that all efficacies of the composition must flow from the powers of the component parts: therefore according to our assumption the compo-nent parts of our body will have to have powers, out of which composi-tion the capacity to think results?

Certainly!

But the powers of these component parts, what nature and quali-ties do we want to attribute to them? Should they be similar or dis-similar to the activity of thinking?

I don't quite grasp this question, was **Simmias'** answer.

A single syllable, said **Socrates**, has this in common with the whole speech, that it is audible; but the whole speech has a meaning, the syllable does not: Is this not true?

Right!

While every syllable only provokes an audible, but meaningless feeling, notwithstanding an intelligible meaning arises from their sum total, which acts on our soul. The efficacy of the whole results here from the powers of the parts, which are dissimilar to them.

This is understandable.

With respect to harmony, order, and beauty, we perceive the same. The pleasure, which they affect in the soul, arises from the effects of the component parts, any of which can excite neither pleasure nor displeasure.

Good.

Once more, this is an example that the activity of the whole can originate from powers of the component parts, which are dissimilar to them.

I grant it.

I don't know if I perhaps am not going too far, my friend!, but I imagine, that all activities of corporeal things could originate from such powers of original substance which are totally dissimilar to them. Color, for example, can perhaps be broken down into such impressions, which have nothing of color, and motion itself perhaps originates from such powers of primary matter, which are anything but motion.

This would require a proof, said **Simmias**.

But it is not necessary now, that we take any more time with this, said Socrates, it is sufficient that I explain by example what I understand by the words: the efficacy of the whole could originate from the powers of the component parts, which are dissimilar to them. Is this clear now?

Perfectly!

According to our assumption, therefore, the powers of the component parts would either be cognitions themselves, and, therefore, of the power of the whole, which should originate from them similarly, or be totally of a different quality and therefore be dissimilar. Is there a third?

Impossible!

But answer me this, my dear!, If a different power is supposed to originate from simple powers in the composition, where can this difference be found? Apart from the thinking being, the powers of the whole are nothing other than the individual powers of the simple component parts, as they alter and limit each other by action and reaction. From this standpoint, therefore, the dissimilarity doesn't occur, and we must once more take our refuge in the thinking being, who visualizes the powers in connection and pulled together differently, than the thinking being would think of them individually and without connection. One sees an example of this in colors, in addition to harmony. Bring two different colors together in a space so small, that the eye can't distinguish them: they will still always remain separated in nature; and remain isolated, but nevertheless our perception will compose a third color from them, which has nothing in common with those colors. Taste has a similar quality, and, if I'm not mistaken, all our feelings and sensations generally. They certainly couldn't become other as such through combination and connection than they are individually; but surely to the thinking being, who cannot clearly distinguish them, they appear differently than they would appear without combination.

This can be granted, said **Simmias**.

Therefore can the thinking being have its origin in simple powers, which don't think?

Impossible, since we saw before, that the ability to think can't have its origin in a whole that consists of many parts.

Entirely correct!, answered **Socrates**: the combination of the simple powers, from which a dissimilar power of the composition is supposed to originate, assumes a thinking being, to whom they appear differently in combination than they are individually; therefore, the thinking being can't possibly originate from this composition, from this combination. Therefore, if feeling and thinking, in a word, imagination is supposed to be a power of the composition: don't the powers of the component parts have to be similar to the power of the whole, and, as a consequence, also be powers of imagination?

How would it possibly be otherwise, since there can be no third?

And the parts of these component parts, must these not also have the same activities of imagination, as far as their divisibility can infinitely reach?

Indisputably! Because every component part is again a whole, which consists of smaller parts, and our rational arguments can be continued as long, until we come to the fundamental parts, which are simple and don't consist of many.

Tell me, my dear **Simmias**! Don't we find in our soul an almost infinite collection of concepts, perceptions, inclinations, and passions, which preoccupy us continually?

Certainly!

Where are these to be found in the parts? Either strewn, some in this part, others in that part, without ever being replicated; or is there at least just one among them, which unites and grasps all these cognitions, desires, and aversions in itself, as many of them as are to be found in our soul.[156]

Necessarily one of the two, **Simmias** answered, and in my thinking, the first case might be impossible; since all conceptions and inclinations of our soul are so closely tied together and united, that they must necessarily be present somewhere together.

We are coming to a meeting of the minds, my dear **Simmias**! We would neither remember, nor reflect, nor compare, nor be able to think, indeed, we would not even be the person that we had been a

moment before, if our conceptions would be divided among many and
were not encountered together somewhere in their closest connection.
Therefore, we must at least hypothesize one substance which unites all
concepts of the component parts. But will this substance be able to be
composed from parts?

Impossible, otherwise we need again a combining and contrasting,
in order that from the parts becomes a whole, and we come back to
the point, from where we have started.

It will therefore be simple?

Necessarily.

Also unextended? for the extended thing is divisible, and the divisible is not simple.

Right!

There is, therefore, in our body at least one single substance,
which is not extended, not compound, but is simple, has a power of
intellect, and unites all our concepts, desires, and inclinations in itself.
What hinders us from calling this substance our soul?

It is all the same, my excellent friend!, answered **Simmias**, whatever name we give it. It is enough that my objection isn't valid, and all
the rational conclusions, which you put forward for the imperishableness of the thinking being, are now irrefutable.

Let us still consider this, the former answered: if many of the same
substances were together in a human body, if we wanted to regard all
the fundamental elements of our body as substances of this nature,
would my reasons for imperishableness thereby lose somewhat of
their coherence? Or would such an assumption not rather compel us
to permit many imperishable spirits, instead of one, and therefore to
allow more than we required for our purpose? Since each of these substances would comprise, as we saw previously, the whole sum total of
all concepts, wishes, and desires of the whole man and, therefore, with
respect to the realm of knowledge, their power would not be able to be
more limited than the power of the whole.

Not possibly more limited.

And how about clarity, truth, certainty, and a life of discovery? Put
many confused, inadequate, and indistinct ideas next to each other—is
a clear, complete, and distinct idea thereby produced?

Apparently not.

If a mind doesn't intervene, which compares them and forms an
even more perfect perception of them through reflection and delibera-

tion: they don't cease even in all eternity to be many confused, inadequate, and indistinct ideas.

Right!

The component parts of man, therefore, would have to have conceptions, which are just as clear, just as true, just as complete, as the conceptions of the whole; since from less clear, less true conceptions, etc., no conception of the whole can be brought out by composition, which would have a greater degree of these perfections.

This is not to be denied.

However is this not to say, instead of one rational spirit, which we would place in every human body, we completely accept without necessity an endless multitude of spirits?

Certainly!

And this multitude of thinking substances itself will most likely not be of equal perfection with each other; for such useless multiplications don't take place in this well-ordered universe.

The supreme perfection of its Creator, answered **Simmias**, lets us conclude this with certainty.

Therefore, one among the thinking substances which we put in the human body, will be the most perfect among them, and consequently have the clearest and most enlightened ideas: Is this not true?

Necessarily!

This simple substance, which is unextended, possesses intellect, and is the most perfect among the thinking substances which reside in me, and contains all the ideas in itself of which I am conscious, in clearness, truth, certainty, etc.—is this not my soul?[157]

Nothing else, my beloved **Socrates**!

My dear **Simmias**!, now is the time, to cast a glance back on the path, which we have traveled. We have hypothesized that the ability to think is an attribute of the composition, and how wonderful!, we bring out from this assumption itself, the directly opposite proposition, through a series of rational arguments, namely, that feeling and thinking would necessarily have to be attributes of the simple and not the composition: is this not an adequate proof, that that assumption is impossible, self-contradictory, and therefore to be rejected?

No one can call this into question.

As we have seen, continued **Socrates**, everything which can belong to the composition can be broken up into the fundamental concepts of extension and motion; extension is the material and motion is the source, from which the changes originate. Both appear in the composition in a thousand manifold forms and exhibit the infinite series of wonderful structures in corporeal nature, from the smallest atom, up to that magnificence of the heavenly spheres, which are regarded by the poets as the seat of the gods. All agree, that its material is extension, and its efficacy is movement. But to experience feelings, comparisons, decisions, desires, wants, pleasure, and displeasure, demands a totally different permanence from extension and movement, a different fundamental substance, different sources for the changes. Here, in a simple fundamental being much must be conceptualized, that which exists outside each other must be brought together, the manifold things must be contrasted against each other, and things which are different must be compared. What is scattered in the wide space of the corporeal world, focuses itself here, to form a whole, and what exists no more is brought into comparison in the present moment with what is yet to become.[158] Here I detect neither extension nor color, neither rest nor motion, neither space nor time, but an internally-active being, which visualizes, connects, separates, compares, and chooses extension and color, rest and motion, space and time, and is capable of still thousands of different qualities, which don't have the least in common with extension and motion. Pleasure and displeasure, desires and aversions, hope and fear, felicity and misery, are not changes of position of little particles of dust. Modesty, charity, good will, the delight of friendship, and the sublime feeling of piety are something more than the flow of blood, and the throbbing of the arteries, which usually accompany them. Things of such different type, my dear **Simmias**!, of such different attributes cannot be confused with each other, without the most extreme carelessness.

I am totally satisfied, was **Simmias'** answer.

Still a small comment, answered Socrates, before I turn to you, my **Cebes**! The first thing that we know of the body and its attributes, is it something more than the manner in which it presents itself to our senses?

Be somewhat clearer, my dear **Socrates**!

Extension and motion are concepts of the thinking being, by which it knows reality outside of it: Is this not true?

Granted!

We may have the most reliable reasons, to be certain, that the things outside us are not different than they appear to us without impediment: but doesn't the idea, regardless of what was just said, always lead the way, and the affirmation that its object is real, follow afterwards?

How is it possible otherwise?, answered **Simmias**, since we cannot be informed of the existence of things outside ourselves, other than by their impressions?

In the sequence of our knowledge, therefore, the thinking being always leads the way, and the extended being follows. We find out first that concepts, and consequently a thinking being, are real, and from them we conclude the actual being of the body and its attributes. We can thereby also convince ourselves of this truth, because the body, as we saw previously, could form no whole without the operation of the thinking being, and motion itself, without linking the past together with the present, would not be motion. We may consider the matter from whatever aspect we choose, we are always aware of the soul with its operations first, and then the body follows with its changes. The act of thinking always precedes that which is merely thought.

This concept seems fruitful, my friend, said **Cebes**.[159]

We can divide the entire chain of being, **Socrates** continued, from infinity to the smallest particle into three levels. The first level thinks, but cannot be thought of by others: this is the only one, whose perfection surpasses all finite concepts. The created minds and souls make up the second level: These think and can be thought of by others. The corporeal world is the last level, which can be thought of only by others, but cannot think.[160] The objects of this last level are always the lowest in order, in the sequence of our knowledge, as in existence outside us, while they always assume the reality of a thinking being: do we want to grant this?

We can't do otherwise, said **Simmias**, after what has been said previously everything has to be admitted.

And nevertheless, continued **Socrates**, the opinion of men for the most part takes the reverse of this order. The first, of which we believe to be certain, is the body and its changes; this controls all our senses so much, that we consider material existence for too long to be the only existence, and everything remaining as its attributes.

I rejoice, said **Simmias**, that you make it clear to us, that you yourself, have walked this false path.

Absolutely, my dear!, answered **Socrates**. The first opinions of all mortals are similar to each other. This is the place of anchor, from which they all begin their journey together. They err, seeking the truth up and down on the seas of opinions, until reason and reflection, the children of Jupiter, shine in their sails, and announce a happy landing. Reason and reflection lead our mind away from the sensuous impressions of the corporeal world back to its country, into the realm of thinking beings, for the time being to its equal, to created beings, which on account of their finiteness, also can be thought of and clearly conceived by others. From this they elevate it to that original source of thinking and thinkable, to that All-Knowing, but All-Unknowable Being, about whom we know so much, to our consolation—that everything which is good, beautiful, and perfect in the corporeal and spiritual world, has its reality from Him, and is preserved by His omnipotence. More is not needed for our peace of mind, for our felicity in this life and in the other life, than to be convinced, moved, and touched by this truth in the deepest recesses of our heart.

Third Dialogue

After some silence, **Socrates** turned to **Cebes** and said: My dear **Cebes**!, since you have attained more correct ideas of the nature of immortal beings, what do you think of the fable teachers, who more often than not depict a god as jealous of the merits of a mortal, and to be hostile to him merely from envy?

You know, **Socrates**, what we have learned to think of such teachers and their inventions.[161]

Hatred and jealously, those base passions, which dishonor human nature so much, must directly contradict Divine Holiness.

I am convinced of it.

Therefore, at this point you believe confidently, without the least doubt, that you, we, and all our fellow men are not envied, not hated, not persecuted by this All-Holiest Being who created us, but are loved most tenderly by Him?

Right!

In this firm conviction, the least fear can never come over you, that the Almighty would doom you to eternal torment, and guilty or innocent, would allow you to be eternally miserable?

Never, never! exclaimed **Apollodorus**, to whom the question was not even directed, and **Cebes** was content to agree.

We will accept this proposition, continued **Socrates**, **that God doesn't condemn us to eternal misery**, as the measuring rod for the certainty of our knowledge, when we talk of future events, which depend solely on the will of the Almighty. From the nature and the attributes of created things, nothing can be concluded in this case with certainty: for from these follow only those propositions which are unchanging as such, and, therefore, they depend on the knowledge of the All Highest, not his consent. We must turn to divine perfections in such investigations, and try to figure out what agrees with them, and what contradicts them. When we are convinced, that the future event would not be in accordance with divine perfections, we can reject it, and deem it impossible, as if it contends with the nature and the essence of the examined thing itself.[162] It is a similar question, my **Cebes**!, which we now have to examine at the instigation of your objection. You concede, my friend, that the soul is a simple being, which has its own existence independent of the body: Do you not?

Correct!

You admit further, that it is be imperishable?

I am convinced of that.

So far, continued **Socrates**, our concepts of the nature of extension and idea have guided us. But now doubts arise about the future destiny of the human spirit, which depends so far only on the will and the consent of the Almighty. Will He let the human spirit continue in a waking state for eternity, conscious of the present and the past? Or has He decreed it to sink into a state similar to sleep with the departure of the body, and never to awake. Was this not what still seemed uncertain to you?[163]

Just this, my **Socrates**.

Sleep, fainting, dizziness, ecstasies, and a thousand other experiences teach us that a total deprivation of all consciousness, of all awareness of one's senses, would not be totally impossible, at least for a short time. Certainly, in all these cases, the soul is still trapped in its body, and must adapt to the condition of the brain, which offers nothing other than imperceptible, fading contours in all these weakened states. From this, we can draw no conclusion about the state of our soul after its separation from the body; because then the connection between these different substances is revoked, the body ceases to be the instrument of the soul, and the soul must follow entirely different laws than those prescribed here on earth. Meanwhile, it is enough for our uncertainty, that a complete lack of consciousness doesn't contradict the nature of a spirit; for if this is the case, our fear seems not entirely without reason.[164] —But if we wish to be freed from this terrible doubt, can we ask anything more than the certainty that our anxiety would run contrary to the intentions of God, and could have been chosen just as little, as the eternal misery of his creatures?

Certainly, was **Cebes**' answer, if we don't look for a conviction, which runs contrary to the nature of the thing investigated. When I asserted my doubts, my dear friend! I have indicated several reasons to you which are taken from the designs of the Creator, which make your doctrinal system highly probable: However I wish to hear it from your mouth, and my friends wish it with me.

I'll try, said **Socrates**, to accommodate you. Answer me, my **Cebes**!, if you are afraid with death to lose all your consciousness in eternity, all feeling of your being, perhaps can you determine, that this fate is in store for the whole human race, or only a part of it? Are we all snatched away by death, and in the language of the poet, from death to the arms of his elder brother, eternal sleep? Or are some of the inhabitants of the earth to be awakened to immortality by the heavenly Dawn? As soon as we grant that a part of the human race is allotted true immortality: then **Cebes** probably doesn't doubt one moment, that this supreme bliss would be reserved for the righteous, the friends of the gods and man?

No, my **Socrates**! The gods don't mete out eternal death as unjustly as the Athenians mete out temporal death. Moreover, I am of the opinion, that in the wisest plan of creation, similar beings have similar determinations, and consequently a similar destiny must be in store for the whole human race. Either they all awake to a new consciousness—and then Anytus and Melitus[165] themselves cannot doubt, that the oppressed innocent person would expect a better fate than his persecutors—or they all end their determination with this life, and return to the state from which they had been drawn at birth; their roles do not go further, than the stage of this life: in the end the actors leave the stage, and become again, what they had been in day-to-day life otherwise. I hesitate, my dear friend!, to follow up these thoughts; since I realize it would lead me into obvious inconsistencies.

It doesn't matter, **Cebes**!, answered the former: we must also address those who don't blush with shame so easily at an absurd conclusion. Similar beings, you have maintained, my worthy one!, must have similar determinations in the wisest plan of the Creator?

Yes!

All created beings, which think and will, are similar to each other?

Certainly!

Even if this one thinks more justly, truly, perfectly, and can comprehend more objects than another: nevertheless there is no boundary line, which separates them into different classes, but they rise in imperceptible degrees above each other, and form a single species: Is this not true?

This must be granted.

And if there are still higher spirits above us, which exceed each other in imperceptible degrees of perfection, and approach the Infinite Spirit gradually, don't they all belong, as many of them as are created, to a single species?

Right!

As their attributes are not substantially differentiated, but only according to degree, as in a in a continuous series, they rise gradually: thus their determinations must also be similar in essence, only be differentiated from each other in imperceptible degrees. For is anything random in the great plan of the creation? Nevertheless the determinations of the beings harmonize in the most precise way with its perfections?[166]

Without doubt!

Oh! my friends! the question which we investigate here, begins to become of infinite importance in the great plan of creation. The outcome doesn't only concern the human species, it concerns the general realm of thinking beings. Are they destined to true immortality, to eternal continuation of their consciousness and clear self-awareness? Or do these benefits of the Creator cease after a short enjoyment, and make room for an eternal oblivion? In the decree of the Almighty, as we saw, the question had been decided in this universality: will we not, with our investigation, also have to consider it in this universal light?

So it seems.

But the more universal the object becomes, continued **Socrates**, the more absurd becomes our anxiety. All finite spirits have innate capabilities, which they develop through exercise and make more perfect. Man works on his inborn capabilities to feel and to think at a speed worthy of astonishment. With every sensation a multitude of cognitions stream in to him, which are inexpressible to the human tongue; and if he juxtaposes the sensations to each other, if he compares, judges, decides, chooses, rejects—he multiplies this multitude into infinity. At the same time, an unceasing activeness unfolds the capabilities of the spirit innate in him, and develops wit, understanding, reason, inventiveness, feelings of beauty and goodness, magnanimity, charity, sociability, and all the perfections, which still no mortal on earth has been able to refrain from acquiring. Grant you, that we call some men stupid, foolish, senseless, wicked, and cruel: comparatively, these labels can make sense sometimes; but no fool has yet lived, who has not exhibited some signs of reason, and no tyrant has yet lived, in whose breast would not still have glimmered a spark of charity. We all acquire the same perfections, and the difference only exists in **more** or **less**. We all acquire them, I say, my friends!, for even the most ungodly person has never succeeded in acting directly contrary to his determination. He may strive, he may resist with the greatest stubbornness; his resistance itself has an innate desire for reason, which is originally good, and will only be corrupted through improper use. This improper use makes the man imperfect and miserable; but nevertheless the exercise of the original drive for the good advances towards the final goal of his being, without his gratitude and against his will. In such ways, my friends!, no man has yet lived in benevolent society with his neighbors, who has not left the earth more perfect than when he walked on it. The same nature exists with the whole series of thinking beings; as long as they feel, think, will, desire, abhor with self-awareness, they always develop the capacities innate to them more and more; the longer they are so occupied, the more efficient their powers become, the more ready, quick, and unstoppable their actions become, the more capable they are of finding their bliss in the contemplation of true beauty and perfection. And how? my friends! do all these acquired, godly perfections pass away, like light foam on the water, like an arrow flies through the air, and leave no traces behind that they had ever been there?[167] In the nature of things, the smallest atom cannot be lost without miraculous annihilation: and these splendors are supposed to disappear forever? Should these perfections be so regarded, in view of the Being from whom they were possessed, without consequences, without benefits, as if they had never belonged to Him? What kind of idea of the plan of creation does this opinion assume! In this all-wise plan, the good is of infinite benefit, and every perfection is of endless consequences: however, only for the perfection of the simple, self-conscious being, to whom a real perfection in actual understanding can be attributed. However, that which we perceive in compound things, is perishable and changeable, like the thing itself, to which they inhere. In order to make this clearer, my friends!, we must take into consideration the difference between the simple and the compound once again. Without reference to the simple being, to the thinking being, as we have seen, neither beauty, order, harmony, nor perfection can be attributed to the composition. Indeed, without this connection, they cannot even be gathered together, to form a whole. Also they had not been created in the great design of this universe for their own sake: since they are lifeless and unconscious of their existence, and as such are not capable of any perfection. The final goal of their existence is rather to be sought in the living and feeling part of creation: the lifeless serves the living as an instrument of sensations, and bestows on it not only the sensuous feeling of manifold things, but also concepts of beauty, order, symmetry, method, final purpose, perfection, or at least bestows the material for all these concepts, which the thinking being develops afterwards, by virtue of its inner activity. In the composition, we find nothing existing in itself, nothing which continues, and is of some permanence, such that one can say in the second moment, it would still be what it was in the previous moment. While I look at you here, my friends!, it is not only the light of the sun, which reflects from your faces in a constant stream; but, in the meantime, your bodies have undergone infinite changes in their internal form and structure: all parts of it have ceased to be what they were; they are in constant transformation and flux of changes, which incessantly sweep them away with it. As the blessed sages of former times already noted,[168] corporeal things are not, but come into being and pass out of being: nothing is durable or permanent in them: but everything follows an unstoppable river of motions, thereby compound things are incessantly created and destroyed. Homer also understood this, when he names Ocean the Father, and Thetis the Mother of all things: he wanted to point out that all things in the visible world come into being through a process of constant change and remain not a moment in their previous place, as in an ocean flowing away.

But if the composition in itself is not capable of enduring: how much less will its perfection endure, which can never be attributed to it in itself, as we have seen, but only in relation to the feeling and thinking beings in creation? Hence we see in lifeless creation beauty wither and bloom, that which is complete decay and appear again in another form, apparent disorder and regularity, harmony and discord, pleasantness and adversity, good and evil alternate with each other in infinite diversity as required for the need, use, convenience, pleasure, and felicity of living things, for whose pleasure they had been created.

The living part of creation contains two classes, sensuously feeling and thinking natures. Both have this in common, that they are of continuous being and always can possess and enjoy a self-subsisting perfection. With all animals which dwell on the earth, we find that their sensations, their knowledge, their desires, and their innate instincts agree in the most miraculous way with their needs, and collectively aim at their preservation, comfort, and increase, also, in part, to the benefit of their posterity. This harmony dwells within them; for all these sensations and instincts are properties of the simple incorporeal being, which is aware of them in itself and in other things: thus they possess a true perfection, which can't be referred to in their relation-

ship to others outside them, but instead has its constancy, and its con-
tinuance in itself. If lifeless things are there partly for their sake, so
that they should find entertainment, pleasure, and comfort: then they
too are able to enjoy these benefits, to feel like and dislike, pleasure
and displeasure, comfort and adversity, good health and misery, and
thereby to become internally perfect or imperfect things. If lifeless
things have been the means used by the All Wise Creator: then the
animals certainly belong to his designs; because a portion of the lifeless has been created for their sake, and they possess the ability to enjoy, and thereby to become concordant and complete in their inner
nature. However, we observe no constant progress to a higher degree
of perfection as we see them on the earth before us. They receive those
gifts, skills, and instincts which are necessary for their preservation
and propagation without instruction, without reflection, without exercise, without intent and desire of knowledge, as it were, directly from
the hand of the Almighty. They do not acquire more, even if they live
centuries, or infinitely increase and reproduce themselves. They also
can neither improve nor worsen what they have received and can't
communicate it to others: but carry it on only in the way in which it
has been implanted in them, as long as it is beneficial to their circumstances, and afterwards they seem to forget it again. It is true that
some domestic animals can learn a little through human instruction
and be trained for war or housebroken: but they show sufficiently by
the manner in which they accept this instruction well enough that
their life here on earth is not intended to be a steady progress towards
perfection; but that a certain degree of capability, which they reach,
also is their final goal, and that they never strive further by themselves, never are internally driven to take up lofty things. Now certainly this lack of progress, this stupid contentedness with that which
is achieved, without wanting to ennoble or elevate themselves above
it, is an indication that they were not the final goal in the great design
of creation. But as inferior purposes, at the same time they deliver
means, and are helpful to things of worthier and more sublime determinations in fulfillment of the final purposes of God. But the source of
life and sensations in them is a simple self-existing being, which has
something constant and continuous among all the changes which it
suffers in the course of things: hence the attributes, which it acquires
by learning, or as a direct gift from the hand of the Almighty, befit it
characteristically, never again entirely disappear naturally, and must
be of unceasing consequences. Since this feeling soul never perishes

naturally, it also never ceases to advance the purposes of God in nature, and it is always more and more efficient with every duration of its existence to help bring its Creator's great final aim to fulfillment. This is according to the infinite wisdom with which the plan of this universe has been designed in the counsel of the gods. Everything is in continuous work and effort to fulfill certain purposes in this plan; an endless progression and series of operations are prescribed to every true substance, which it must gradually bring to fruition, and the acting substance becomes at all times more efficient by the last operation to perform the next which follows. According to these principles, the spiritual essence, which animates the beasts, is of infinite duration, and also continues in eternity fulfilling God's intentions in the series and subsequent steps, which have been assigned to it in the universal plan.

Whether these animal, simply sensuous and feeling natures lose their lowly station with the passage of time, and beckoned by a sign from the Almighty, will lift themselves aloft into the spheres of spirits, is something that can't be determined with certainty; however, I am very inclined to believe it.[169]

The rational natures and spirits in the great universe, as well as especially man on this earth, occupy the most distinguished place. Nature adorns herself in her maiden beauty for this under-lord of creation on earth. The lifeless serves man, not only for his use and comfort, not only for his nourishment, clothing, lodging, and safe abode, but especially for his enjoyment and education; and for this purpose, the most sublime spheres, the most distant stars, which scarcely can be discerned with the eye, must be useful to him for this purpose. Friends, if you want to know his destiny here on earth, just look at what man does here below. He brings onto this stage neither skill, nor instinct, nor innate talent, neither defense nor protection, and appears poorer and more helpless with his first appearance than the irrational beast. But the effort and the ability to make himself more perfect, these most sublime gifts of which a created nature is capable, variously replace the loss of those animal drives and skills which are capable of no improvement, no higher degree of perfection. He barely enjoys the light of the sun and stars, and already the whole of nature labors to make him more perfect: the former sharpens his senses, imagination, and ability to remember; the latter exercises his noble powers of cognition, works on his understanding, his reason, his wit, his astuteness; the beauty in nature forms his taste and refines his feelings; the sublime excites his admiration, and elevates his ideas, as it were, over the spheres of this transitory world. Order, concord, and symmetry serve not only for his rational enjoyment, but utilize his powers of mind in proper harmony, which is beneficial to their perfection. Soon he enters into society with his fellow men, in order to mutually facilitate the means to felicity: and behold! Lofty perfections multiply and form in him in this society, which, until now, were enfolded as in a bud. He acquires duties, rights, privileges, and obligations, which elevate him into the class of moral nature—ideas of justice, equity, respectability, honor, respect, posthumous fame come into being. The limited impulse for love of family is broadened into love of the fatherland, to the whole human race, and benevolence, charity, and magnanimity spring from the innate seed of sympathy.

Gradually this interaction, sociability, conversation, and encouragement ripen all moral virtues to maturity, they kindle the heart to friendship, the breast to bravery, and the mind to the love of truth. A competitiveness of favors and favors in return, love and requited love, an alteration of seriousness and jest, profoundness and cheerfulness, are spread over human life, which excel all solitary and unsocial pleasures in sweetness. Hence, the possession of all the goods of this earth, even the enjoyment of the most fervent pleasures don't please us if we can only possess and enjoy them in solitude; and the most sublime and splendid objects of nature delight the social animal, man, not so much as a sight of his fellow man.[170]

If this rational creature now attains a true conception of God and his attributes, oh!, what a bold step to a higher perfection! From community with his fellow creatures he steps into community with the Creator and discovers the relationship in which he, the entire human race, and all living and lifeless things stand to the Originator and Sustainer of the whole. The great order of causes and effects in nature now becomes also an order of means and purposes for him. What he until now enjoyed on earth, was as if thrown to him from the clouds; now these clouds part, and he sees the friendly benefactor who has bestowed all these benefits on him. What he possesses in body and mind as qualities, gifts and skills, he recognizes as gifts from this kind Father; all beauty, all harmony, all good, all wisdom, prudence, means, and ultimate goals, which up to now he discerned in the visible and invisible world, he contemplates as the thoughts of the All-Most-Wise, which are given to him to read in the book of creation in order to raise him to a higher perfection. To this loving Father and Educator, this gracious Regent of the world, he simultaneously consecrates all the virtues of his heart, and they win a divine brilliance in his eyes, because he knows that through them, and through them alone, he can please the All Good Creator. Virtue alone leads to felicity, and we cannot please the Creator in any other way than by striving towards our true felicity. In this state of mind, what a height has man reached on earth! Look at him, my friends, the well-meaning citizen in the city of God, how all his thoughts, wishes, inclinations and passions harmonize among themselves, how they all aim to the true well-being of the creature, and to the glorification of the Creator! Oh! if the world would have to show only one particular creature of this perfection, would we hesitate to seek the final goal of creation in this imitator of divinity, in this object of divine pleasure?

Certainly all features of this picture don't touch on men in general, but only a few noble people who are an adornment to the human race; but this is perhaps the dividing line between men and higher spirits. It is enough that they all belong to the same class, and to me their difference exists in the more or less. From the most unknowing creations, up to the most perfect among the created spirits, all have their own determination, befitting of the wisdom of God, and appropriate to their own powers and capabilities, to make themselves and others more perfect. This path is marked out before them, and no one of even the most perverse will can completely stray from it. Everything which lives and thinks cannot refrain from exercising its powers of cognition and desire, to develop, to change in capabilities, therefore to approach perfection more or less, with stronger or weaker steps. And this goal, when is it reached? It never seems so perfect that the way to further progress could be obstructed: as created natures never can reach a perfection above which nothing can be thought. The higher they climb the more unseen distances remove the clouds from their eyes, which spur on their steps. The goal of this striving exists, like the nature of time, in continuous progress. Through the imitation of God one can gradually approach His perfections, and the felicity of spirits exists in this approach; but the path to divine perfection is infinite, and cannot be completely traversed in all eternity. Therefore the striving in human life knows no boundaries. Every human desire aims as such to the infinite. Our desire for knowledge is insatiable, our ambition also—even lowly greediness torments and disturbs us, without our ever being able to satiate it. The feeling of beauty seeks the infinite; the sublime charms us simply by the unfathomability which adheres to it: pleasure disgusts us, as soon as it reaches the borders of satiation. Where we see limits which are not to be surpassed, there our imagination feels itself as forged in chains, and even the skies seem to enclose our being in too narrow a space: therefore, we gladly give our imagination free rein, and place the borders of space in infinity. This endless endeavor, which projects its goal out ever farther like a jewel beyond its grasp, is appropriate to the nature, the attributes, the determination of the spirits, and the wonderful works of the Infinite One contain enough material and nourishment to maintain this endeavor in eternity. The more we penetrate into its secrets, the more wider vistas open up to our eager eyes; the more we explore, the more we find to investigate, the more we enjoy, the more inexhaustible is the spring.

We can, therefore, continued **Socrates**, accept with good reason, that this striving toward perfection, this increase, this growth in inner excellence, is the determination of rational beings, and consequently also the highest final goal of creation. We can say that this universe, vast beyond all measure, had been created so that there are reasonable beings, which progress from step to step, gradually increase in perfection, and in this increase may find their felicity. The Supreme Being cannot possibly have chosen and brought into the plan of the universe, which has pleased Him above all, that these beings stop dead completely still in the middle of their course, not only stand still, but are all at once be pushed back into the abyss, and should lose all the fruits of their efforts. As simple beings, they are imperishable; as natures existing for themselves, their perfections are also continuous and of infinite consequences; as rational beings, they strive towards a continuous growth and progress in perfection. Nature offers them adequate material for this infinite progress; as the ultimate goal of creation they can pursue no other purpose, and, because of that, are not intentionally interrupted in the progress or possession of their perfections. Is it befitting wisdom to create a world, such that the spirits which are put there may contemplate its wonders, may be blissful, and on the other hand, a moment later, to withdraw even the capability of contemplation and felicity from these spirits forever? Is it befitting wisdom to make the final goal of its miracles, a phantom of felicity, which always comes into and passes out of being? Oh no, my friends!, providence has not given us a desire for everlasting felicity in vain. It can and will be satisfied. The goal of creation continues as long as the creation; the admirers of divine perfections continue as long as the work, in which these perfections are visible. As well we serve the

Regent of the world here on earth, while we develop our capabilities: in like manner we will also continue in that life after death under His divine care, exercising ourselves in virtue and wisdom, constantly making ourselves more perfect and efficient, fulfilling the chain of divine purposes which extend from us into infinity. To stop anywhere on this path, contends openly with divine wisdom, goodness, or omnipotence, and would be pleasing to the Most Perfect Being as little as the most intense misery of innocent creatures in His design of the plan of the world.

How pitiful is the fate of a mortal, who has robbed himself of a comforting expectation of a future through wretched sophistries! He can't think about his situation and must live as in a daze, or despair. What is more terrifying to the human soul than annihilation? And what is more wretched, than a man who sees annihilation closing in on him, and in hopeless fear, awaits it and believes it to be at hand. In prosperity, the horrific thought of non-existence slinks in between the most cheerful images, like a serpent between flowers, and poisons the enjoyment of life; and in misfortune it strikes man totally hopeless to the ground, while it wears away the only comfort for him which can sweeten his misery, the hope of a better future. Yes, the conception of an impending annihilation so much opposes the nature of the human soul that we cannot reconcile it with its next consequences, and wherever we turn, we come across a thousand absurdities and contradictions. What is this life with all its trials and tribulations, especially when its pleasant moments are spoiled by the fear of an inevitable annihilation? What is a continuation of yesterday and today, which will exist no more tomorrow? An extremely despicable trifle which rewards us very wretchedly for the trouble, work, worry, and burdens with which it is maintained. And, nevertheless, to him who has nothing better to hope, this trifle is everything. To follow through on his doctrine, the present existence would have to be the highest good to him, which nothing in the world can counterbalance. The most painful, the most tormented life would have to be infinitely preferable to death, to the total annihilation of his being.[171] His love for life absolutely couldn't be conquered by anything. Which motive, which consideration, would be powerful enough to tempt him to expose his life to the slightest danger? **Honor and posthumous fame?** These shadows vanish, when one speaks of the real physical goods which may be compared with them. **If it concerns the welfare of his children, his friends, his fatherland?** And if it were the welfare of the whole human race; to him a few moments of the most miserable pleasure is all that he has to comfort himself, and hence, is of infinite importance: how can he risk his life? What he risks cannot be compared at all with that which he hopes to preserve. For life is, according to the thinking of this sophist, in comparison with all other possessions, infinitely great.

But have there been no heroic spirits who would sacrifice their life for the rights of humanity, for freedom, virtue, and truth without being convinced of their immortality? Oh yes! And also there are those, who will put their life at stake for far less laudable reasons. But certainly the heart, and not reason, has brought them there. They have done it from passions, and not from principles. He who hopes for a future life and locates the purpose of his existence in the progress to perfection can say to himself: Behold! You have been sent here, to make yourself more perfect by advancement of the good: you may therefore promote the good, even at the expense of your life, if it cannot be obtained otherwise. If tyranny threatens the destruction of your fatherland, if justice is in danger of suppression, if virtue suffers, and religion and truth are persecuted:—use your life wisely, die, in order to preserve for the human race these precious means to felicity![172] The merit, to have promoted the good with so much self-denial, gives an inexpressible value to your life, which simultaneously will be of infinite duration. As soon as death grants to me that which life cannot, then it is my duty, my calling, in accordance with my determination, to die. Only then can the value of this life be declared and be brought into comparison with other possessions, when we consider it as a means to felicity; as soon as we think we lose all our existence with this life, however, it ceases to simply be a means. Life becomes the ultimate goal, the final aim of our desires, the highest possession we can strive for, which is sought for, loved, and desired for its own sake, and no possession in the world can come into comparison with it, for it surpasses all other considerations in importance. Therefore, I cannot possibly believe that a man who thinks this life is all there is, could sacrifice himself for the welfare of his fatherland, or for the welfare of the entire human race, according to his principles. Rather, I am of the opinion that, for example, as often as the preservation of the fatherland, for example, unavoidably requires that a citizen would lose, or even merely come in danger of losing his life, according to this assumption, a war must ensue between the fatherland and this citizen— and what is most curious, a war which is just on both sides. For doesn't the fatherland have a right to demand that any citizen should sacrifice himself for the general welfare? Who will deny this? But this citizen has the directly opposite right, if he thinks life is his most important possession. He can, he may, yes, according to his principles, he is obliged to seek the destruction of his fatherland, in order to lengthen his all-too-precious life a few days. According to this assumption, to every moral being inheres a definitive right to cause the destruction of the entire world, if his life, that is his existence, can only be prolonged.[173] All his fellow creatures have the same right. What a general uprising! What rebellion, what confusion in the moral world. A war which is right on both sides, a general war of all moral natures, where each in truth has right on his side; a conflict, which as such, cannot be settled according to justice and good will, even by the most upright judge of the world: what can be more absurd? If all the opinions about which men ever argued and about which they doubted were brought before the throne of truth: what do you think, my friends! Would this Deity not be able to instantly decide, and irrevocably establish, which proposition would be true and which false? Entirely indisputable! For in the realm of truth there is no doubt, no seeming, no hypothesis and opinion; but everything is decidedly true, or decidedly erroneous and false. Everyone will also grant me this, that a doctrine which can only exist if we accept self-contradiction, irresolvable doubts, or undecided uncertainties in the realm of truths, must necessarily be false: for in this realm of truth, the most perfect harmony prevails everywhere, which nothing can interrupt or disturb. Justice has the same quality: before its throne all disputes and arguments about justice and injustice are decided by eternal and unchanging rules. Before the throne of justice, no court case is disputable and uncertain, there no legitimacies doubtful, two moral natures are never found who have an equal right in one and the same matter. All these weaknesses are an inheritance of a shortsighted humanity, which doesn't understand arguments and counterarguments properly, or cannot weigh them against each other. In the understanding of the Most Supreme Spirit, all duties and rights of the moral being stand in the most perfect harmony, as all truths. All conflict of obligations, all collision of duties, which can throw a limited being into doubt and uncertainty, find their irrevocable resolution here. An equal justice and injustice is not less absurd in the eyes of God, than equality of proposition and counterproposition, or being and non-being both belonging to the same object at the same time. What are we therefore to say of an opinion, which, through the most coherent conclusions, opinion, which, through the most coherent conclusions, leads us to incoherent and invalid concepts? Can it be sanctioned before the throne of truth? My friend, **Crito**, some days ago was not willing to concede to me that I am obligated to the republic and the laws, to submit to the punishment, which had been imposed on me. If I'm not mistaken about his way of thinking, he seemed to have misgivings only because he considered the verdict unfair which had been handed down to me. If he knew that I were actually guilty of the crimes of which I had been accused, he would not doubt that the republic would be entitled to take my life, and that it is incumbent on me to suffer this punishment. The right to act corresponds at all times to an obligation to suffer.[174] If the republic, as every other moral person, has a right to punish the one who offends it, and if the lighter punishment doesn't suffice, then to sentence him even to death: then the offender also must be bound, according to the rigor of justice, to suffer this punishment. Without this obligation to suffer, the right to punish wouldn't make sense. In the physical world, there is rarely an act without a suffering: just as rarely, in the moral world, can a right of a person be imagined, without an obligation on the part of this person. I don't doubt, my friends!, that **Crito** and you all here agree with me. But we could not think so, if life means everything to us. To follow this false logic, the most heinous criminal would not be obliged to suffer the well-deserved punishment. If he had incurred the sentence of death from the republic, he would be authorized to destroy the fatherland, which wants his demise. To change what has happened can't be done; life is his supreme good: how can he prefer the welfare of the republic to his life? How can nature prescribe a duty to him, which doesn't aim to his highest good? How can he be obligated to do something, or to suffer something, which is at odds with his total felicity? He will, therefore, not be forbidden, it would even be incumbent on him, to destroy the state with fire and sword, if he can thereby save his life. But how would the villain acquire this authority? Before he committed the punishable offense, he was, as a man, linked to the welfare of humanity, as a citizen, to advance the welfare of his fellow citizens. What could henceforth free him from this obligation, and could have given him the opposite right against it, to destroy everything around him? What has caused this change in his duties? Who dares to answer: **The committed crime itself!**

Another calamitous result of this opinion is that its supporters are ultimately obliged to deny the providence of God. According to their thinking, the life of man is confined between the narrow borders of birth and death: they can look over life's path with their eyes and ignore their immortality. Thus they have sufficient knowledge to judge of the ways of providence, if there is one. But they observe much in the events of this world, which apparently doesn't accord with the conception which we must have of the attributes of God. Many things contradict His goodness, many His justice, and at times one could believe that the fate of man would have been designed by a cause, which would find pleasure in evil. In the physical part of man, they discover pure order, beauty and harmony, the wisest purposes, and the most perfect agreement between means and ends: purely visible proofs of divine wisdom and goodness. But in the social and moral life of man, at least as much of it as we can survey, the traces of these divine qualities are entirely unrecognizable. Triumphant vice, evil deeds awarded, persecuted innocence, and oppressed virtue often prevail; the innocent and just suffer not less seldom than the evil-doer; treason succeeds as often as the wisest legislation, and an unjust war succeeds as well as a just war or any other beneficial undertaking which contributes to the betterment of the human race. Fortune and misfortune encounter good and evil without noticeable difference, and, at least in the eyes of these sophists, must seem to be distributed among men entirely unintentionally with regard to virtue and merit. If a wise, kind and just Being was concerned about the destinies of men, and regulated them according to His pleasure: would this wise order, which we admire in the physical world, not reign in the moral world as well?

Indeed, some might say: "These complaints simply arise from discontented minds, whom neither the gods nor men could please. Even if all their wishes were fulfilled, and they were placed on the peak of felicity, they would find in the dark recesses of their hearts enough selfishness and evil temper to complain about their benefactors. In the eyes of a moderate and contented man, the goods of this world are not as unequally distributed as is believed. For the most part, virtue has an inner serenity as a companion, which is a sweeter recompense than fortune, honor, and riches. Innocence which is defeated would perhaps seldom desire to be in the place of the enraged person who oppresses it. Innocence would have to pay all too dearly through inner turmoil for the apparent fortune and honor. Generally, he who pays more attention to the feelings of men rather than to their opinions, will not find their state as lamentable as they portray it in their common speech and conversation." So some may allege, in order to salvage the ways of a wise providence in nature.[175] But all these reasons have weight now, when all is not over for us when this life ends, when our hopes extend before us into infinity. In this case, it can, yes, it must be far more important for our felicity when we struggle here on earth with misfortune, if we learn and apply patience, constancy, and submission to the Divine Will, than if we forget ourselves in fortune and prosperity. Even if I end my life by means of a thousand martyr-doms, what does this do? If my soul has only acquired the beauty of suffering innocence thereby, it is paid for all its pain with interest. The agony is brief, and the reward is of eternal duration.[176] But what com-pensates him, who forsakes his whole existence among these tor-ments? And with his last breath also lets go of all the beauties of his spirit, which he acquired through this struggle? Is the fate of such a man not cruel? Can He be just and kind who decrees it so? And as-suming that the consciousness of innocence would counterbalance all the painful feelings of the agony of death, which the innocent suffers at the hands of his persecutor: should that violent criminal, that of-fender of divine and human justice pass away in such a way, without ever being torn away from the blind stubbornness of heart in which he lived, and without acquiring more just ideas of good and evil? Without becoming aware one day, that this world is ruled by a Being, who finds pleasure in virtue? If there is no hope for a future life, then providence is to be justified as little with respect to the persecutor, as the perse-cuted.

Unfortunately, many are enticed by these seeming difficulties to deny providence. The Maximum Being, they imagine, is not concerned about the fate of humanity at all, notwithstanding his attention to the perfection of man's physical nature. Virtue and vice, innocence and guilt, he who serves it and he who blasphemes it, the absurd and con-demnable opinions to which one necessarily strays to as soon as he forsakes the path of truth, they say, are perfectly equal to the general spirit of the age. I consider it superfluous, my friends! To say more about the unreasonableness of these opinions, since we are all certain that we stand under Divine Care, and receive the good from His hands, as well as the evil, only with His permission.

However, we know a more certain and easier way to find out of this labyrinth. In our eyes, the moral order of this world denies the perfection of its Creator as little as the physical order. As disorders in parts of the physical world, such as storms, tempests, earthquakes, floods, plagues, etc., resolve into perfections of the immeasurable

whole: similarly, in the moral world, in the fate and events of the social man, all earthly defects resolve into eternal perfections, temporary
sufferings into unceasing felicity, and brief tribulations into permanent well-being. To consider the fate of one single man in his own particular light, we must be able to look at his life in its entire eternity.[177]
Only then could we examine and judge the ways of providence, when
we could bring the concept of the eternal existence of a rational being
under one point of view commensurate with our weakness. But then,
be certain, my loves! We would neither censure, nor murmur, nor be
dissatisfied; but, rather, would completely adore and admire the wisdom and goodness of this World Ruler.

From all these proofs taken together, my friends!, the most reliable assurance of a future life awakens, which can completely satisfy
our mind. The ability to feel is not an attribute of the body and its fine
structure, but has its existence in itself. The essence of this existence is
simple and consequently imperishable. Also, the perfection which
these simple substances acquired, must be of unceasing consequences
in regard to themselves, and makes them more and more efficient to
fulfill the purposes of God in nature. Particularly our soul, as a being
which is reasonable and striving toward perfection, belongs to the
class of spirits which embody the ultimate purpose of creation, and
never ceases to be an observer and admirer of divine works. The beginning of its existence is, as we see, a striving and progress from one
degree of perfection to another: its being is capable of perpetual
growth; its impulse has the most evident predisposition to infinity;
and nature provides an inexhaustible spring for its thirst, which can
never be quenched. Further, the spirits have, as moral beings, a system of duties and rights, which would be full of absurdities and contradictions, if they were inhibited on the path to perfection and turned
back. And, finally, the seeming disorder and injustice in the fate of
men refer us to a long series of consequences, in which everything resolves itself, which seems a labyrinth on earth. He who fulfills his duty
here on earth with steadfastness in defiance of misfortune and en-
dures adversity with surrender to the Divine Will, must finally enjoy
the recompense of his virtues; and the wicked cannot pass away, without being brought in one way or the other to the recognition, that evil
deeds are not the way to felicity. In a word, all attributes of God, His
wisdom, His goodness, His justice would be contradicted if He had
created rational beings, which strive for perfection only for a limited
time.

Any one of you might say: "Good, **Socrates**! You have shown us that we have a future life to console us: but tell us also, where will our departed spirits sojourn? Which region of the aether will they inhabit? With what will they busy themselves? How will the virtuous be rewarded and the wicked be brought to repent?"

If anyone asks me this, I answer: Friend, you demand more of me than is my calling. I have led you through all the twists and turns of the labyrinth and show you the way out. Here ends my task. Other guides may lead you further. Whether the souls of the godless have to suffer frost or heat, hunger or thirst, whether they toss and turn in the morass of Acherusia, in gloomy Tartarus, or must spend their time in the flames of Phlegethon until they are purified;[178] whether the blessed breathe in the purest air of heaven on a radiant earth of pure gold and precious stones, and sun themselves in the brilliance of the sunrise, or if they rest in the arms of everlasting youth and are fed with nectar and ambrosia: all this, my friend!, I know not. If our poets and fable teachers know it better: may they assure others of it. Perhaps it is not harmful, if some people's imagination is occupied and exerted in such a way. As far as I am concerned, I content myself with the conviction that I will exist eternally under Divine Care, that His holy and just providence will reign over me in that life as in this, and that my true felicity exists in the beauties and perfections of my spirit: these are temperance, justice, freedom, love, benevolence, knowledge of God, promotion of His intentions, and surrender to His Holy Will. These beatitudes await me in that future, to which I hasten, and I don't need to know more to set out upon the path, which leads me there, with confident courage. You, **Simmias**, **Cebes**, and my other friends!, you will follow me, each in his time. Inflexible fate now beckons me, as perhaps a tragic playwright would say. It is time that I go into the bath; for I consider it as more decent to take the poison after the bath, so as to spare the women the trouble of washing my corpse.

As **Socrates** had finished speaking, **Crito** began to speak and said, Let it be! But what do you have to leave behind for these friends or me, regarding your children or domestic affairs? How can we live to please you?

If you live in such a way, **Crito**!, he said, as I have recommended to you for a long time, I have nothing new to add. If you have self respect, you will live to please me and yourselves, even if you don't promise it: but if you neglect yourselves, and don't want to follow the path which has been pointed out to you today and previously: then make all the promises in the world, it will mean nothing.

Crito answered: We will strive with all our powers to obey you, my **Socrates**! How shall we deal with you after your death?[179]

As you please, answered **Socrates**, when you have me dead. Hopefully you won't forget the real Socrates?

At the same time, he looked at us smiling, and said: I cannot persuade **Crito**, my friends, that the real **Socrates** is he who now talks, and has conversed with you awhile; he still believes that the corpse, which he soon will get to see, and which at the very moment is only my garment, is **Socrates**, and asks how he should bury me. All the reasons which I cited to up to now to prove that I, as soon as the poison has worked, remain with you no more, but will be transported to the dwellings of the felicitous, seem to him mere fabrication, to console you and myself. Be so kind, my friends!, and now guarantee to **Crito** the opposite of that which he has guaranteed to the judges. He vouched for me that I would not escape. However, you must be my guarantees to him, that I, myself, right after my death, don't care whether he burns my body or sees fit to bury it in the earth, without grieving so much, as if the greatest misfortune befalls me. He mustn't say at my funeral: "**Socrates** is laid on the bier, **Socrates** is carried away, **Socrates** is buried." You should know, he continued, my worthy **Crito**!, such speeches are not only contrary to the truth, but also an insult to the departed spirit. Rather, be of confident courage and say my corpse is laid to rest. For the rest, you may bury it as you please and in a manner which you believe is in accordance with the laws. Upon this, he went into a neighboring chamber to wash. **Crito** followed him and told us to wait. We stayed and discussed that which we had heard, repeated, reflected on, and considered some arguments, to convince ourselves properly of them; but the rest of the time we were occupied with the inconsolable expectation of the great misfortune which approached us. We felt as if we lost our father and from now on must live in the world as orphans. When he had bathed, his children were brought in: (he had three, two small, and one grown) and the women of his house stepped in. He conversed with them in the presence of **Crito**, said to them what he had to say, then let the women and children take leave, and came back to us. The sun was about to set, for he had spent a somewhat long time in the neighboring chamber. He sat down, but said very little; for soon after the officer of the Eleven Men came, sat next to him, and said: O **Socrates**! I am aware of something in you entirely different than in other condemned men. They are in the habit of being outraged and cursing me when I announce on the command of the authorities that it is time to drink the poison; but you always seem to me, and especially now, to be the most serene and most gentle man who ever entered this place. I know indeed, that now you are not angry with me, but with them (you know them), who are to blame. You are probably fully aware now, **Socrates**! what kind of dispatch I have to bring to you. Fare you well, and endure with patience what is not to be changed. He said this, turned around, and wept. **Socrates** looked after him, and said: Live well, friend! We will obey you. But to us he said: What an upright man! He has often visited me and talked now and then with me. He is a very good and honest man. See how sincerely he weeps for me now! But, **Crito**! Indeed we must obey him: let the poison to be brought here, if it is ready; if not, let it be prepared.

Why so are you in such a hurry, my **Socrates**? replied **Crito**: I believe that the sun still shines upon the mountains and has not set yet. Others are accustomed, after the announcement, to wait a long while before they take the cup of poison, and allow themselves time to eat, to drink and to partake of love. We can still draw out the time a good while.

Crito!, answered **Socrates**, let them who consider every respite as a gain do that, but I have my reasons to do the opposite. I believe to gain nothing if I delay, and would only seem ridiculous to myself if I was begrudging and miserly with my life now, since it is mine no more. Do my will and don't detain me.

Hereon **Crito** signaled the lad who stood next to him. The lad went out, took some time with the mixing of the poison, and brought in the man who had the cup of poison in his hand, to extend it to **Socrates**. **Socrates** saw him coming, and said: Good man, give it here! But, what must I do with it? You will know. Nothing other, answered the former, than walk to and fro after you drink it until your feet become heavy; then lie down: that is all. And with that he passed the cup to him. **Socrates** took it, dear **Echecrates**!, with such composure, without trembling, without flushing or changing his countenance in the least, looked at the man with his eyes wide open, and said: What do you mean? May one not spill a few drops as an offering to the gods? It is just as much as necessary, answered the former. So be it, answered **Socrates**; but I can still direct a prayer to them. **You who call me, you gods!, grant me a happy journey!** With these words, he raised the cup to his lips and emptied it, peacefully and calmly.

Until now, many of us still could hold back our tears, but as we saw him raise, drink, and empty the cup, it was not possible. For myself, the tears didn't trickle, but poured forth like a river, and I had to hide my face in my coat, to be able to weep undisturbed, not for him, but for myself, that I had the misfortune to lose such a friend. **Crito**, who still could not hold back his tears even before I started to cry, stood up and paced around in the jail; and **Apollodorus**, who cried almost the entire time, began then to wail and lament out loud, such that all our hearts broke. Only **Socrates** remained unmoved and called to us: What are you doing, faint-hearted ones? For this reason I have just sent the women away, so that they might not wail and whimper here: for, I have been told, one must try to give up the ghost among blessings and good wishes. Be quiet and act like men!

When we heard this, we were ashamed of ourselves and stopped crying. He walked to and fro until his feet became heavy and lay down on his back, as the slave had advised him. Soon afterwards, the man who had given him the poison felt him with his hands, and observed his feet and hips. He squeezed Socrates' foot and asked if he felt it. No, he said. He squeezed his thigh, but let go again and informed us that it was cold and stiff. He touched him again, and said: as soon as it gets to his heart, he will pass away. Now his abdomen began to become cold. Socrates uncovered himself, for he had been covered, and said to **Crito**: (these were his last words:) **Friend!, don't forget to sacrifice a rooster to the god of convalescence, for we have a debt to him**.

Crito answered, it shall be done. Have you otherwise nothing more to leave behind? No answer followed on this. A short time after he convulsed. The man uncovered him completely and his gaze remained fixed. When **Crito** saw it, he shut Socrates' mouth and eyes.

This was the end of our friend, Oh **Echecrates**!, a man, who among all men we knew, indisputably had been the most honest, wise, and just.

Appendix to the Third Edition of the *Phädon*, 1769

Appendix, Concerning Some Objections, Which Have Been Made to the Author

Several friends of the truth have had the good will to allow me to see their comments and remarks about the above dialogues, partly in personal letters and partly in writings available to the public. I have used quite a few of them beneficially in this second edition. I have changed passages here and there, have explained myself more clearly in some places, and commented on other places with notes. These are the only thanks which these worthy men expect from me. But I have not been able to remove everything which seemed objectionable to my critics. Partly their arguments have not convinced me, and partly their demands exceed my powers. Permit me to explain myself in regard to some of their comments.

Actually, I must confess that, in my view the critics have been indulgent, rather than harsh. I can't complain about any unreasonable criticism, perhaps rather about the unreasonable praise. My own knowledge of myself assures me that it is exaggerated. Excessive praise usually has the intention more of demoralizing others, than of spurring them on in their subject matter. I have never let it cross my mind to create an epoch in philosophy or to become famous through my own system. Where I see a well-trodden path before me, I don't seek to blaze a new trail. If my predecessors have defined the meaning of a word, why should I diverge from it? If they have brought a truth to light, why should I pretend that I know it not? The reproach of sectarians doesn't deter me from accepting from others, with a grateful heart, those criticisms which I find useful and necessary. I confess, the spirit of the sectarian has damaged the progress of philosophy, but it can, in my opinion, be more easily bridled by the love of truth than the quest for novelty.

In the first dialogue, where I claim to have followed Plato more closely, they allege that I took propositions from **Wolff**[180] and

Baumgarten[181] without proof, which not every reader absolutely takes for granted.[182] Then what are these propositions? Perhaps, **that the powers of nature are constantly active**? I believe this proposition to be as old as philosophy itself. It has always been known that an active thing, if it isn't hindered, produces an effect appropriate to it, and if it finds resistance, it reacts to this resistance. It is therefore never at rest. By the word to be **real**, whereby one signifies existence, is reasonably understood that everything which is, also be **real**—that is, it would have to do something. A power which doesn't act is a power which doesn't exist, for **ability, capability**, etc. are merely possibilities, conceptions, which don't have an object prior to them, as when real powers are discussed, which are applied in a certain way, in so far as they don't contradict their nature through other applications. One says, for example, of a man in business, he **could** also write poetry, that he possesses the **capability** to do that excellently. If this expression should be truthful, it must have the following meaning: that the spiritual powers of this man, which now are occupied with the management of a middle-class office, etc., also don't contradict an application through which good poems could be composed.[183] When it is said of a power that it only acts given a **certain opportunity**; the question arises: and when this opportunity is absent, what happens? —Then this power doesn't act at all?—Thus, is it a **mere possibility** to act, in the absence of the opportunity, and nevertheless this mere possibility should also exist?—The opportunity can only change the application of the powers, while this application can't change by the power itself; but depends on the connection in which it stands to other things. However, the opportunity can **awaken** no power, which has ceased to act, nor can it annihilate a power that exists. Therefore, if it is said: every power must be continuously active; it is obvious that only primal, original powers are discussed, not their application to specific types of objects, whereby **capabilities** come into being. From time to time these capabilities are also called powers, if somewhat improperly; however it is obvious that they might not always be active. This happens, as the subject has been touched on before, as far as we are able to grasp the original power that it, by its very nature, must be **applicable** to a certain type of object, but not always must be **applied**. So, thought can be entirely inactive for a long time in a sleeping person, the powers of discovery entirely inactive in a person occupied with the senses, and the powers of judgment inactive in a person who is delusional. But then the original power, from which these capabilities are merely derivations (which from time to time are also called powers), is nothing less than inactive. These ideas are so clear to common sense, that they need no proof, and philosophers of all times must have thought them, only verbalized them differently sometimes.

Is perhaps this sentence like Wolff: **that everything change-able remains for not a moment unchanged**? Not at all, the writings of **Plato** are full of this. All changeable things, says this philosopher in the **Theaetetus** and in many other places, are constantly changing forms and never remain similar to themselves. He attributes no real existence to them, but a coming-into-being.[184] They do not exist, he says, but come into being through movement and change, and pass away. This is a fundamental principle of Platonic doctrine, and hereon he bases his theory of the true existence of universal unchanging conceptions, his distinction between knowledge and opinion, his teaching of God, and of felicity—his whole philosophy.

All schools of antiquity were engaged in proving or disproving this proposition. One knows the allegory of the tree, which casts its shadow on flowing water. The shadow always seems to be the same, although the surface, on which it is cast, constantly moves on. So, said the followers of Plato, things seem to have permanence to us, even though they are constantly changing. That these teachings occur also in **Wolff** and **Baumgarten** is no surprise, since they had to be investigated by every philosopher since the time of Heraclitus and Pythagoras. I would have remained in antiquity completely, if I hadn't allowed the use of any newer propositions than these.

I supposedly based my entire demonstration on the proposition **that to perceive, think and will are the only actions of the soul**, and this proposition supposedly isn't accepted outside of the school with which I associate. Yes, adds a critic, even if this proposition is admitted of the soul, **as soul**; nevertheless, it cannot hold true of the soul as **substance**. As substance it must also still have a moving and resisting power, which has absolutely nothing in common with the thinking power, he says. With this distinction one of my main proofs is supposedly overthrown, because the soul can remain active **as substance** after death, without perceiving, thinking, and willing as soul.[185]

We shall see! My proof, they say, is based on a proposition, which is not true, and I? I believe the proposition is true, but my proof is not based on it.[186] Whether a substance could have only **one** fundamental power, or could have several, if thinking and willing flow from **one**, or several fundamental activities of reason; whether the soul moves or doesn't move the body; if the soul is entirely disembodied after death—I can leave these and several related investigations as undecided. It is true, I have taken one viewpoint for myself; but the proofs for the immortality of the soul should be tangled up with as few other matters of dispute as possible. The ability or the power to think and to will I call soul, and my entire proof is based on the following dilemma: thinking and willing are either attributes of the composition, or of that which is simple. The former is investigated in the second dialogue. In the first dialogue I consider them as attributes of the simple being. The attributes of a simple being are either fundamental activities, or modifications of other activities. One must grant, that thinking and willing must not merely be modifications of other powers but original activities. One or several, that is not important; simple beings themselves may have still other powers outside of thinking and willing, moving, resisting, pushing, or attracting, as many as one wants, and for which names can be devised. It is sufficient, that thinking and willing are not simply changes of these unnamed powers, but are fundamental activities different from them. However, all natural powers can only change determinations, only alternately make modifications with each other, but they can never transform fundamental attributes and activities of the material objects existing as such into nothingness; therefore the power to think and will, or the powers to think and will, can never be annihilated by natural changes, even if they leave behind so many powers different from them. Such an ability to create, or to annihilate, belongs only to a miraculous Almighty.

That nothing actually could be annihilated by all the powers of nature, as far as I know, has still never been questioned by any philosopher. A natural operation, one has always said, must have a beginning, a middle, and an end, that is to say, some time must elapse, before it is completed. This part of time may be as small as one wants, it never denies the nature of time, and contains successive moments. If the powers of nature are to produce an effect; they themselves must gradually approach this effect and prepare it before it occurs. But an effect, which cannot be prepared in advance, which must occur in an instant, ceases to be natural, and cannot be produced from powers which must do everything in time. All these propositions were not unknown to the ancients, and they seem to me to exist distinctly in the argument of Plato[187] **of the opposite states [conditions] and the transition from one to the other**. Therefore, I conveyed them to my readers in the manner of Plato, but with the clarity appropriate to our times. They are, indeed, reasonably clear to common sense; but, in my opinion, they obtain a high degree of certainty only through the **doctrine of continuity**. I gladly seized the opportunity to make my readers familiar with this important doctrine, because it leads us to proper conceptions of the changes of the body and the soul, without which one cannot consider death and life, mortality and immortality from the proper view point.

But how? One asks, can a change proceed at all without total annihilation? Doesn't the determination of a thing have to be annihilated, if the opposite determination is supposed to be active in it? And how is this possible, if the powers of nature can annihilate nothing? I believe the word **annihilate** is misused here. If a hard body becomes soft, or a dry body becomes wet; the hard thing or dry thing is not annihilated, and the soft thing or wet thing is not created. So, without any annihilation, the long can become short, the short long, the cold warm, and the warm cold, the beautiful ugly, and the ugly beautiful. All these modifications are connected with each other by gradual transitions, and we see clearly, that they can alternate with each other without any annihilation or creation. Generally, the opposing determinations, which are possible in a thing through natural changes, are all of the type such that also a mean occurs between both extremes. Fundamentally, they are differentiated from each other only by the more and less. Let certain parts be changed in their situation, let these parts be brought closer together, those parts farther from each other; then the beautiful becomes ugly, the long becomes short, etc.—these ideas are obscured, and those are made distinct, these desires are weakened, and those inclinations strengthened, thus you have changed the insights and the character of a man. All this can happen through a gradual transition, without any annihilation, and such changes, of course, are possible for nature. But two opposing determinations, which have no mean between them, can never follow each other naturally, and I know no law of motion, which would contradict this statement. Father **Boscovich**[188] [189]who has put the law of continuity in an excellent light, deserves to be read again on this subject.

But why all these thorny inquiries in a Socratic dialogue? Are they not too sophisticated for the simple-minded manner of the Athenian philosopher [Socrates]?

I answer: one seems to forget, that I emulate Plato, and not Xenophon.[190] The latter avoided all the subtleties of the dialectic and portrayed his teacher and friend as following unsophisticated common sense. With regard to moral matters, this method is acceptable; but in metaphysical inquiries, it doesn't go far enough. Plato, who was favorable to metaphysics, made his teacher into a Pythagorean philosopher and portrays him as initiated in the most hidden secrets of this school. When Xenophon bumps into a labyrinth, he lets the wise man timidly sidestep, rather than take a risk. Plato, however, leads Socrates through all the twists and turns of the dialectic and engrosses him in the investigations, which are far above the realm of the common understanding of men. It can be, that Xenophon remained truer to the sense of the philosopher who fetched philosophy down from the heavens to us. Nevertheless, I had to follow the method of Plato, because this matter, in my opinion, permits no other treatment, and I prefer to be inventive, than give up some of the rigor of the argument. Sophistry has appeared in our day in many different guises. One moment armed with subtleties, the next under the guise of sound reason, the next as a friend of religion, shortly after with the arrogance of a know-it-all Thrasymachus, then again with the innocent mood of a Socrates who knows nothing.[191] With all these skills of Proteus,[192] sophistry has tried to make the doctrine of the immortality of the soul uncertain and to mock the arguments in favor one moment, the next to refute them in earnest. How should the friends of this truth defend it? Through Socratic ignorance one can enrage the dogmatist but can't settle anything. Nobody is convinced by mockery of them. Therefore, no other way remains for you, than to expose the tricks of the skeptics as such and to convince them of the truth as best you can.

I explicitly admit in the preface that I put arguments in the mouth of Socrates, which could not have been well known to him, in accordance with the status of philosophy at his time. I even name the modern philosophers, from whom I have borrowed the most. Therefore, it could not have been my intention to extract something from their achievements about the doctrine of immortality, and to attribute it to the ancients. Generally, my Socrates is not the Socrates of history. The historic Socrates lived in Athens, among a people who were the first to be concerned about true philosophy, and indeed at that time not for very long yet. Neither the language, nor cognitive minds, were developed for philosophy yet. He was a student of philosophers who seldom glanced into their souls, who had made everything, rather than themselves, the subject of their observations. Hence, the greatest darkness still must have reigned with respect to the doctrine of the human soul and its determination. The brightest truths could merely be seen glimmering in the distance, without knowing the paths which led to them. A Socrates himself in such a time could do nothing more than direct his eyes steadily to these unique truths, and be guided in his moral conduct by them. The evidence of philosophical conceptions and their rational connection is an effect of time and the persistent efforts of many cognitive minds, which look at the truth from different view points, and thereby shed light on it from all angles.

After so many barbaric centuries, which followed on that beautiful dawn of philosophy, centuries, in which human reason must have been a slave to superstition and tyranny, philosophy has finally experienced better days. All areas of human knowledge have made considerable progress through a successful observation of nature. We have learned to know our soul itself better on this path. Through a precise observation of the soul's actions and sufferings, more data have been gathered, and from it, more correct conclusions can be drawn, by means of a proven method. Through this improvement of philosophy, the noblest truths of natural religion have attained a certain degree of development, which obscures all the insights of the ancients and throws them back into the shadows. It is true, that philosophy has not yet reached its bright midday, which our grandchildren[193] perhaps will catch sight of some day; but one must be very jealous of the achievements of his contemporaries, if one doesn't want to concede great merits to the moderns in respect to philosophy. I have never been able to compare Plato with the moderns, and to compare both with the muddled thinking of the Middle Ages, without giving thanks to providence that I had been born during these happier days.

As I had to re-examine the immortality of the soul, and it caused me some trouble to differentiate faith from conviction, the thought occurred to me: by which arguments would a Socrates be able to prove immortality in our time to himself and to his friends?[194] A friend of reason, as he was, would most certainly have gratefully accepted from other philosophers, what in their doctrine is founded on reason, regardless of what country, or religious party they might belong to. In regard to the truths of reason, one can agree with someone, and nevertheless find various things unbelievable, which that person accepts on faith. Since the brotherly tolerance of the political world is praised so much today; the friends of truth must first foster brotherly tolerance among themselves. What concerns faith, we want to leave to the conscience and peace of mind of each individual, without appointing ourselves as judges on that point. Out of true charity we don't want to argue, where the heart speaks louder than reason; and we have confidence in the All-Merciful God, that He will justify anything, if our conscience justifies it to us. But we want to share in the truths of reason in a more than fraternal fashion, we want to enjoy them collectively, like the light of the sun. If it has, brother!, illuminated you, rather than me; be pleased, but not proud of it, and what would be even more inhuman, don't try to block the light from me.

Who has brought this or that truth to light, was he of your fatherland, of your faith? Well! It is comfortable to stand in a closer relationship with the benefactors of humanity. But, nevertheless, what your fellow citizens, your co-religionists created is not less than a benefit which is bestowed on us all. Greek wisdom benefited the barbarians, and helped you, who just recently came out of barbarism, to be freed from barbarity.[195] Wisdom knows a universal fatherland, a universal religion, and even if it tolerates different beliefs, it doesn't sanction the hostility and misanthropy of these differences, which you have laid as the foundation of your political institutions.—Thus, I think, a man like Socrates would think in our days, and seen from this viewpoint, the mantle of modern philosophy, which I hang on him, may not appear so unseemly.

Subsequent considerations have prompted the proof in the second dialogue that matter cannot think. Descartes has shown that extension and ideas are of entirely different natures, and that the attributes of the thinking being can't be explained by extension and motion. This proof was sufficient for him, that the same substance could not be attributed to them [extension and ideas], for according to a well-known principle of this philosopher, an attribute, which cannot be clearly understood by the idea of a thing, cannot belong to this thing. But this principle itself has met with manifold opposition, in regard to what befalls the attributes of the extended and thinking being; so the proof was required that they are not only of disparate nature, but contradict each other. Regarding attributes which directly contradict each other, we are certain that they cannot belong to the same object; but regarding attributes which merely have nothing in common with each other, this did not yet seem so settled.

When I had to prove the immateriality of the soul, I ran into this difficulty, and even if I am of the opinion that the proposition of Descartes, which I mentioned just now, cannot be doubted: I still looked

around for a manner of proof which could be handled with less difficulty, in accordance with the Socratic method. A proof of **Plotinus**,
which several moderns have further elaborated, seemed to promise
me this convenience.

"In every soul," concludes **Plotinus**,[196] "a life is present (inner
consciousness). But if the soul is supposed to be a corporeal being;
then the parts of which this physical being consists, either one, or only
a few, or none of them, must have a life (inner consciousness). If only
one single part has life; this part is the soul. More parts are superfluous. But if every particular part should be robbed of life; then such a
part also cannot be preserved by the composition; since it is not possible to form life from many lifeless things, and many things without
mind cannot form mind."

Subsequently, Plotinus repeats the same conclusion, with some
modification: "If the soul is corporeal, what is its relationship to the
parts of this thinking body? Are the parts also souls? And are the parts
of these parts? This goes on and on continuously; so one sees that
mass contributes nothing to the essence of the soul, which would be
the case, if the soul had a corporeal mass. In our case, the soul would
be completely present in every part, because in a corporeal mass no
part can be equal to the whole in capacity. But if the parts are not
souls, then likewise from parts which are not souls, no souls can be
composed." These reasons have all the appearance of truth; but they
are not totally convincing. Plotinus assumes as unquestionable, that
no living whole can be put together from non-living parts, and that no
thinking whole can be put together from unthinking parts. But why
can an ordered whole be composed from unordered parts, a harmonic
concert from non-harmonic notes, a powerful state from weak
individuals?

I knew also, that according to the system of this school,[197] to which
I supposedly adhere too much, motion supposedly originates from
such powers, which are not motion, and extension supposedly originates from attributes of substances which are entirely different than
extension. Therefore, this school certainly cannot agree with the
proposition of Plotinus in all cases, and, nevertheless, in respect to the
thinking being it seems to be completely valid. A thinking whole con-
sisting of unthinking parts is contradictory to common sense.

Therefore, in order to be convinced of this proposition, what still
had to be investigated was which attributes could belong to the whole,
without belonging to the component parts, and which could not. First,

it is obvious that such attributes, which are due to the composition and arrangement of the parts, don't necessarily belong to the component parts. Figure, mass, order, harmony, elastic power, the power of gunpowder, etc. are of this type. Then, it is also found, that often attributes of the component parts produce phenomena in the whole, which according to our perception, are completely distinguished from the parts. The compound colors appear to us to be different than the primary colors. We feel the compound emotions quite differently than the simple emotions of which they consist. Particular fragrances, which are mixed together, produce an entirely different-seeming smell—occasionally they produce a very unpleasant smell. On the other hand, a pleasant smell can be obtained by mixing together foul smelling gums. (see Halleri, Physiol. p. 169-170.)[198] The triad in music, if the notes are sounded at the same time, creates an entirely different effect, than the separate tones, of which it consists.

The attributes of the composition, therefore, to which the component parts don't necessarily belong, flow either from the arrangement and combination of these parts themselves, or are simply phenomena. That is to say, the attributes and effects of the component parts, which our senses cannot separate and differentiate from each other, appear to us differently in the whole than they really are. At this point, I applied this consideration to the proposition of **Plotinus**.

The power of reason cannot be an attribute of this type; since all these attributes are apparently effects of the power of reason, or presuppose the same to it. The composition and arrangement of the parts require a comparison and juxtaposition of these parts, and the appearances are not to be encountered as much in the things outside us, as in our thought. Both types are, therefore, effects of the soul, and cannot form its being. Therefore, no thinking whole can be composed from unthinking parts.

Also, the other part of the proof required a further elaboration. There have been philosophers who attributed indistinct concepts to the atoms of the body, out of which then, according to their opinion, clear and definite concepts come into being in the whole. Here, my intent was to prove that this is impossible, and that the smallest of these atoms would have to have conceptions as clear, as true, as alive, etc., as the whole man. For this purpose, I made use of the proposition which Mr. Plouquet[199] so nicely elaborates, **that many weaker degrees taken together form no greater degree**. Namely, there is a mass of quantity (quantitas extensiva), which exists in the quantity of parts from which it is put together, and is also called the **degree**. If many parts are added, then the mass of the first type increases, but to increase the degree requires intensification, not a greater extension. If lukewarm water is poured into lukewarm water; then the mass of water is increased, but not the degree of warmth. Many bodies, which move with equal velocity, if combined, make up a greater mass, but no greater velocity. The degree is as great in each part as in the whole, therefore the mass of the parts cannot change the degree. If this were to happen; then the effects of the mass must be concentrated in a one, because in such a way the intensification can be increased proportionally, as the extension decreases. Many weak lights are able to illuminate **one** place brighter, many magnifying glasses can set **one** body on fire more intensely. The more characteristics one and even the same subject perceives in an object, the clearer the image of this object becomes to the subject. It follows from here very naturally, that all indistinct concepts of atoms which are next to each other, taken together, cannot form a distinct concept, indeed not even a less indistinct concept, if they aren't concentrated in a subject, collected and, as it were, viewed by the same simple being from a higher standpoint.

The main arguments of my third dialogue are borrowed from Baumgartner's **Metaphysics**[200] and Reimarus' **Noblest Truths of Natural Religion**.[201] I have already mentioned in the preface, that I haven't found the proof anywhere else about the harmony of our duties and rights. As well, I assumed that in certain cases the death penalty is legal. However now the Marquis Beccaria in his treatise on **Crime and Punishment**[202] seems to put this proposition in doubt. Since this philosopher is of the opinion that the authority to punish is based solely on the social contract, from which then the injustice of the death penalty follows, therefore, in this second edition, I have sought to refute this opinion in an explanatory note. The Marquis himself cannot abstain from considering the death penalty unavoidable in some cases. In fact, he wants to make a kind of law of necessity of it; but the law of necessity itself must be based on a natural authority, otherwise it is a mere act of violence. In general, the proposition that all contracts in the world generate no new right probably is not to be called into question; however, they transform imperfect rights into perfect rights. Therefore, if the authority to punish were not based on natural law, such a right couldn't be produced by a contract. But if it is assumed, that the right to punish without a contract would be an imperfect right—even though I consider this absurd—nevertheless, my proof loses nothing of its coherence; for before the judge's seat of conscience, the imperfect rights are just as strong, the imperfect duties just as obliging as the perfect. An imperfect right to punish someone by taking his life presupposes, at the least, an imperfect obligation to suffer this punishment. But this obligation would be absurd, if our soul were not immortal.

In the **New Library of the Beautiful Sciences** (V.VI.),[203] a detailed announcement and evaluation of the *Phädon* is found which contains excellent comments. The prefatory thoughts about the philosophical dialogue by the reviewer, could serve as a model of how a critic must first justify himself as an expert before he becomes a master.—The proof against the collision of duties is cited, saying that it contains a circular argument. "It is said (P.331), that it is a duty for someone to abdicate the preservation of our lives. It can only mean that we believe to know higher purposes than life itself. If this were proved false; then those duties are lost, and with them at the same time the contradiction." I believe not to be disproved by this in any way. The proof can take different paths, which lead to the goal without going in a circle. One proceeds from man's obligation to society. This can be proved regardless of the immortality of the soul and is based on metaphysical principles like all moral truths. One hopefully wouldn't take me to task to elaborate on this, because it would obviously lead me too far afield, and these propositions have already been elaborated sufficiently by others. But no human society can exist, if the whole society doesn't have the right in certain circumstances to sacrifice the life of one of its people for the common good. Epicurus, Spinoza, and Hobbes couldn't deny this proposition, even if they wanted to recognize no higher purposes than life itself. They realized that social life couldn't occur among men if this right wasn't granted to the whole. But since the conceptions of right and duty were not sufficiently developed, it wasn't noticed that this right also assumes the duty on the side of the citizen, to sacrifice himself for the welfare of the whole, and that this duty of nature would not be corresponding, if the soul is not immortal.

As occurred in the last dialogue, I can also assume the justice of punishing an offense, which, in fact, must also be in store for man in the state of nature, as was explained. Indeed the reviewer makes the following comments in opposition to my arguments. "The right of retribution in the natural state of affairs, and the right to punish in civil society are, in fact, two different rights. The first applies simply to the person who has committed an offense, to take away his power and will to offend us again in the future: the other concerns the rest of the persons in society who have not committed an offense against us; to deter them from the crime, by the practical knowledge of the physical misfortune which they have to expect by committing it. The first is simply based on the right to defend oneself, or is rather coherent with it; but in the case of the state of nature, the offender retains the right to oppose our reprisal. The right to punish in civil society is based on the voluntary transference of one's total rights to society. Thus, through this, the right of the offender to defend himself against reprisal which comes from the entire society is annulled, etc." But I can't see how these differentiations can be granted to him. The right of retribution in the natural state? I know no right of mere retaliation, or reprisal, in human nature, that does evil, because evil occurred, whereby the physical evil is increased, without promoting the moral good. And why should man in the state of nature not be allowed to have the intent to deter others from offenses? Does this belong to a social contract? Does man first have to give up only a part of his rights to society, before he shows others that he has the right of retribution?—Finally, the right which is accorded the offender to oppose the revenge obviously annuls the harmony of moral truths, and establishes a case where right can be equal on both sides, where might makes right, a **natural duel**. I consider a proposition, which perpetrates disorder in the system of moral truths, as no less absurd, than if the harmony of metaphysical truths should be disrupted thereby. To avoid this discord, we must accept the duty of the offender to suffer punishment in the state of nature.—Were the offender, in the state of nature, to have the right to defend himself, then it would also have an effect on society. For, if the offended gave up his right of retribution and the offender relinquished his right of defense, then they would cancel each other, and no punishment could occur. It is, therefore, not possible to liberate the moral world from contradictions, if one doesn't want to permit life beyond death.

However, that there are cases in which the death penalty is the only means to prevent future offenses, even Beccaria had not called into question, even though he justifiably thinks that these cases in which the death penalty applies are not as widespread as is practiced in the prevailing penal laws. Generally the punishment keeps pace with the crime. If the crime knows no limits, likewise the punishment knows no limits, and there is no degree so high, which they cannot reach. There are also no determined barriers between torture and death, which one could apply to penal justice; therefore, if in some cases it is permitted to torture someone for punishment, there must also be cases, in which it is permitted to punish someone with death—because the transition from torture to death is gradual, it is never interrupted by fixed boundaries.—Yet what the reviewer states subsequently—that, indeed, conclusions can be drawn from the nature of things and applied to the law, but that from the law conclusions cannot be drawn and applied to the nature of things—does not seem so necessary to me. A circular argument is forbidden. Why should I not be able to draw conclusions from the law, and be able to apply them to the parts of the organization of nature, with which the reviewer disagrees?

Bibliography

Mendelssohn, Moses. *Jerusalem: Or on Religious Power and Judaism*. Translated from German by Allan Arkush. (Hanover, NH, 1983.)

Altmann, Alexander. *Moses Mendelssohn: A Biographical Study*. (Philadelphia, 1973.)

Samuels, Moses. *Memoirs of Moses Mendelsohn, the Jewish Philosopher; including the Celebrated Correspondence, 'On the Christian Religion,' with J. C. Lavater, Minister of Zurich*. Second Edition. (London, 1827.)

Schmidt, James. "Introduction" to *Moses Mendelssohn: The First English Biography*, a republication of the 1825 Samuels *Memoirs*. (Bristol, 2002.)

Neher, André. *Jewish Thought and the Scientific Revolution of the Sixteenth Century: David Gans (1541-1613) and His Times*. Translated from French by David Maisel. (New York, 1986.)

Arkush, Allan. *Moses Mendelssohn and the Enlightenment*. (Albany, 1994.)

Hensel, Sebastian. *The Mendelssohn Family (1729-1847) From Letters and Journals*. Second Revised Edition, translated by Carl Klingemann and an American Collaborator. Two volumes. (New York, 1881.)

Grunwald, Max. *Vienna*. Jewish Publication Society of America's Jewish Community Series. (Philadelphia, 1936.)

Notes

1. I have chosen to translate the "Appendix to the Third Edition," since it contains virtually everything that is in the "Appendix to the Second Edition," and then some (translator's note).

2. *Was meinest du, Simmias? würden wir einen Menschen nicht höchst lächerlich finden, der die Mauern von Athen niemals verlassen hätte, und aus seiner eigenen Erfahrung schliessen wollte, dass keine andere Regierungsform, als die demokratische, möglich wäre?*

3. The bulk of material presented here on Mendelssohn stems from Alexander Altmann's definitive and insightful English-language study, *Moses Mendelssohn: A Biographical Study*. 900 pages. (The Jewish Publication Society of America, Philadelphia, 1973, University of Alabama Press, publisher). Unless specified otherwise, any reference to "Altmann" refers to this work.

4. For the most extensive material on Gans in English, see André Neher's *Jewish Thought and the Scientific Revolution of the Sixteenth Century: David Gans (1541-1613) and His Times*. Translated from original 1974 French edition by David Maisel (Oxford University Press, 1986).

5. Abravanal was able to establish numerological connections between the 1492 banishment and the fall of the Third Temple. When his calculation for the coming of the Messiah in 1503 was found wanting, he found successful employment under the Venetians, negotiating the international spice trade. The modern authority on, and proponent for, Abravanel was B. Netanyahu (the father of the former Israeli Prime Minister, Bibi Netanyahu). His 1953 study is titled *Don Isaac Abravanel*.

6. English translations are those of David Maisel, as found in Neher's work on Gans.

7. Forty years later, Mendelssohn, the intellectual grandson of Hasid, would find his main collaborator in Vienna to be Hasid's biological grandson, Joseph von Sonnenfels. (Though Sonnenfels had converted to Christianity, his statue was still removed by the Nazis, during the 1938 Anschluss.)

8. Braunbehrens, Volkmar. *Mozart in Vienna, 1781-1791*. (NYC, 1989.) Braunbehrens brought to light that, in 1781, Mozart was the only non-Jew in the Fanny Itzig Arnstein household.

9. Friedrich Nicolai's report in his *Allgemeine Deutsche Bibliothek* (Berlin & Stettin, 1786). As cited in Altmann, p. 27.

10.   The story that dates the introduction by Gumpertz of Mendelssohn to Lessing early in 1754 appears to stem from Friedrich Nicolai's memory as of 1786. See Altmann, p. 36.

11.   Lessing's house at 68 Spandauer Strasse later became Mendelssohn's residence for the whole of his married life (that is, from 1762 to 1786).

12.   Sulzer's letter to Künzli, as quoted by Harnack, as cited by David Beeson's *Maupertuis: An Intellectual Biography* (Oxford, The Voltaire Foundation, 1992.)

13.   I treated Mylius' attempted travel to America and meeting with Franklin as an early attempt by Kästner to set up direct collaboration with Franklin. Shavin, David. "Leibniz to Franklin on 'Happiness'," p. 45-73 of *Fidelio*, Vol. XII, No. 1 (Spring 2003). The premature demise of Mylius likely contributed to the deep bond between Lessing and Mendelssohn.

14.   English translation by Paul Gallagher, "'Pope a Metaphysician!' An Anonymous Pamphlet in Defense of Leibniz." p. 45-59 of *Fidelio*, Vol. VIII, No. 4 (Winter 1999).

15.   To Michaelis' credit, after Lessing had proved to Michaelis that Mendelssohn indeed was the author, Michaelis gracefully announced in the October 2, 1755 *Göttingische Anzeigen* that a non-scholar, and a Jew, had written the *Philosophical Dialogues*, and that this was a pleasant surprise.

16.   The four short dialogues were published at the end of "Part 1" of the 1761 *Philosophical Writings*. See the English translation of Daniel O. Dahlstrom (Cambridge University Press, 1997, p. 96-129).

17.   Moses Mendelssohn. *On Sentiments*, published at the beginning of the 1761 *Philosophical Writings*. In Dahlstrom's translation, p. 7-95.

18.   Mendelssohn includes, in the fourth letter of his first section, *On Sentiments*, an extensive paraphrase from "a modern philosopher whose thoughts, nevertheless, deserve our attention." Fritz Bamberger identified Mendelssohn's reference here as to the first of Sulzer's two works.

19.   Daniel O. Dahlstrohm identified this as a reference to the preface of Volume I of Noel-Antoine Pluche's 1732 *Spectacle de la nature*.

20.   Mendelssohn's letter to Lessing, January 10, 1756.

21.   For example, Nicolai's *Treatise on Tragedy*. Of note, Mendelssohn brought to Lessing's attention Winckelmann's 1755 *Thoughts on the Imitation of the Works of the Greeks in Painting and Sculpture*, which would later be the impetus for Lessing's *Laocoön*.

22.   I treated Bach's "Musical Offering" as an epistemological intervention in tandem with the concerns of Kästner, Mylius, and Lessing in 1747. Shavin, David. "'Thinking through Singing'—The Strategic Significance of J. S. Bach's 'A Musical Offering'," p. 60-84 of *Fidelio*, Vol. IX, No. 4 (Winter 2000). Mendelssohn would likely have had broad reasons for his sessions with Kirnberger.

23.   Altmann, p. 68.

24. However, it did gain its own notoriety. It was reprinted in Philadelphia by Benjamin Franklin's German-newspaper partner, Anton Armbrüster. Further, an English translation was distributed in at least seven editions in 1758, in London, Boston, New York, and Philadelphia. It has been shown that the Jewish founder of the Union Society of Savannah, Georgia, Benjamin Sheftall, excitedly displayed the sermon in 1759 to his long-time associate, a Lutheran minister. (See Holly Snyder's *A Tree with Two Different Fruits: The Jewish Encounter with German Pietists in the Eighteenth-Century World. William and Mary Quarterly.* October, 2001. Thanks to my colleague Steven Meyer for calling this to my attention.) The Sheftalls were in love with the ideas of the sermon, the ideas of what would come to be the United States. Benjamin's twenty-four-year-old son, Mordechai, would later apply the spirit of the sermon in his unique civil and military leadership in the American Revolution. (And a century after the sermon, Mordechai's son, as an old man, would dress up in his father's uniform and make a one-man Unionist parade in antebellum Savannah!)

25. Mendelssohn's *Morgenstunden.* Translated by and found in Altmann, p. 578.

26. Mendelssohn's July 5, 1763 letter is in the Isaak Iselin-Archiv 28 of the *Staatsarchiv Basel.* This portion is to be found, translated, in Altmann, p. 145.

27. See Note (p) in the *Philosophical Writings*, edited and translated by Daniel O. Dahlstrom (Cambridge University Press. 1997, pages 84-87).

28. Leibniz's 1676 dialogue *Pacidius to Philalethes*, part of Leibniz's writings collected and published as *The Labyrinth of the Continuum*, translated by Richard T. W. Arthur (Yale University Press, 2001, p. 129-131).

29. His grandmother, the Countess Bückeburg, was very close to Leibniz's patron, Sophie, and to his student, the Crown Princess Caroline (married to the future King George II). His father, raised in the midst of Leibniz's battles for control of the English court, would attempt a major Leibnizian intervention upon Frederick II. This was in 1738 when Frederick was still a prince and was falling under the sway of Voltaire for the first time.

30. Wilhelm had extended an offer to Mendelssohn to join his court. Years later, in 1774, Mendelssohn finally did meet with Wilhelm, and they worked together on projects for several years. Mendelssohn's description of Wilhelm: "...[T]he finest Greek soul in a rough Westphalian body....He loved hard and dangerous physical exercises, the sciences, great deeds....Death for the sake of freedom and justice, the future life, and Providence were the topics of his ordinary conversation. I never heard a man talk with more warmth about the truths of natural religion. Free from all the prejudice that leads to discord and hatred of men, he was permeated to the degree of enthusiasm with the true, beneficial teachings of religion." Found in Altmann, p. 283.

31. Altmann, p. 163, cites Jakob Auerbach, 1887, in the *Zeitschrift für die Geschichte der Juden in Deutschland*, to the effect that "Levi was the only mourner at Leibniz' unceremonious funeral in 1716, and it was through him that the exact location of Leibniz' grave could be established later." However, it

was likely that he was the only Hanoverian there, who later could show the funeral site. For example, Leibniz's nephew from Leipzig, Simon Loeffler, travelled to Hanover for the funeral. (Regarding "unceremonious": King George I was nearby, but he and his court avoided the funeral of their longtime court minister, he who had concluded the negotiations that made George I a king of England.)

32. The whereabouts of Levi's initial letter is not known. The thrust of his comments may be inferred from Mendelssohn's response. See Altmann, p. 162-3.

33. This is cited by Altmann, p. 152, as, Goethe edition Inselverlag, 12:21-24.

34. See note 6.

35. Moses Mendelssohn's Treatise on the Incorporeality of the Human Soul (Vienna, 1785).

36. See Altmann, p. 177-178.

37. Altmann locates the particular section as the fifth volume of d'Alembert's *Melanges de litterature, d'histoire et de philosophie* of 1768. See Altmann's discussion, p. 178-179.

38. See Altmann, p. 178-179.

39. He, and his older brother, Duke Karl Eugen, seemingly had an array of problems with upstart commoners who displayed genius. This famously included: (a) refusing to hear the young Mozart before he became famous and then demanding to see him three years later, when he was famed as a prodigy; (b) the arrest of the young poet, Friedrich Schiller; and (c) factional warfare against Mendelssohn's collaborators in Vienna in the early 1780s.

40. Duke Ludwig Eugen to Moses Mendelssohn, June 27, 1767. See Altmann, p. 200-201.

41. J. G. Hamann's *Golgotha* attacked Mendelssohn for atheism. On the rest, Altmann cites the account of J. H. Schulz's work in the *Bibliothek der Deutschen Aufklärer des achtzehnten Jahrhunderts* (edited by Martin von Geismar, vol. 3, 1846).

42. For example, David Friedländer, who became an Itzig son-in-law and who co-founded the Berlin Jewish Freeschool with Isaac Daniel Itzig, would later publish the *Phädon* editions of 1814 and 1821—the first in Germany since Mendelssohn's fourth and last edition in 1776. Herz Homberg, who worked on the last book of Mendelssohn's *Pentateuch* translation, became his representative in Vienna for the education projects. Hartwig Wessely's poetry celebrated the translation project. Many others grouped around Mendelssohn, and their ongoing educational and translation projects were the seedbed of the next 150 years of Haskala.

43. These quotes are from the translation by Bayard Quincy Morgan, found in The German Library edition, *Nathan the Wise, Minna von Barnhelm, and Other Plays and Writings* (NYC, 1998).

44. A fragmentary essay found in Lessing's *Sämtliche Schriften*, edited by K. Lachman, vol. 16, p. 444, of the 3rd edition. The quote is found in Altmann, p. 578. (Clearly, Lessing's approach found an immediate and inspired voice in Mozart's 1782 *Abduction from the Seraglio* opera.)

45. Undated letter. See Altmann, p. 579-80.

46. From the "Notes and Additions" section of Mendelssohn's 1785 *Morgenstunden*, as translated in Altmann, p. 581.

47. This is covered in some greater detail in my article, "Philosophical Vignettes from the Political Life of Moses Mendelssohn," p. 29-45 of *Fidelio*, Vol. VIII, No. 2 (Summer 1999). Mendelssohn's literary efforts heavily intersected the movement that, among other matters, shaped the uniqueness of the American republic.

48. His concluding paragraph has a footnote reference to his active concern over an early 1783 debate in the U.S. Congress—apparently to a clause in a bill that read: "The Christian religion shall in all times coming be deemed and held to be the established Religion of this Commonwealth." James Madison helped defeat this bill, importantly with the support of the Christian ministers in the legislature. This, and the quality of debate over the issue of citizenship over the next several years, suggests that Mendelssohn's plea did not fall on deaf ears.

49. Mendelssohn, Moses. *Jerusalem: Or on Religious Power and Judaism.* Translated from the German by Allan Arkush (Hanover, NH, 1983, p. 138-39).

50. Mendelssohn's August 16, 1783 letter to Elise Reimarus, who served as the go-between with Jacobi. (Elise, her brother, and her father all knew Lessing from the 1760s in Hamburg. Their friendship continued when Lessing moved to Brunswick.)

51. Dr. Marcus Herz's account, published January 24, 1786, as part of the "Preface" to Mendelssohn's defense of Lessing, *An die Freunde Lessings.* Translation as found in Altmann, p. 740.

52. Thomas Abbt (1738-1766) was Mendelssohn's closest correspondent from 1761 until his death in November 1766. He was educated at the University of Halle, 1756-58, under the theologian, S. J. Baumgarten. The aesthetical work of the more famous brother, A. G. Baumgarten, was promulgated by Abbt. It is probable that, under S.J. Baumgarten, Abbt would have also studied the aesthetic writings also of Kästner, Sulzer, and Mendelssohn.

53. Johann Joachim Spaulding's 1748 *Betrachtung über die Bestimmung des Menschen* had just been republished, when, on Jan. 11, 1764, Abbt wrote to Mendelssohn, suggesting that Mendelssohn work out his "thoughts and doubts," using Spalding's work as a touchstone. In 1748, in the wake of official attacks upon Leibniz, Spalding had presented a tame Leibnizian argument that, beyond the pleasures of the body, and beyond those of the mind also, there is the happiness of others; and so, there is a virtuous God. Otherwise, Mendelssohn and Spalding would have known each other, as both had been participants in Berlin's "Wednesday Society" discussion group.

54. In this work, Abbt was "Euphranor" and Mendelssohn was "Theodul." First, Abbt wrote his *Doubts Concerning the Determination of Man*, to which Mendelssohn answered with his *Oracle Concerning the Determination of Man*, both in the early months of 1764.

55. Vom Verdienst, 1765.

56. Typical of Mendelssohn's graceful expression, he balances what he clearly thinks is Leibniz's superior treatment with the humility needed to attempt to capture properly all the very real issues involved in translating from a profound and ancient language.

57. In particular, Plotinus' treatise *On the Immortality of the Soul (Ennead* IV. vii*)*, as developed with Leibniz's concept of monads. (See Altmann, page 154.)

58. John Gilbert Cooper's 1749 *Life of Socrates* was published in London. One passage (page 21f) must have served as a model for Mendelssohn's own life, and he was impressed enough to use it in full: "Socrates therefore from the beginning labored under these disadvantages and difficulties, which to others would have been insurmountable. He had the prejudices of education first to overcome in himself, the custom-protected ignorance of others to enlighten, sophistry to confute, malice, envy, calumny, and continual insults of his adversaries to endure, poverty to undergo, power to contend with and what was the greatest labor of all, the vulgar terrors and darkness of superstition to dissipate; all of which, we shall find in the sequel, he overcame with the true wisdom of a philosopher, and the disinterested virtue of a patriot, the patience of a saint, and the resolution of a hero, at the expense of all worldly pleasure, wealth, power, fame, and lastly life itself, which he cheerfully laid down for the sake of his country; sealing with his blood a testimony of the love he bore to his own species, and the unchangeable duty to the Creator and Governor of all things." (Altmann, pages 159-60.) Benno Boehm's *Sokrates* has more extensive comparisons between Mendelssohn and Cooper.

59. Diogenes Laertius' *Life of Socrates*: "And some say that the Graces in the Acropolis are his work; and they are clothed figures." Laertius cites the *Silli* of Timon to abet his contention. It counts in favor of the testimony here that Timon was not an advocate of Socrates. Also, since Timon, arguably, had connections to those who might have known about Socrates' particular work in sculpture, one might consider this one of Laertius' more likely anecdotes. Timon was a third century BC philosopher from Phliasia, whose study in Megara and Elis suggests that his sources there were the schools established soon after Socrates' death by, respectively, Euclides and Phaedo. (Both individuals are cited by Plato as among the few who attended Socrates at his death.) Timon settled in Athens, where he wrote his three satiric books, called the *Silli*.

60. Phidias (circa 490-430 BC) was the lead sculptor and planner of the Parthenon in Athens during the major projects of the so-called Periclean "Golden Age." He is most famous for the statue works of "Athen Parthenos", executed between 447 and 439 BC. Zeuxis (464- ? BC) was known for his

paintings. Myron worked in bronze, managing to portray athletes twisted in action, yet in balance. His most famous known work is the "Discus Thrower."

61. Laertius: "And Demetrius, of Byzantium, says that it was Criton who made him leave his workshop and instruct men, out of the admiration which he conceived for his abilities."

62. Anaxagoras (circa 500-428 BC) is cited by Socrates in Plato's *Phaedrus* (270A), as the philosopher who had the most competent approach, in that he started his physics with "nous" (noetic mind) governing the universe. Despite being friends with Pericles, he was convicted of impiety, and exiled from Athens, c. 432 BC. His student, Archelaus, instructed Socrates, no later than the 430s. Theodorus (465-398? BC) was a geometer from Egypt's "Greek" colony, Cyrenaica (now Shahhat, Libya). He ended his studies with Protagoras to pursue geometry. In Plato's *Theaetetus*, he introduces his theme by describing his student, Theaetetus, as being most like Socrates. Prodicus of Ceos, followed the tradition of Protagoras, and was, for Plato, the sophist par excellence. He was overly-proud of his learning and charged high fees. In Plato's *Protagoras*. Socrates first meets Prodicus in 432 BC at the gathering of sophists in Callias' house. In *Cratylus*, Socrates refers to his deficient knowledge, having only taken Prodicus' one-drachma course (instead of the 50-drachma course). Finally, Evenus of Paros is cited in Plato's *Apology* as a money-earning sophist, having been hired to teach the children of the wealthy Callias. Later, in the *Phaedo*, sport is made of Evenus as a philosopher that has not faced up to mortality. Socrates recruits Callias' son Philebus away from such as Evenus.

63. Cicero (106-43 BC) was perhaps the best hope among the Romans to properly assimilate the accomplishments of the Greeks. He made it a point to rediscover the grave of Archimedes, whose murder by Roman soldiers in 212 BC epitomized the barbaric end of a scientific culture. Cicero himself was assassinated in 43 BC, in the wake of the burning of the Alexandrian Library and the destruction of much Greek learning.

64. In the preceding three paragraphs, Mendelssohn also had his eye on his own situation, in dealing with fundamentalists on one side, and sophists such as Voltaire and Maupertuis on the other.

65. Mendelssohn clearly felt the similarities of his position in Berlin with this description of Socrates' position. This paragraph was also the subject of the first major attack upon his *Phädon*. (See "Introduction" on Duke Ludwig Eugen.)

66. Friedrich Schiller, a generation later, expressed this in terms of being both a patriot of one's country, and a citizen of the world.

67. The 432 BC rebellion against the increasingly colonial policies of Athens was, effectively, the opening of the 431-404 BC Peloponnesian Wars.

68. The eighteen-year-old Alcibiades, raised in Pericles' household, was the prime candidate to come to rule Athens. Plato sets his *Alcibiades* dialogue in the months just prior to this expedition, where Socrates undertakes to steer

Alcibiades toward true leadership. See Plato's *Symposium* (219E-220E), for Alcibiades' description of the expedition.

69.   The *Varia Historia* of Claudius Aelianus (175-235 AD)

70.   Aulus Gellius (130-180 AD) lived and wrote in Rome and Athens. (However, as this story is in Plato's *Symposium* dialogue, over 500 years earlier, it is hard to figure that Gellius was not relying upon the same.)

71.   Mendelssohn then would have Socrates initiate his public organizing at the onset of the Peloponnesian War, when Pericles has walled in the population against the Spartan invasion. Socrates was then 38, the same age as Mendelssohn when the *Phädon* was published.

72.   Plato's *Theaetetus* (149A-151B), has Socrates most explicit and developed discussion of his midwifery of ideas (and his testing for a real birth, or just a "wind-egg"!).

73.   This was a key policy for Mendelssohn in his own political and ecumenical practices. Later, his reforms of 1782, for secular rights of citizens in an ecumenical framework, and his hopes for the new American Congress, reflected this.

74.   In Plato's *Apology* (21A), Socrates tells the court how the impetuous Chaerephon asked the oracle whether anyone was wiser than Socrates. Hence, Socrates felt compelled to investigate whether others, and particularly the leaders of society, were so lacking in wisdom. A version is also to be found in Xenophon's *Apology of Socrates*.

75.   Xenophon's *Banquet* is set in 421 BC—not to be confused with the 416 BC *Symposium* banquet portrayed by Plato.

76.   From Xenophon's *Symposium* (or *Banquet*), II, 17-19, where Socrates responds to Antisthenes' jibe about the shrewish Xanthippe. Also in Laertius, XVII.

77.   Xenophon's Memorabilia, or Recollections of Socrates (Book 2, Chapter 2).

78.   424 BC.

79.   Plato's *Laches* dialogue (181B).

80.   Mendelssohn found in Laertius, VII, that Socrates saved Xenophon at Delium. Confused stories have been passed down about the battle of Delium. However, it is almost certain that Xenophon was too young for duty at Delium. Strabo, writing around 20 AD, may be in part the source here, though he claims that Socrates saved the life of Xenophon's son Gryllus. (It were possible that someone at Delium saved Xenophon's father, Gryllus, who was the right age to be fighting there.) The clearest testimony, from Plato's *Symposium* (221 A-B), is Alcibiades' eyewitness account, that Socrates saved General Laches at Delium. While Plato is writing a dialectical drama, and not narrative history, it is unlikely he would have so drastically altered this sort of detail.

81.   Aristophanes (c. 445-c. 385) had been writing plays for about four years at that point. His initial success was the anti-war *Acharnians*, winning first prize in 425 BC. With his sarcastic wit, he was the Voltaire of his day; and

Mendelssohn would have been naturally suspicious of the motives of the Aristophanes' supporters. His play, *The Clouds*, entertained an Athens of 423 BC, jaded from eight years of unsuccessful war. See Plato's *Symposium* for his hilarious treatment of the hiccupping Aristophanes.

82.　Diogenes Laertius: "Some people believed that he assisted Euripides in his poems; in reference to which idea, Mnesimachus speaks as follows: '*The Phrygians* are a new play of Euripides,/But Socrates has laid the main foundation.' And again he says: 'Euripides: patched up by Socrates.' And Callias, in his *Captives*, says: 'Are you so proud, giving yourself such airs?' 'And well I may, for Socrates is the cause.' And Aristophanes says, in his *Clouds*: 'This is Euripides, who doth compose/Those argumentative wise tragedies.' " Laertius (XXIV) writes that Euripides (C. 484-406 BC) and Socrates (15 years younger) attended lectures of Anaxagoras. Both men also knew Protagoras at some point.

83.　422 BC.

84.　Of course, Plato composed his *Alcibiades* dialogue, *after* the charges and rumors against Socrates were in circulation. In his *Alcibiades* dialogue, Plato portrays Socrates' historic mission of intervening on and educating the potential future leader of Athens, as Socrates' "eros" for Alcibiades. "Eros" is usually what we understand as erotic love, and certainly is not the brotherly love, "philos," nor the universal love of God for man, "agape." However, Plato is ruthless here in portraying "eros" in the more general sense, as love focused upon a one—whether it be some one person, thing, or idea. Usually love focused upon a one can be obsessive, but here it is Socrates' unique mission to intervene on history, before the civil wars destroy Greece. Baser readings of Plato's play, that missed the historically specific character of the setting, were not infrequent.

85.　Critias (c. 460-403 BC), Plato's relative on his mother's side, appears in Plato's *Timeaus* and his *Critias*. Plato describes in his *Seventh Letter* how and why he refuses to join with Critias' political rule. Xenophon describes Critias as one of the worst of the short-lived "Thirty Tyrants" of 404 BC. Mendelssohn is drawing from Xenophon's *Memorabilia*: "Listen then: Socrates was well aware that Critias was attached to Euthydemus, aware too that he was endeavoring to deal by him after the manner of those wantons whose love is carnal of body." But Critias wouldn't listen, so Socrates, in the "presence of a whole company and of Euthydemus [remarked] that Critias appeared to be suffering from a swinish affection, or else why this desire to rub himself against Euthydemus like a herd of piglings scraping against stones. The hatred of Critias to Socrates doubtless dates from this incident...." Regarding Critobulus, the son of Crito, see the *Memorabilia*, Book I, Ch. 3, 8-9. Xenophon witnesses Socrates' warning when he hears that Critobulus has kissed the fair son of Alcibiades, and warns about the uncontrolled pleasures of Aphrodite.

86.　This was a sensitive issue for Mendelssohn, as his nemesis, Voltaire, had circulated various reports, alleging homosexuality on the part of the King,

Frederick the Great. Voltaire also explicitly defamed Plato's account of Socrates' relationship with Alcibiades in a poem to Frederick!

87.   The naval battle of Arginusae in 406 BC, a precious victory for Athens, was turned into the last victory of Athens before her final collapse. The trial that ensued highlights that Athens, more than anything else, collapsed from the inside.

88.   The Spartans were victorious at Aegospotami in 405 BC, leading to the complete defeat of Athens in 404 BC.

89.   Here Mendelssohn's story, starting from the appearance of Charicles, is from Xenophon's *Memorabilia, Or Recollections of Socrates* (Book I, Ch. 2, 31-38).

90.   Plato's *Apology* (32 C-D). Leon, for all that is known, was a reputable citizen. Socrates relates the story, pointing out that the tyrants had a practice of ordering such evil tasks primarily to corrupt otherwise innocent citizens.

91.   Anytus, Melitus, and Lycon formally brought the charges against Socrates. For Plato's treatment of Melitus, see the *Apology*, and of Anytus, see his *Meno* dialogue. Anytus (along with his partner Thrasybulus) was funded by the suddenly wealthy Ismenias to create the "democracy" of 403 BC. Ismenias was later executed as a Persian spy. In 402 BC, Anytus was the Athenian host for the visit of his political ally, Meno of Thessaly—whom Socrates identifies in the *Meno* (78D) as "the ancestral friend of the Great King." Meno's mission to Anytus was part of his family's traditional role as the Persian king's agent in Thessaly. Meno, as described in Xenophon's *Anabasis*, would next betray the Greeks in their invasion of Persia. So, Ismenias, Meno and Anytus display the footprints of the Persian King, Artaxerxes II. In 399 BC, Anytus would lead two lesser figures—the poet Melitus and the orator Lycon—in the prosecution of Socrates.

92.   In the the *Alcibiades* dialogue, Socrates' prime student in 432 BC was Alcibiades. In 415 BC, just prior to General Alcibiades' flight-forward into the ruinous assault upon Syracuse, the sacrilegious mutilation of the Hermes statues occurred. Plato's treatment of Alcibiades in the *Symposium* dialogue, situated in 416 BC, suggests that his behavior was an abreaction, having fallen away from the historic mission that Socrates had assigned him, back in 432 BC, before the war. (Note therein—Plato has Alcibiades compare Socrates to the Silenus statue, with an ugly exterior and true inner beauty, an image that plagues Alcibiades. Perhaps he is suggesting that the mutilation involved opening up ugly exteriors of the statues.)

93.   Actually, the charges against Alcibiades, and his subsequent flight, only came after the initial foray against Syracuse had miscarried.

94.   Mendelssohn's hypothesis is totally coherent with Plato's treatment in *Philebus*, where Socrates recruits Protarchus, the scion of the family responsible for preserving the sanctity of the Eleusian mysteries, to a scientific treatment of the inner truths of the mysteries.

95.   The charges are certainly reported in Plato and Xenophon; however Mendelssohn's wording is very close to that of Laertius, whose claim to

accuracy is that the charges "are preserved to this day, says Favorinus, in the Temple of Cybele...." Favorinus, an orator and sycophant in the court of Emperor Hadrian (117-138 AD), was close to Plutarch, the priest of the Oracle of Apollo at Delphi. Favorinus seems to have had access to the Temple of Cybele (the Roman earth-mother goddess), where, evidently, the Athenian state archives eventually resided.

96. Hermogenes, brother of Callias and uncle to Philebus, reports in Xenophon's *Apology*, that he urged Socrates to write such a speech, not that he had written one. However, Laertius cites a speech written by Lysias. Since Lysias was a major financial backer of Anytus' collaborator, Thrasybulus, there was some irony involved in a defense speech written by friends of the prosecution! It were likely that one faction of Socrates' opponents preferred to manage the conviction of Socrates, without martyring him. See Plato's *Phaedrus* for his treatment of Lysias' honeyed sophistry.

97. Xenophon's *Apology*.

98. Evidently, Mendelssohn's own translation of Plato's *Apology* (35 C-D).

99. Plato's *Apology* (36E). However, the references, before the quote, to Plato attempting to speak at the trial, and to a 33-vote majority, are not from Plato. The *Apology* of Plato refers to a switch of thirty votes that would have altered the guilty verdict. (Assuming the traditional 500 judges, the vote was inferred to be 280-220.)

100. Plato's *Apology* (38C-39B).

101. Lucius Annaeus Seneca (4 BC- 65 AD). Dr. Martin Luther King, Jr. also studied Seneca and Socrates on these matters, e.g., in his preparation of his *Letters from a Birmingham Jail.*

102. Xenophon's *Apology* is the source for the last two stories, on weeping and on Apollodorus.

103. Mendelssohn proceeds to quote and summarize the whole of Plato's *Crito* dialogue.

104. Socrates' dream woman quotes Achilles in Homer's *Iliad* (Book IX, 363), where he contemplates leaving the battle and going home to Phthia.

105. Here is the germ of Mendelssohn's more developed argument in Book III of the *Phädon*, where the lack of immortality of the soul pits the individual against his whole society in the fevered struggle for his own physical existence.

106. Corybantes were frenzied dancers of the Phrygian goddess Cybele. Plato has Socrates crown his reasoned argument for a higher law, with this totally juxtaposed image of two cases of possession: his by reason, the dancers by flutes!

107. After Socrates execution in 399 BC, Phädon has journeyed from Athens to Phliasia (west of Corinth), perhaps on his way back to his home town of Elis, where he would set up a school of philosophy. Phliasia was a town with a Pythagorean school, probably led by Echecrates, who was himself a student of Plato's good friend, the geometer and statesman, Archytas. Aristoxenus lists as

students of the Pythagorean Philolaus, who also live in Phliasia: Echecrates, Phanton, Diocles and Polymnastus. Phliasia was known for a disproportionately high contribution of men to two of the crucial battles against the Persian invasion— Thermopylae and Plataea. Otherwise, according to the account of Aulus Gellius (ii, 18), Phädon had been brought to Athens originally as a prisoner, and was freed when Cebes paid his ransom.

108. It is the proper name "Theoria," but perhaps "festival of the Mission" would be better. Greek "theoria" means spectacle but also means the ambassadors who go to the event, and the mission to the event. Here the festival is for sending off the mission to Delos.

109. Athens usually had nine archons, or chief magistrates, elected on an annual basis. Judicial matters would fall under their authority.

110. Plural "listeners" because Echecrates' students of his school are present; but it also works for Plato to invite in any auditors of his dialogue.

111. Apollodorus of Phalerum had followed Socrates from approximately 402 to 399 BC. That Plato portrays Echecrates as "in the know" about Apollodorus' behavior is one way that Plato suggests that the Pythagoreans of Phliasia were following Socrates' actions. Otherwise, Apollodorus was also portrayed as overly emotional in the *Symposium*, which was situated several years earlier than the *Phaedo*.

112. Crito was Socrates' oldest friend and most dependable supporter. The other Athenians were, after some fashion, students of Socrates. Of some note: Hermogenes, brother of Callias and son of the Peloponnesian general, Hipponicus, also appears in the *Cratylus*. He would be the source for Xenophon on the trial of Socrates. Aeschines of Sphettus was a rhetorician and a writer of Socratic dialogues, who would become poor in Athens and then join the court of Syracuse. (Plato had to contend there with Aeschines for Dionysius II's attention.) Antisthenes, a veteran of the Peloponnesian War, set up a school in Athens that, notably, taught the different classes of Athenians. Menexenus is portrayed in a spurious dialogue of the same name as being from a family of politicians. In Plato's *Lysis*, he is the friend of Lysis, and an admirer of Ctessipus.

113. Crito had represented to Socrates (in Plato's *Crito* dialogue) that Simmias, and also Cebes, had come with funds to help him escape. In Thebes, Simmias and Cebes were students of Philolaus, a Pythagorean from Croton (or possibly Tarentum). Philolaus, an astronomer and philosopher, is said to be the teacher of Archytas, who was Plato's source for Pythagorean treatises. Otherwise, Simmias is credited by Diogenes Laertius with the composition of 23 (lost) dialogues.

Euclides' school in Megara provided shelter for Plato and his associates, who left Athens after the execution of Socrates. Plato's *Theaetetus* dialogue has Euclides, decades later, relate to Terpsion the story that he had heard from Socrates about the courageous young student, Theaetetus.

114. Plato seems to enjoy taking his digs at the rhetorician Aristippus, with whose influence over Dionysius I of Syracuse Plato would have to contend. In the opening of his *Meno* dialogue, set around 402 BC, Plato has Socrates compare Meno's desire for knowledge with his desire for his lover, Aristippus—with the implication that both were too shallow. Meno would soon betray the Athenians to the Persians. Here, in 399 BC, Aristippus seems to be off with a new love, away from the trial and execution of his supposed friend, Socrates.

115. The "Eleven" were chosen by lot, and supervised the prisons, including executions.

116. Mendelssohn found Plato's sense of drama finely wrought. Surely, the Socratic "leg-rub" would have enchanted him. At a moment of meeting his friends on his last day, the image of Socrates philosophizing on his leg pain captures both his totally being at one with himself, and the paradoxically conjoined pleasure and pain just described by Phädon. An opening theme is announced.

117. Socrates had alluded to Evenus in his "Apology"—as an example of sophists who sell their wares, and Callias' willingness to employ such to attempt to train his boys.

118. Meaning, not just the "most splendid music" of philosophy, but the setting of words to verse. Given the musicality of ancient Greek words, there was also an innate component of this versification that would include what we, today, refer to, more simplistically, as music.

119. The leg-rub and the putting of both feet onto the ground demarcates the wonderful example of Plato's staging. From the pleasure-pain paradox to Socrates' mention of Aesop, which prompts Cebes to ask about the versification, and allows Socrates to engage Cebes and Simmias on the difference between Evenus and Socrates as philosophers—Plato's voice-leading has allowed Socrates to engage the two Pythagorean-trained interlocuters on their views of death. Now, consider: did Socrates innocently bring up Aesop, or not?

120. Philolaus was a young man when the whole of the Pythagorean leadership was attacked and burned. For Plato and Archytas, he was their key link to the Pythagoreans. Importantly, he held that the earth moved around the sun. (Both as a youth and as the great German philologist, August Böckh published on Philolaus' astronomical work.) Plato studied Philolaus' writings from works provided by Archytas, and significant portions of Philolaus are reflected in Plato's title character, Timaeus. Besides teaching Cebes and Simmias in Thebes, he is counted by Aristoxenus as the teacher of the Phliasians—Phanton, Echecrates, Diocles and Polymnastus. Socrates saw Cebes and Simmias as a link to this precious source; and Plato had this in mind in crafting his dialogue to take place before the Phliasian Pythagoreans.

121. Socrates' words become those of Mendelssohn here. He was particularly attracted to this part of Plato's *Phaedo*, and the possibility of dealing with some of the cynicism in his own culture. In Letter 14 of his essay, *On Sentiments*, and in his *Rhapsody, or Additions to the Letters on Sentiments*,

he takes significant pains to counter the utilitarian arithmetic of the pro-suicide views of Maupertius' 1750 *Essai de philosophie morale.* Even if one could prove there was more negative than positive in life, such calculations did not address one's relationship with one's Maker. "[O]ne must surely wonder at philosophers who have wanted to compute the sums of pleasant and unpleasant sentiments in human life and compare them. The author of the *Essay on Moral Philosophy* imagined this consideration in a very facile manner." See Daniel Dahlstrom's translation of Mendelssohn's *Philosophical Writings* (Cambridge University Press, 1997, p. 147).

122.   The unresolved issue of the brutal burning of the Pythagoreans was the key spectre behind all intellectual and cultural warfare of the period. How to account for how they served as sentries and how they were replaced was a deeply resonating issue. And the impact of Socrates' choice to deal with this is powerful—perhaps to be compared with the effect of Lincoln's *Gettysburg Address* on the relationship that we owe the soldiers who have fallen before us, delivered by one who is not long for this world.

123.   Mendelssohn's monotheistic addition, making explicit what he thinks is implicit with Socrates.

124.   Mendelssohn expands upon Plato's notion of man's obligation to his lord, by developing the previous allusion to philosophy as the most excellent music. Man has a mission to compose the finite, himself, in tune with the infinite. This argument, beginning with "Perhaps if a spark of righteousness...", is where Mendelssohn first diverts from Plato's text in any substantial fashion.

125.   Here Mendelssohn ends his expansion, and returns to Plato's action, with the objection of Cebes.

126.   Though a joke on one level, the *Apology* defense speech should be read to grasp the magnitude and significance of this statement about Socrates' last project—to now convince his friends. To give this further dramatic emphasis, Mendelssohn chose to set off this line.

127.   As we learn later, one drink proved sufficient for Socrates. So, by this brief "comic" interlude, Plato is able to suggest (retrospectively) that when Socrates spoke, he wasn't simply "overheating," but he conveyed passion without the extraneous friction.

128.   This "esoteric" discussion is demarcated from the later "exoteric" discussion, with a different mission in the dialogue.

129.   Approximately here begins Mendelssohn's second major insertion of the "First Dialogue," to develop Philolaus' idea as to how man may catch a glimpse of truth.

130.   With Simmias' second invocation of "the voice of Jupiter" (and, in general, with the more frequent refrains of "Jupiter") by Simmias, Mendelssohn marks the consistent and developing quality of Simmias' character. It denotes the increasingly higher-ordered (though as yet unanswered) questions that Simmias has identified for himself to work on. Finally, Mendelssohn proceeds to have Socrates address "the voice of Jupiter" as we would investigate a flute

or a work of art. Schiller would develop this aesthetic theme, of beauty leading one towards truth.

131. Mendelssohn uses the undeveloped, but opaque character of Apollodorus to provide Socrates with the perfect foil. It is one thing to be sensuously attached to the sounds of great ideas, and another to internalize and to develop higher ideas. He links the problem of the overly-emotional Apollodorus to the problem of pursuing truth and immortality.

132. An initiation festival for those who would delve into the mysteries.

133. The case has been made for the initiates. But how do they deal with the greater public's concerns? It is one thing for them to agree with Socrates' argument about death; it is another how they might deal with the greater public, e.g., those who voted at Socrates' trial. With the philosophical understanding hammered out, how would natural science proceed?

134. Pure Mendelssohn! He has Socrates first call for the standard invocation of a divinity, but after deliberation, concludes that seeking "the truth with a pure heart" is what the sole Deity gives man. Mendelssohn, in this short insertion, weds monotheism to humans relying not upon invocations, but upon internal deliberation and work!

135. And typical Mendelssohn: deliberate changes in conduct are always before our mind and too rarely acted upon; but Mendelssohn offers it as being in the same rich world as all other natural changes—with the (Leibnizian) optimistic orientation that all actual problems are indeed solvable.

136. By asking Cebes whether he would like to be severed in two, Mendelssohn makes the case for a serious idea—whether a Platonic idea or a Leibnizian monad—in a playful and effective manner.

137. Mendelssohn uses Apollodorus almost as a marker for the witness of his play, or his reader. Apollodorus was transfixed when last heard from, and now he is in the fight to figure out matters.

138. Here, and in the analyses to follow, Mendelssohn adopts the language of the "great machine." Julien de la Mettrie's influential 1748 work, *L'homme machine*, had prompted much discussion along these lines. Mendelssohn had concerns about the mechanistic influence of la Mettrie, the King's royal reader, upon Frederick the Great and the court.

139. Cebes' re-introduction of the omnipresent: Their discussion is intensely non-"academic," as their teacher's imminent death forces them to be changed forever by this discussion. Socrates' hint is that his power of dialectics is open to one and all, so they shouldn't be so defensive about accepting their mission. (Mendelssohn actually makes somewhat less of this than does Plato at this point.) But the edge has been put on the issue: Let Socrates, again, cover both options, but let his listeners pay more attention to how to lead such investigations.

140. Socrates worked on statuary in the public works of Periclean Athens. Thus, he traced his lineage to the patron of sculptors, Daedalus. Also, Plato's use of the

rolling mechanism is taken as supporting evidence for the advanced mechanisms used in actual Greek stage productions.

141.   A sharp-edged analogy. It was the democracy (though, admittedly, as a front for the Persian Empire) that was putting Socrates to death that day. Implied here is that deeper deliberations upon the soul might also allow for a more scientific approach to governing. Socrates' comment has a thematic resonance with the previous allusion to "barbarians."

142.   It is worth noting that "natural" was from the Greek word, "phusis"—from whence we understand, "physics." Plato, Leibniz and Mendelssohn knew this as a higher concept than what we today commonly consider as mere matter. To the extent we take "phusis" as dead matter bumping against each other, we also remain inside the womb, or stuck inside a decaying Athens.

143.   Some seventeen years earlier! *Symposium* (210E-211A).

144.   Here, Mendelssohn greatly augments Simmias' speech over what Plato had him say at this point, so as to deal with the witty cynicism that Voltaire had cast upon European culture, and particularly upon Mendelssohn's Berlin.

145.   Here, Mendelssohn concludes this particular augmentation of Plato's work, with this identification of two issues: "the truth losing its strength"; and whether the mind could do work that would systematically address this, such that one could "remember all these reasons vividly, and to feel the power of truth." Mendelssohn uses Simmias' concern as the theme for the second dialogue. (Mendelssohn's project was, famously, taken up by Friedrich Schiller in his treatment of the aesthetic education of man.)

146.   Part of the dizzying effect of this section upon Socrates' audience, and upon readers, is that Simmias has inverted Socrates' argument. Instead of treating what we don't know as a caution not to extrapolate based upon pedestrian principles, now, what we don't know is a glimmer into the stultifying complexity of life that we won't ever know. The former allows for a transcendental soul defining physical realities, the latter reduces man's soul to the mystery of a never-to-be-fathomed complex clockwork.

147.   Echecrates breaks in upon the narrator, making explicit the deep concern of Plato's and Mendelssohn's audiences—that they too doubt their capacities in such matters.

148.   Socrates' character was prepared ahead of time for such a disarray—similar to the battle-field qualities that Mendelssohn describes in his biographical sketch of Socrates.

149.   Better to fight for the real life of Socrates, his principled ideas, than to mourn the loss of his body. (Lincoln's inversion in his *Gettysburg Address*—"It is rather for us to be here dedicated...."—is appropriate, transforming the fragile concerns about mortality into living actions for immortality.) It is time for Socrates' mourners to show their real regard for Socrates. Mendelssohn, as does Plato, links the issue of immortality with their power to reason. Phaedo's hair rivals Socrates' leg-scratching for memorable dramatic images.

150. Iolaus was Hercules' nephew, who, importantly, served as his charioteer when he went to fight the nine-headed Hydra. As Hercules cut off a head, two more grew in its place, and so Hercules was being entwined by the snake. The Iolaus came with a torch to sear each cut-off neck closed, ending the doubling of the heads. Evidently, Phaedo wanted Socrates to perform this service in the face of multiplying arguments. But Socrates will make it clear that Phaedo had more to learn from him than how to end multiplying arguments.

151. Athens was in southern Attica. Just north of Attica was a long island, Euboea, separated by a channel of water, Euripus. In this narrow strait, the waters become quite constricted near Chalcis.

152. Mendelssohn has amplified on Plato's argument, from "I please myself at times with the thought...." to this last sentence. His "flattering images" took shape a decade later, in 1776, "That all men are created equal, that they are endowed by their Creator with certain inalienable rights; that among these are life, liberty, and the pursuit of Happiness." The head of the committee that wrote those words, Benjamin Franklin, had met with Mendelssohn's collaborators in Hannover and Göttigen to study Leibniz's concept of "felicity" or "happiness" in the same summer of 1766 when Mendelssohn was completing his *Phädon*.

153. Socrates' introduction of the shocking image of himself, as guilty of making arguments to please opinion, underlines his commitment to recruit his friends—who are not in Socrates' precise situation—to fight for the truth regarding the soul.

154. This is a prime example of Mendelssohn improving upon Plato with "modern" thought—by which Mendelssohn meant Leibniz.

155. If Mendelssohn were referring to Crito's proposal that Socrates escape, that discussion (in *Crito*) was from a previous morning. However, earlier this same morning (in *Phaedo*), Socrates had shown little patience when Crito had interrupted to convey the jailor's concern that an over-heated discussion might cause extra cups of poison to be needed. Mendelssohn, as Plato, used that to put into relief the greater importance of Socrates' mission with Cebes and Simmias. Perhaps Mendelssohn now has the amiable and long-suffering Crito reappear with relative trivialities, so as to underline the importance of dealing with the remaining doubts.

156. In his "Preface," Mendelssohn cites the preceding argument, that the soul was not in any of the parts of a composite body, as being based upon a student of Plato. This is in Plotinus' *On the Immortality of the Soul* (*Ennead* IV. vii). Now, he proceeds to develop a most graceful presentation of Leibniz's concept of the monad.

157. And so concludes Mendelssohn's development of Leibniz's concept of the monad. Leibniz's student, Raphael Levi, wrote to Mendelssohn of his amazement that Leibniz's fundamental concepts could be so broadly disseminated. (See "Introduction.")

158. Mendelssohn has been casting suggestions as to a Leibnizian physics, where Cartesian and Newtonian motion and extension are not sufficient. Here now is a hint of Mendelssohn's development of the implications of Huyghens' and Leibniz's tautochrone curve—where all locations on the curve are an equal time from the bottom.

159. Mendelssohn has added a brief account of Leibnizian pre-established harmony. And, being happy, Mendelssohn has his Cebes respond with an appropriately graceful pun. Concepts, ideas, bear fruit. Mendelssohn, as Shakespeare in his *Sonnets*, imbues such fundamentals with such fecundity—a very healthy humor results in both cases.

160. This very fecund concept later is characterized as the complex domain of the noetic, the biotic and the abiotic, most notably developed by V.I. Vernadsky in *Problems of Bio-Geochemistry* and Lyndon H. LaRouche, Jr. in the *Economics of the Noösphere*.

161. Mendelssohn, picking up on hints by Plato, is happy to credit the Pythagoreans with moving beyond paganism and beyond any merely punishing god. This important, and overlooked, theological and epistemological advance in the Greek world likely stemmed from currents traceable to Moses and the Egyptian Temple of Amon.

162. Mendelssohn's articulated Leibnizian methodology addresses the conceits of Voltaire and Newton. Scientific investigations don't start from the pretense of making no hypotheses, and simply extrapolating from "the facts." That the world is bent toward justice is a pre-condition for our capacity to think and know.

163. Mendelssohn has altered the issue as posed in Plato's text, where Cebes is concerned about the wearing down of the soul through many cycles of transmigration. Here, Mendelssohn examines the state of the soul without the body and so avoids what might be unnecessary complications with the issue of transmigration.

164. Mendelssohn avoids confusion by separating the possibility of the unconscious spirit from our tendency to extrapolate from bodily considerations (e.g., of extension and motion) to unsound conclusions about the spirit—a good example of his Leibnizian method.

165. In the *Apology*, Socrates had expressed such a likelihood, a matter his accusers, Anytus and Melitus, could not allow.

166. Mendelssohn's application of Leibniz's principle, that nature acts continuously (sometimes pictured by others as a "Great Chain of Being"), includes the causal feature of a lawful ordering.

167 This poignant passage harkens back to Mendelssohn's description of the loss of his first child, Sara, only eleven months old. He wrote to Abbt on May 1, 1764: "My friend, the innocent child did not live in vain.... Her mind made astonishing progress in that short period. From a little animal that cried and slept she developed into a budding intelligent creature. One could see the blossoming of the passions like the sprouting of young grass when it pierces

the hard crust of the earth in spring. She showed pity, hatred, love, admiration. She understood the language of those talking to her, and tried to make her own thoughts known to others." Mendelssohn, two decades later, with six living children, would still remember his Sara with tears.

168. Heraclitus would be the most notable exponent of this view.

169. Mendelssohn was, undoubtedly, familiar with Leibniz's thoughts on the souls of animals. This, and the inspired section to follow, are beautiful examples of Mendelssohn's capacity to put Leibniz's profound concepts into impassioned speech.

170. Man, for Mendelssohn, encapsulates all the potential for development of the glories of the non-living world, e.g, the light of the stars and astronomy, with the exponentially greater glories of the living world, especially with other humans. Similarly, Socrates, in Plato's *Republic*, amazes Glaucon with all the glorious epistemological development from astronomy, only then to cast it as one of many such rich subjects (such as music) that the statesman must master to even begin to deal with the multiply connected human being properly.

171. Mendelssohn proceeds to draw out the paradox of his ruler, Frederick the Great, who, from 1756-63, had successfully led Prussia through much bloody warfare against great odds. However, Frederick was prone to Voltairean cynicism and soul-less materialism. During the period of the composition of the *Phädon*, it was not clear what lessons Prussians would draw from the devastation of the Seven Years' War. Might a leader harboring such a diseased soul be permitted to call upon others to die for a cause? (Contrast this, e.g., with Nathan Hale's reported last statement, before his execution a few years later: "I regret that I have but one life to give for my country.") Mendelssohn's developed argument, which he had proudly called attention to in his "Preface," would resonate most vividly throughout Prussia and Europe.

172. Mendelssohn has put into Socrates' mouth perhaps the most direct statement of his last mission, given the threatened destruction of Athens and Western civilization. Schiller developed Mendelssohn's argument in terms of the "sublime," as in his treatment of Joan of Arc.

173. Compare this with Mendelssohn's early (1756) *Sendschreiben an einen jungen Gelehrten zu B.*: "One who denies immortality must prefer to see the entire creation perish, if only he can preserve himself. When it is a question of life and death, his egotism has no limits, since neither God nor nature can oblige him to agree to his own annihilation." (Altmann identifies this as the "collision of duties" argument. Cited by Altmann, p. 155-6.)

174. "Suffer", in Greek, is the proper antonym of "act." (The English word "passive" is derived from the Greek word for "suffer". And the older sense of the English word "suffer" was the antonym of "act.") Here, Mendelssohn knows that acting and suffering are bound together etymologically.

175. Such was the level of the argument, e.g., from Voltaire on one side, and Spalding on the other, prior to Mendelssohn's treatment. (See "Introduction.")

176. Friedrich Schiller captured this line in his treatment of the sublime in his play, *The Maid of Orleans*: "Brief is the pain, eternal the joy." Ludwig von Beethoven then treated Schiller's phrase as a musical canon.

177. This was the formulation of the line of attack that Lessing suggested to Mendelssohn, as a sequel to Voltaire's cynical *Candide*.

178. Mendelssohn begins, for the first time in Part 3, to turn back to the ending of Plato's *Phaedo*. He alludes to Socrates' guidance for the journey of the soul, including Achersia, Tartarus, Pyriphlegethon and much more (108D-114C). Mendelssohn chooses an alternate course.

179. Mendelssohn (and Plato) has Crito articulate a feeling that many observers of this scene also share: We've heard the argument about the soul, but we act as if we had not. This underlines Socrates' injunction made a moment ago, not to "neglect yourselves." The Greek term was used repeatedly by Plato's Socrates, without the negation, translating as to "take concern for yourself." However, Socrates always meant something like "work deliberately and ceaselessly over your true self, your soul—failure here will create tragic results."

180. Christian Wolff (1679-1754) was a Professor of Math and of Philosophy at the University of Halle, and for a period, at the University of Marburg. He made a career out of categorizing, and so, watering down, Leibniz's work. Mendelssohn worked beyond Wolff's version of Leibniz no later than 1754, when his Pope, A Metaphysician!, was forged in collaboration with Lessing, in an alliance to put an end to the lazy optimisms of Alexander Pope and Christian Wolff. Generally, mention of Leibniz at this time was avoided by scholars when allusion to propositions of Wolff could be cited instead.

181. The Leibnizian, Alexander Gottlieb Baumgarten (1714-1762), was a student and then a professor at the University of Halle. He was famous for his work on aesthetics. Mendelssohn's collaborator, Abbt, was taught by Baumgarten's brother. Abbt also wrote the biography of Alexander Gottlieb, the 1765 *Baumgartens Leben und Charakter*.

182. *Göttingische Anzeigen* review (1767, no. 124: 985) reads: "When the author puts our modern philosophy into the mouth of Socrates and makes him talk like an eighteenth-century philosopher, Socrates recedes into the background, and I see the Wolff/Baumgartian philosopher." Or the January 16, 1767 letter by Friedrich Gabriel Resewitz to Mendelssohn's publisher, Friedrich Nicolai: "It is somewhat out of tune, when Socrates uses arguments that require knowledge or, at least, presuppositions of our present time...." (From no later than 1755, Mendelssohn had known and criticized Resewitz's views—e.g., that our mind makes us happy because it visualizes pleasant objects.)

183. Mendelssohn's chosen example references his own circumstances! As such, Mendelssohn plays with his audience: If the reader can admit he is holding in his hands the *Phädon*, an admired German work of art, written by a Jew who never could attend university and who manages a silk factory, then Mendelssohn becomes a living example that "the powers of nature are constantly active," and that the principle is "as old as wisdom itself." (Such

graceful methods of weaving profound ideas into the "normal" fabric of life, was typical of the classical and accessible creations of Mendelssohn and Lessing.) Mendelssohn's encapsulated image prefigures that of the republican man of the American Revolution.

184. Plotinus says, Iam vero neque corpus omnino erit ullum, nisi animae vis extiterit. Nam fluit semper et in moto ipsa corporis natura versatur, citoque periturum est universum, si quaecunque sunt sint corpora. (Mendelssohn's note.)

185. This might have been argued by Isaak Iselin, an Enlightenment spokesman in Switzerland, to whom Mendelssohn had submitted the first draft of the First Dialogue in 1763. (Iselin's "Patriotic Society of Bern" had solicited Mendelssohn's membership, plus a literary work.) In 1767, Iselin wrote Mendelssohn after he had read the full published work. Though that July 30, 1767 letter is lost, Mendelssohn's September 10, 1767 response indicated that Iselin had argued for the possibility that the soul could survive without a faculty for thinking. (To a third party, Iselin had labeled Mendelssohn's *Phädon* as "casuistry"! However, upon further examination of the *Phädon*, he found a deeper agreement.)

186. Leibniz's analysis of the soul in terms of his concept of monad, is meant here. (See, e.g., his *Monadology*.) However, after fifty years of suppression of—and twenty years of direct political assaults upon—Leibniz and monads, Mendelssohn is perfectly willing to play with his "Leibniz-baiting" critics, along such lines as: Yes, that is the school that I follow, and though the power of the ideas are undoubtedly of this school, the proof presented stands on its own.

187. In the Phaedo. (Mendelssohn's note.)

188. In his Discourse, *de lege continui*, and in his *Princ. Phil. Nat.* (Mendelssohn's note)

189. The dissertation of Ruggiero Giuseppe Boscovich (1711-1787) on the "law of continuity" was published in Rome, 1754, as *De continuitatis lege, et ejus consectariis*. In 1759, in the *Literaturbriefe*, Mendelssohn reviewed Boscovich's follow-up work on this subject, *Philosophiae naturalis Theoria redacta ad unicam legem virium in nataura existentiu*, (Vienna, 1759) finding interest in Boscovich's presentation on the "law of continuity." Later, in 1769, Boscovich led an expedition to California as a part of a worldwide collaboration of scientists for measuring the transit of Venus.

190. Xenophon's *Memorabilia, or Recollections of Socrates* and his *Apologia Socratis* are more narrative than dramatic.

191. Mendelssohn sounds as if he is referring to specific sophists of his time. Among some possible candidates, one might include the "friend of religion," J.B Kölbele, whose 1764 *Outline of Religion* was a series of letters to "Mademoiselle R.," a young girl. The next year, he followed with an attack on Mendelssohn's 1763 prize essay on metaphysics, which would qualify Kölbele also for the "mask of sound reason" category. (Kölbele possibly recognized

Mendelssohn's reference to him, as he followed with an *Antiphädon*, published before this "Appendix.") Those armed with subtleties might well include Voltaire and Maupertius, and Euler's 1752 thuggery against König, paired with his 1761 *Letters to a German Princess* could suggest "the arrogance of a know-it-all Thrasymachus."

192.   Proteus was a prophetic god who served Poseidon; and was capable of changing his shape at will.

193.   Of some note, two of Mendelssohn's own grandchildren were the composers Felix Mendelssohn and Fanny Mendelssohn Hensel. Their brother-in-law was the brilliant mathematician, Lejeune Dirichlet, a follower of Karl Gauss, and one who might be said to have caught a sight of the bright mid-day!

194.   In this and the next paragraph, Mendelssohn reveals his thinking, in choosing Socrates for his unique treatment. In the description of his "Socrates" project, and the resultant perspective for resituating the strengths of Western civilization outside of denominational quibbles, one can recognize some of the immediate fruits: Lessing's 1779 *Nathan the Wise* and Mendelssohn's 1782 citizenship projects for Vienna and Berlin—along with 1783 work, *Jerusalem*, explicating the happy and healthy relationship between state and religion.

195.   The European Renaissance, only three centuries earlier, was highly dependent upon the Greek texts preserved first in the Alexandria Library, and then in that of Baghdad—both lands of the "barbarians."

196.   *Ennead.* 4 L. VIII. (Mendelssohn's note.)

197.   For Leibniz, motion and extension are derivative of substance. It is significant to Mendelssohn that Plotinus' terms are sufficient for the argument on the immateriality of the soul, while Descartes' are too dependent upon certain ascribed doctrines. (Also, Mendelssohn once again has some fun at the expense of those that would treat his *Phädon* as merely suppressed Leibnizian ideas, repackaged in the mouth of Socrates.)

198.   Albrecht von Haller's 1747 *Primae Lineae Physiologiae* (First Lines of Physiology). A Swiss physiologist, botanist and poet, Haller (1708-1777) was the professor of anatomy, medicine and botany at the University of Göttingen, 1736-1753. He had studied with Leibniz's closest collaborator, Johann Bernoulli, and was a regular correspondent of Mendelssohn's friend, Johann Georg Sulzer.

199.   Gottfried Plouquet (1716-1790) studied Leibniz and Wolff. Mendelssohn refers to Plouquet's 1764 *Methodus calculandi in Logicis praemissa commentatione de arte characteristica* in his 1764 review of J.H. Lambert's *Neues Organon*. Mendelssohn was interested in, from Leibniz's early work (e.g., *De Arte Combinatoria*), his universal characteristic, and the possibility of a scientific language whose structure and signification reflected that of the discovered world. (It were likely that Mendelssohn was also familiar with, and sympathetic with, Ploucquet's paper on monads—part of the famous 1747 Berlin Academy contest, and with his 1750 inaugural disputation, "Against La Mettrie's Materialism.")

200. Alexander Gottlieb Baumgarten's *Metaphysica* (Halle, 1739).

201. *Abhandlungen von den vornehmsten Wahrheiten der natürlichen Religion,* 1755, was written by Herman Samuel Reimarus (1694-1768), a professor of Hebrew and Oriental languages in Hamburg. (Earlier, around 1760, Mendelssohn had also favorably reviewed his work on the instinct of animals.) The Reimarus home served as Hamburg's cultural center. Later, Lessing would frequent his home during his stay in Hamburg (1767-1770), and become good friends with Reimarus' son and daughter. After Lessing's death, the daughter Elise transferred her regular correspondence with Lessing to their mutual friend, Mendelssohn. (The famous controversy over the suppressed writing of Reimarus, his *Apologia in Defense of the Rational Worshippers of God,* arose several years after the *Phädon,* when, in 1774, Lessing began publishing them anonymously as the *Fragments of the Unnamed.*)

202. Cesare Beccaria (1738-1794), of Milan, wrote his 1764 work, *Dei delitti e delle pene,* against arbitrary feudal practices, such as the torture-confessions and secretive accusations, made famous by the still-active court of the Inquisition. His argument, for basing punishment upon some proportionality with the crime, was within the confines of Beccaria's study of British social contract theory. Mendelssohn obviously thought it worthwhile to deal with this new celebrity's argument. As Mendelssohn refers to Becarria not as a "Marchese," but as a "Marquis," it is likely that he had seen Andre Morellet's 1765 French translation of Becarria's work. Again, a secondary source might have been Voltaire's 1766 *Commentaire sur le livre, Des Delits et Des Peines.*

203. The anonymous review in the 1767 *Neue Bibliothek der Schönen Wissenschaften und der freyen Künste* was written by Christian Garve (1742-1798). Altmann cites Mendelssohn's collaborator, David Friedländer, for the identification of Garve as the author (*Ibid.* p. 785, footnote 78, which refers to *Moses Mendelssohn Gesammelte Schriften Jubiläumsausgabe,* Vol. 3.1, page 409.) The reviewer had called Mendelssohn's Leibnizian treatment of Plotinus' argument, "a masterpiece." Garve graduated in 1766 from the University of Leipzig and delivered his habilitation there in 1769. (Later, in the spring of 1782, Garve's relative and collaborator, the Prussian councilor E.F. Klein, would work closely with Mendelssohn, in the wake of the American Revolution, in the push for reforms for Jews.)